Praise for *How to Work a Room*

"When it comes to connecting with others, some of us are naturals. But those who aren't—and that's most of us—thank heaven for Susan RoAne. This newly updated version of her classic work shows how to converse and connect with people you meet at social events, trade shows and conventions—as well as in new meeting places like Facebook, Pinterest and LinkedIn. If you want to learn how to enter a room and build a network of people you can help and who can help you, read this book and heed its many lessons."

—Daniel H. Pink, *New York Times*
bestselling author of *Drive* and *To Sell Is Human*

"This is Susan RoAne's original masterpiece on steroids! While her classic advice remains pertinent, the 25th-anniversary version recognizes that as the world gets smaller, the rooms get larger. A must-read for all communicators!"
—Harvey Mackay, author of the *New York Times*
#1 bestseller *Swim with the Sharks Without Being Eaten Alive*

"Buy this book if you want to be a savvy socializer. Buy a second one for a shy friend. Buy a third one as an ebook, so you're never without it."
—Guy Kawasaki, former chief evangelist of Apple
and author of *APE: Author, Publisher, Entrepreneur*

"Everyone expects that politicians know how to 'work a room.' That simply isn't true. This book is an excellent handbook for people in politics and in all walks of life. Whether the setting is business, political or social, RoAne's guidelines serve anyone who has to meet with the public."
—Willie Brown, former mayor of San Francisco

"I didn't think it was possible to top the groundbreaking insights and strategies Susan RoAne first introduced in the original edition of *How to Work a Room*; yet that's exactly what she has done with the silver anniversary edition of this life-changing book. If you want to learn how to shine in any room, you'll not find a more effective guide than this invaluable, must-read book!"
—Ivan Misner, Ph.D., *New York Times*
bestselling author and founder of BNI

"The ability to connect with colleagues, clients and coworkers is essential for success. Susan RoAne's revised classic will guide you through any room, whether it's a room full of associates or strangers."
—Connie Glaser, author of *GenderTalk Works: 7 Steps for Cracking the Gender Code at Work*

"Ever dreaded entering a roomful of strangers? If this has happened to you, then buy this clever, informative and accessible book by Susan RoAne, the best conversationalist I know."
—Robert Spector, author of *The Nordstrom Way to Customer Service Excellence*

"*How to Work a Room* is a classic! Susan RoAne provides insights into interpersonal excellence and savvy social etiquette that they don't teach you in school! Unless you plan to survive on an island . . . by yourself—BUY THIS BOOK."
—Dan Maddux, executive director/CEO of American Payroll Association

"Susan RoAne (aka 'The Mingling Maven®') has done it again! RoAne applies her sage advice, engaging wit, and personal charm, along with her empathy and support, to help others. *How to Work a Room* is a 'must-read' book for those of us who want to enhance our most unique human quality—the ability to converse, connect, and embrace others locally and globally."
—Bernardo J. Carducci, director of the Indiana University Southeast Shyness Research Institute, fellow of the American Psychological Association, and author of *The Shyness Breakthrough*

Also by Susan RoAne

Face to Face:
How to Reclaim the Personal Touch in a Digital World

How to Create Your Own Luck:
The "You Never Know" Approach to Networking,
Taking Chances, and Opening Yourself to Opportunity

What Do I Say Next?
Talking Your Way to Business and Social Success

The Secrets of Savvy Networking:
How to Make the Best Connections for
Business and Personal Success

HOW TO
WORK
A ROOM®

The Ultimate Guide to Making Lasting Connections— in Person and Online

SUSAN ROANE

WILLIAM MORROW
An Imprint of HarperCollinsPublishers

Grateful acknowledgment is made to the following copyright holders for permission to reprint the following:

"Sleaze Factor" © 1988. Reprinted with permission from Chronicle Features.—Chapter 7, page 93.

"Working the Room" © The New Yorker Collection 1997. Bernard Schoenbaum, from cartoonbank.com. All rights reserved.—Chapter 11, page 161.

"Thank You Notes" *Rhymes with Orange* © 1988 by Hillary Price. Reprinted with permission from Universal Press Syndicate.—Chapter 14, page 218.

"Cathy" © 1988. Reprinted with permission from Universal Press Syndicate.—Chapter 16, page 240.

"Laptop" © The New Yorker Collection 2002. Michael Maslin, from cartoonbank.com. All Rights Reserved.—Chapter 17, page 262.

Cell Phone © The New Yorker Collection 1999. Charles Barsotti, from cartoonbank.com. All Rights Reserved.—Chapter 18, page 275.

"It Keeps Me from Looking at My Phone" © The New Yorker Collection 2013. Liam Walsh, from cartoonbank.com. All rights reserved.—Chapter 18, page 282.

HarperCollins books may be purchased for educational, business, or sales promotional use. For information please e-mail Special Markets Department at SPsales@harpercollins.com.

Paperback edition was published by Warner Books in 1988. A Quill edition was published in 2000. A Collins edition was published in 2007.

FIRST ORIGINALLY PUBLISHED EDITION

Library of Congress Cataloging-in-Publication Data has been applied for.

ISBN 978-0-06-229534-7

15 16 17 18   OV/RRD   10 9 8 7 6 5 4

This book is rededicated in memoriam to the spirit of three special people:

To Joyce "Mumsy" Siegel, whose memory I'll forever hold dear: for constant support, sounding board brilliance, laughter and wisdom.

To Ida B. Harvey, my "assistant mother," who taught me that "beauty is only skin deep, but ugly . . . is to the bone."

To Sally Livingston, my "femtor" who coined the term to describe herself—my female mentor—who was a guiding spirit, my networking teacher, a role model and cheerleader.

To my dear friends old and new who have graced my life; you know who you are.

And to those whose words of wisdom, kindness and support continue to echo eternally and internally. Thank you.

CONTENTS

Get Set!

Go!

ACKNOWLEDGMENTS

The best part of writing a book is drafting the acknowledgments because writing a book still feels like giving birth to an elephant. And I was never alone each time.

Over the years, thousands of people gave me their time, energy, insight and humor in personal interviews, conversations, emails and audience feedback. Friends, clients and colleagues, as well as people I meet on airplanes, at events, in line at the supermarket or "treading on the mills" at the health club, continue to be generous with their whys, wisdom, wherefores, wit, wonderment and wows. I'm grateful to the people who took the time to share their stories and experiences for this book.

And thanks to my friends, who support me, believe in me (once again), let me hibernate and become who Ruthe Hirsch calls "Esther Sequester." I am especially grateful to Aileen Jett RoAne, my late, dear, former mother-in-law, who was the first person to tell me that I could and should write a book. Thanks to Dr. Geraldine Alpert for her wisdom; to Patricia Teal, Mark Chimsky, Laura Friedman, Griggs RoAne,

Lois Keenan, Patricia Fripp, Toni Boyle, Diane Parente, Pam Martens, Gail Edenson, Leigh Bohmfalk, Allison Fortini Crawford, Robert Spector, Helen Bohaczyk, Anne Paterlini; Susan Belling, Sandy Hufford and Donna Schafer— my Saturday Breakfast Club; Arlynn Greenbaum, my New York host and friend; Lisa Miller Beckstead, who was a most supportive roommate during the initial writing of my "firstborn"; Nicole Wells Johnson for her bringing her skills and sunny disposition to my business and allowing me to be her wedding greeter; Sherwood and Jonathan Cummins, who work my muscles and help me work through situations that I've captured in the book; Mike McEvoy, Harold Hingle and Tim Eatherton for my web presence; Bonnie Hughes for all; my brother, Ira Rosenberg, for clever quips and current sports tips; Victoria "G.G." Kellman for more than I can express; the Berringers for allowing me to be part of the family and Grandma Susan to their girls; my Foxcroft/Adams family of Durban for sharing their South Africa with me; and to the entire Skov clan and Shayne, Patrick, Olivia and Annika— being your Grandma Susan is a joy!

To Lana Teplick, chief of staff and best friend, for her wisdom, total support, timely reminders and her "oh, wows!" for many years.

To Judith Briles, who first recognized that *How to Work a Room* should be a book and who continues to help other emerging authors at Author U.

To Connie Glaser, my cosmic twin, for her continued friendship, laughter and support.

To Carl La Mell, the chairman of the board of The RoAne Group, for his great "BS" detector and CEO-size street smarts and decades of friendship.

To Joann Davis, for believing both in me and in this

book and for making me write the next two books to create the trilogy of connecting and communicating.

To Zach Schisgal, the editor who first acquired this book for Morrow/Harper and gave it a new home and is now a friend.

To Trish Daly, my current editor (and my former student at NYU's Summer Publishing Institute) for her enthusiasm, support and wise advice.

To Becky Gordon, patient transcriber of my hiero-glyphics, to whom I am eternally grateful for her editorial know-how, organizational skills and sense of humor and the Gordon Giggle test. Once again, she helped "birth" the book you now have in your hands.

And I am especially grateful to the transgressors of good taste and good behavior. Unfortunately, I legally cannot name them and so wish I could. We all know who you are. Your inappropriate behavior is a treasure trove of volumes of material you continue to contribute . . . unwittingly.

To my agent, Michael Bourret, a savvy, smart sweetheart of a guy, with a superb sense of humor, for his unfailing en-couragement.

Merci beaucoup, muchas gracias, todah rabah, thank you to the unsung heroes of book sales: the sales reps without whom this book would not be in the stores or in your hands and the booksellers—both online and in your neighbor-hoods around the country—who have been so supportive of my "baby" and kind to me these past twenty-five years.

To my social media *mishpocheh* and blogger pals who helped the get the word out via their blogs, websites, newszines, tweets, posts, "pins" and status updates. You are cyber-super!

And to the readers and members of my audiences, who

have thanked me over these many years to help them manage to mingle more successfully. Without you, I wouldn't be a best-selling author.

To my clients, who realize how important this skill is, I thank you for continuing to hire me to share these strategies with your companies and associations: Without you, I wouldn't be a successful keynote speaker.

PREFACE

You're holding the newly updated Silver Anniversary edition of *How to Work a Room* because twenty-five years is worth celebrating! *How to Work a Room* is my first book, which I describe as my firstborn. That explains why I gave it a tenth birthday party, a "book mitzvah" at thirteen, complete with chopped liver flown in from New York and at twenty-one, a champagne reception.

 To view my video introduction of my brand-new updated edition, scan this QR code or add this URL to your browser: http://youtu.be/FCPn3qpd9Ek.

In twenty-five years so many things about our society and culture have changed. Technology has created a tsunami of gadgets, habits, hardware and options that were unfathomable in 1988. What hasn't changed is basic human nature. Over 90 percent of us are still shy and find a roomful of people—strangers—to be daunting. *How to Work a Room* has been imparting suggestions, techniques and encouragement to mingle and socialize worldwide for a quarter of a century.

Savvy socializing is a still recognized and essential quality in business; as a recent article in *Fortune* stated, "high-profile leaders tend to know how to work a room and many may have learned to like the limelight." But even star CEOs need to be cautious in their room-working, socializing with humility and recognizing the people around them. The *Fortune* article quotes David Waldman, a management professor at Arizona State University, who claims that leaders can be both self-obsessed and humble: "They like to be the subject of the limelight, they have high self-regard and a degree of hubris. But they also recognize that other people around them deserve a lot of praise." This article makes the point that while confidence is an essential leadership quality, we all still need to know how best to navigate through the various rooms in our lives, even those of us who have achieved a great deal of success already.

We must continue to redefine those rooms as they proliferate and grow, both offline and as online sites and clever "apps," which make life more interesting, if not easier. We'll always be attending in-person events: meetings, conferences, fund-raisers, trade shows, reunions, weddings and graduation parties, where our skills and ability of socializing, mingling and schmoozing come into play. To be memorable and ensure our visibility and viability, we'll have to navigate all "rooms."

Unlike the last edition, which mentioned Facebook and LinkedIn, this edition includes the new rooms called Instagram, Pinterest and Google+. By the time this book is published, there will be newer rooms to work. And you will. One of my goals is always to be relevant like my inspiration Joyce (Mumsy) Siegel was. To that end, this edition is a refreshing update.

OVERCOMING OVERWHELM

How to Work a Room has helped countless readers abate that "overwhelm" since 1988. It's my hope and goal that this even more robust and relevant Silver Anniversary edition and I are your caring coaches offering concrete, practical ideas that you can implement immediately as you enter and interact in every room.

Clients, members of my audiences, readers and former "strangers" have made a number of the new suggestions; others have percolated and evolved over time. Some have even awakened me in the middle of the night, demanding to be written.

The book is still in the easy-to-read, easy-to-digest, easy-to-implement format. I kept that which still applies, makes sense and makes the point. Because technology has changed our lives immensely, you'll read about the importance of online sites such as LinkedIn, Pinterest, Facebook and Twitter as "new rooms to work." But these rooms have not eliminated the need for basic social skills: In these pages you'll also encounter users and abusers of Bluetooth devices (perhaps suffering from "Bluetooth decay") and text messengers who violate audience etiquette (one, in particular, known as the "*Wicked* texter").

The need to meet, mingle, make contacts and make conversation is even more important in this twenty-first century's Internet-working world because we have lost some of our face-to-face communication skills. Dr. Nathan Keyfitz's prediction continues to be true. As Harvard professor emeritus of sociology in the mid-1980s, he said, "In the year 2000, we will all be technically adept, but who will succeed will be the people who can talk to other people." Because of our technology-addicted world of cell phones, iPads, instant and text messaging and MP3 players and the constant presence of earbuds in our ears, social skills are on the decline. The good news is that those who have them will shine in any room.

I encourage my audiences to "bring who they are to what they do." So I did what I invite others to do. Because of that, many of the stories are mine. That's why you'll get to meet a terrific group of good folks who have something to say—and they say it.

My original goal was to write this book to help people manage the mingling in their personal and professional lives. It's twenty-five years later and that remains my goal.

With hindsight, I realize that my life has been graced and enhanced by wonderful people, many of whom began as strangers. I met them because of sweet serendipity; you'll get to meet them, too.

It's my hope that you will have equally wonderful, valuable and memorable experiences as you successfully work every room of your life.

My best wishes.

Susan RoAne

HOW TO
WORK
A ROOM®

INTRODUCTION

INVITATION CONSTERNATION

You open your inbox and it's there: an invitation to attend an event. You can tell either by the thud it makes as it drops into your inbox or the feel of the envelope that arrives in your mailbox that it's an invitation to *something*, and you're right. One of your clients is the honorary chairperson for a local charity and she's throwing a huge fund-raiser in four weeks. Not only *should* you go, but many potential clients, opportunities and investors will be there and it's a chance to meet people and promote your business or your career.

Before you even have a chance to think about it, a little voice in the back of your head pipes up, "Wait a minute . . . You'll walk into that enormous ballroom and see thousands of strangers! They'll all know one another, but no one will know you. Who will you talk to? What will you say?" So you gingerly place the invitation in your "wait-and-see" file or computer desktop file or the "circular" one or you may even delete it without a second glance. If it's an Evite, you may RSVP and say you can't attend. But you'll never know what opportunities may have awaited you.

You are not alone! This scenario happens daily in offices and homes across the country. It doesn't matter whether the invitation is for a purely social event, a business gathering of only fifty people or a combination of the two—it's daunting for most of us to walk into a room full of people we don't know, especially when we want to make a good impression.

But every room presents us with one of the best business and social opportunities we'll ever run across. The benefits of being able to work a room with the ease and grace of a mingling maven are enormous.

- You feel better about yourself. You approach business or social gatherings with enthusiasm and confidence, knowing that this is an arena where you will be comfortable, effective and productive.

- You make other people feel more comfortable, which makes them want to know and possibly do business with you and refer business to you because people remember those who make them feel included.

- You make invaluable business contacts, as well as starting friendships that may last your whole life. If you hadn't been able to walk up to people, smile, put out your hand and say "Hi," those opportunities might have been lost.

SAY YES TO OPPORTUNITIES

In my research for *How to Create Your Own Luck*, I learned that those who turn serendipity into success say yes when they want to say no. Because they do that, they are able to parlay possibilities and coincidence into opportunities they otherwise would not have had.

I have rewritten this book to give you the confidence, suggestions and the tools to say yes and to walk into any room and shine—whether the event is social or professional, a convention, a shareholders, meeting, party, TEDx event, reunion, PTA committee meeting or an inaugural ball. This book is designed to help you manage these events successfully, mingle with ease and come away feeling that you have accomplished your own goals—and made other people feel good in the process—and have had a good time.

The focus will be on:

- Identifying the "roadblocks" that inhibit us from circulating with ease and comfort
- Providing a remedy to neutralize each roadblock
- Acclimating yourself in the old and new virtual and techno toy rooms
- Strengthening confidence and projecting your warmth, interest and sincerity, which will invite people to open up
- Implementing practical tips and strategies for starting conversations, establishing communication and building rapport with "strangers" in a variety of situations that you encounter
- Preparing yourself to enter all the rooms of your life
- Building quality business and social relationships
- Sharing the stories of those who have done it and how they have been successful

In this century, those who have the personal touch will profit professionally. Working a room can be your number one marketing strategy. Visibility marketing is some of the best advertising you can get to make a positive, lasting impression—and it's free.

ROOMS WITH STRANGERS: OUR TOP FEAR

All of us "work" rooms. If you've ever been to a wedding, a fund-raiser, a reunion or a meeting, you've worked a room—or wished you could have mingled more comfortably and then come to deeply appreciate how much easier and more pleasant life would be if you developed this skill. People in my audiences and at book signings tell me that the most upsetting thing about these events is that everyone else seems to be completely comfortable. Trust me, they only *appear* to be having a grand time.

Most people don't like entering a room full of strangers for any reason. "A party with strangers" is the number one social fear according to a study on social anxiety reported in the *New York Times*. In a book of phobias that crossed my desk, it was number two on the phobia chart. The number one phobia (just in case it's in a trivia game) is a fear of spiders (arachnophobia). Most of us would rather speak in public than attend an event with people we don't know.

It might even be said that if you didn't have some anxiety about this, *you would not be normal.*

Most of us want to feel comfortable with other people, even strangers, and will do whatever it takes to minimize the anxiety and move through a crowded room with ease and grace. We not only want to be comfortable, but we also want to make other people feel comfortable with us. We want to "manage the mingling" so that we have fun, feel good about ourselves, score some professional points and feel that even "putting in an appearance" is a good use of our time, especially since time is a precious commodity.

TOM HANKS: THE NICE GUY

On a late-night television show, actor/director Ed Burns followed Tom Hanks, who stayed on the set. Ed turned to Tom and said, "I can't believe I am sitting here with you. When I was starting out in this business, I worked as a gofer on *Entertainment Tonight,* and three years before that worked for a company that gave the party for *A League of Their Own.* And you asked me to bring you a cup of coffee." You could see and hear how Ed Burns felt about his career path and how he felt to be sharing the stage with Tom Hanks.

Tom Hanks turned to Ed Burns and said, "Please tell me that I was nice to you." Burns replied, "Yes, you were very nice." Tom Hanks looked relieved and said he was glad. Here is a man with great acclaim, celebrity, career success and wealth and his first concern was that he was nice to this young man who had brought him coffee.

That, in a nutshell, is the right impression we want to leave with the people who cross our paths in the rooms that we "work" and in which we work. We show our character not by how we treat people in a position to help us but in how we treat people who can't—or so we think. Being nice in any room pays off.

WORKING A ROOM ISN'T
NETWORKING AND VICE VERSA

"Working a room" is an old political phrase that conjures up images of overweight men in smoky back rooms pressing flesh and cutting deals. But that's not what we mean by it today; today's definition of *working a room* is "the ability to circulate comfortably and graciously through a gathering of people: meeting, greeting and talking with as many of them as you wish; creating communication that is warm and sincere; establishing an honest rapport on which you can build a professional or personal relationship; and knowing how to start, how to continue and how to end lively and interesting conversations."

Networking is a different, though interrelated, activity. It's a mutually beneficial process in which we *share* leads, ideas and information and it enhances our personal and professional lives and involves follow-up behaviors that create ongoing connections and lasting relationships.

You first have to work rooms and then you network—that ongoing process of life that is a continuous follow-up. Some people confuse the two. There are some people who are excellent minglers and lousy networkers. Others are fabulous networkers for whom the thought of walking into a room full of people and mingling is daunting.

SINCERITY IS THE GLUE

In spite of how some people behave, there is nothing inherently calculated or manipulative (unless you are calculating and manipulative) about working a room. However, if you don't really care for and about people or your warmth, your openness or your desire to connect with them is not genuine, then no technique in the world will help!

This has nothing to do with shyness or being introverted; it's whether or not you *like* people. People sense the truth; they usually know when they are being manipulated because you have an agenda or want to make a sale. They also know when you are making a sincere effort to extend yourself to them and they appreciate it and will forgive an inadvertent faux pas.

My guideline: Go to have fun and enjoy the people at every event. The professional benefits will follow. But *go!*

RISKS AND REWARDS

Working a room is a risk whether you're a CFO or CPA or a C student, no doubt about it. Our egos are on the line and that can be intimidating. It can also be tremendously rewarding and have payoffs on both a personal and a professional level. But not going to events is a greater risk because there is no chance to reap the possible rewards if you don't show up.

This book is about understanding what keeps us from approaching these events with ease and enthusiasm and what we can do to make them comfortable, pleasant, productive, profitable and even fun. It is also about giving ourselves permission to work (never overwork!) every room we enter and to reap the benefits—both personal and professional.

Caveat: This book focuses on social skills and cross-cultural communication, relevant in the United States. It's important to note that *How to Work a Room* has been published in over thirteen countries in a number of languages because people across the globe want to know the art of mixing and mingling. There are other very fine books and websites that specialize on international cross-cultural issues.

PRACTICE DOES MAKE PERFECT

I encourage you to attend as many events as you can and to practice the techniques in this book. Some will work well and others may not be right for you. But as Mom always said, "Can't hurt to try!"

You may find that you already know some of the information in this book or that you already practice some of the techniques. Great! Let the book serve as a reminder and sharpen your skills as you go along. The more you practice, the better you'll be.

And above all—enjoy. When you are having fun, the room "works" you.

GET
READY!

☺   ☺

PASSPORT
TO
OPPORTUNITIES

Technology continues to impact and change our lives in myriad ways. This newly updated Silver Anniversary version of *How to Work a Room* mirrors those changes and is even more relevant, informative and helpful as we leave our cubicles, computers, tablets and smartphones to venture forth into the world of opportunity. This book is your passport to possibilities.

What I've learned in the twenty-five years since I originally wrote *How to Work a Room* is that people of all ages, from all walks of life and backgrounds, can find events uncomfortable and often daunting—be they meetings, sales conferences, parties, retreats, weddings, fund-raisers or even family gatherings.

I've guest-lectured nationwide at universities and Fortune 20 to Fortune 500 companies, to senior executives and young professionals, to provide the strategies, philosophy and techniques of business and personal socializing and mingling. The purpose is not only to ease the discomfort but also to make the most of every event: from making contacts, starting conversations and building relationships to having a good time. Developing good social skills even has a health benefit: According to a "Live Longer and Better" quiz in *Parade* magazine citing a 2012 study in the *British Medical Journal*, people who had a "rich or moderate social network" lived five years longer.

CONVERSATION IS THE LINCHPIN

Talk—conversation—is how we relate, explain, persuade, sell, converse, amuse, learn, collaborate, motivate and connect. No matter what walk of life we pursue, we need to be able to break the ice, approach strangers and start, build and maintain conversations.

- We cannot build strategic partnerships, business and social relationships and business-to-business models unless we communicate.
- We cannot approach team building unless there is an exchange of words among the members of the team.
- We cannot collaborate unless we discuss the issues.
- We cannot enjoy the benefits of brainstorming unless we are conversing.
- We cannot build a base of customers unless we are communicating.
- We cannot sell our services or products unless we listen to our customers, converse with them and solve their problems, according to author Daniel Pink in *To Sell Is Human*.

"Face-to-face contact with bosses, employees, customers will become newly important," according to William Strauss, coauthor of *The Fourth Turning: An American Prophecy in the 21st Century*. That makes mingling, conversing and connecting necessary skills and requires the personal touch.

This Silver Anniversary edition will assist you in working actual rooms, online sites and virtual rooms, as it has more suggestions, tips and ideas. A room full of people, especially of strangers, is *still* a daunting experience—even more so today. Why? Because we spend an inordinate amount of time communicating online, texting, shopping and playing games on our smartphones, we have let our "fingers and thumbs do the talking" and have lost the skill, courage and confidence to deal with the face-to-face. We are addicted to text messaging, email, online gaming, e-commerce and our apps. The consequence is that we have decreased our ability to chat at a business dinner or a social event.

In the 1980s Dr. Philip Zimbardo, founder of Stanford University's Shyness Clinic and currently president of Heroic Imagination Project, discovered that 80 percent of adults identify themselves as shy. In 2000 that figure increased to 93 percent, due in part to technology. We can get money "out of a hole in the wall: the ATM"—that's where kids think money comes from; money growing on trees is history—and, in fact, we can do all of our banking online and never have to exchange pleasantries with a teller.

We can get our stamps via the Internet, our groceries can be self-checked (which I never thought I would do and now it's my check-out preference) or ordered from the web and we can "talk" to people's voice mail without ever having a conversation. These changes impact and decrease day-to-day social conversation skills.

COMFORTABLE IN CROWDS

When I ask my audiences how many of them feel comfortable in a room full of strangers, it is still *rare* that as many as 5 percent raise their hands—even among salespeople. If you are sitting in a meeting; attending a convention, a board retreat or a yearly conference; or are involved in a keynote presentation, you are already in a group with whom you have something in common. You just need some strategies; tips; opening and exit lines; and mostly, the permission to talk to those still unknown colleagues, cronies, contacts, clients, customers and potential friends.

How to Work a Room provides the information and the impetus, along with many new, improved, tried-and-true strategies, examples and ideas to work any room, gleaned from years of conversations with a multitude of audiences and feedback from over a million readers and visitors to my website.

THE BORING TRUTH

I'm often asked how to converse with someone who is disinterested, bored or aloof. One of the realities of life is that we will not click with everyone we meet. Their timing, interests, agendas and values may be very different from ours. But the rooms will be full of other nice, interesting, friendly people who will be open to meeting, conversing and doing business with us.

At a presentation for a professional services firm, one of the partners wondered how he could possibly introduce a person he found boring to a client. His colleague provided the perfect response, "What's boring for you may be fascinating for someone else who shares their interests."

It's so true. When people talk about their favorite recipes or science-fiction books and movies, I struggle to keep my eyes from glazing over, but a foodie or sci-fi fan would find that person to be interesting, even fascinating.

If you are in situations where being able to work—or just feel comfortable in—any room is important professionally or personally, this book is for you. It contains quizzes, quotes, quips and cartoons. If you have a sense of humor, this book's for you. If you suffer from "irony deficiency," especially when you have to attend a conference, party, fundraiser, meet-up or trade show, this book is the perfect antidote!

If we are aware of and prepared for the roadblocks we encounter, we can implement the remedies as we prepare to circulate in the rooms we enter.

This book continues to be my "magic mingling wand" that will help you remedy the roadblocks and turn you into a newly minted Mingling Maven!®

ROANE'S REMINDERS

★ Good social skills positively impact one's well-being and life expectancy.

★ Those who can mingle and make contacts and conversation will shine in any room.

★ Conversation is the cornerstone of team building and collaboration.

★ Face-to-face contact with bosses, colleagues and clients requires a personal touch.

★ When you're in the same room, you already have something in common.

★ No one is boring when you discover their area of passion.

2

THE FIVE ROADBLOCKS: MOTHER'S DIRE WARNINGS

If working a room is so much fun and so profitable, why do our hearts thump, our palms sweat and our eyes glaze over when we think about it? One reason we've established is that 93 percent of us think of ourselves as shy in different situations. When we get invited to a meeting, conference or party, we shy away from the opportunity in order to avoid the discomfort.

Another reason is that many years ago we were taught *not* to talk to strangers. Mom gave us these dire warnings with the best of intentions—"for our own good"—and everybody agreed that we should heed them. The trouble is they worked a lot better when we were six years old than they do now that we are twenty-six, forty-six or sixty-six.

Ask yourself this: Do you like people? If the answer is yes, then read on. You will discover ideas and suggestions that will be helpful in any room. If your answer is no, read on as well. You may discover some suggestions that will change your attitude.

There are five major roadblocks to working a room successfully. Knowing where they come from is the first step to letting go of them.

ROADBLOCK #1
"DON'T TALK TO STRANGERS"

This first roadblock is as American as apple pie. It is often stated as a warning and accompanied by a shaking of the index finger. It made sense when our mothers said this to us and it makes sense when we tell it to our children. We *still* don't want our children to talk to strangers on the way home from school, today more than ever.

But it *doesn't* make sense when we're selling a product at a trade show, beginning our first day on a new job, attending a formal ball or mingling at a professional association meeting or convention where contacts and connections are standing around the room. Yet we often find ourselves standing in the door, feeling uncomfortable, with that imaginary finger shaking in our faces and the message "Don't talk to strangers" flashing across our subconscious. So we don't.

Instead, we choose a nice, quiet spot at the hors d'oeuvres table and start nibbling, get very busy with a cup of coffee or a drink, smile nervously around the room at no one in particular—and have an awful time. Or we hang out on the periphery of the room, hovering close to the walls (hence the term *wallflower*).

Or we walk into a meeting, convention or conference and look around the room for a familiar face. And we'll talk to that person the entire time rather than approach "strangers" in the room.

The problem is that, as a result, we also miss tremendous

business, career and social opportunities. Who knows what wonderful person or valuable contact was standing in that room feeling just as uncomfortable as we were!

Life is too short, and time too precious, to spend an hour or two squandering opportunities and, in the process, having a bad time.

ROADBLOCK #2
"WAIT TO BE PROPERLY INTRODUCED" (THE SCARLETT O'HARA SYNDROME)

Imagine legendary Scarlett, a charming and spoiled Southern belle, standing on the steps of Tara in all its antebellum glory, batting her eyelashes as she drawls, "My, but we haven't been properly introduced." Her beauty and charm notwithstanding, *Gone with the Wind*'s protagonist wouldn't have gotten very far at a company retreat or a professional association meeting. In Scarlett's day and social sphere, everyone was very much aware of proper introductions and there were people, usually older women, who did little else. They would make *sure* you met that gallant, dark-haired man or that stunning belle or the local banker who might be interested in your crop expansion (translated to today: the venture capitalist who'd invest in your mobile-to-mobile app).

But tomorrow has, indeed, become what Scarlett said was "another day," and now you can't count on personal or professional matchmakers to be sure you are introduced around at the professional meeting or reception after the lecture. We are on our own.

It is certainly *easier* and preferable to begin a conversation when you've been formally introduced. At the very least, you have in common the person who introduced you. "How do you know Leslie?" elicits more information about the person you've just met and can lead to other subjects of conversation. Most likely, Leslie shared information about each of you that you can use to start a conversation.

But at most events we can't count on being introduced to anyone, let alone the people we most want to meet. We are on our own when it comes to circulating. We have to walk up to people and introduce *ourselves*, if we don't want to be left standing in the middle of the room, staring at the ceiling or the floor. We might as well be "gone with the wind."

ROADBLOCK #3
"GOOD THINGS COME TO THOSE WHO WAIT" (THE PROM KING/QUEEN COMPLEX)

Let's face it. The world still beats a path to the door of prom kings and queens, but once the prom is over, even the ex-kings and ex-queens can't always afford to sit back and hope that people will seek them out.

There is an old adage, "Good things come to those who wait." Au contraire. Gray hair comes to those who wait and sometimes even varicose veins, if the waiting is done standing up!

THE WAITING GAME

New York Times best-selling author and TV personality Larry Winget has a different approach: "I always want to be the most interesting-looking person in the room and wait for people to talk to me." Larry accomplishes this by wearing colorful and eye-catching cowboy shirts and boots. But for most of us, waiting for people to introduce themselves to us is an exercise in futility. Chances are they won't—because it's just as difficult for them as it is for you. Because 93 percent of us are shy and won't initiate, the "waiting game" is a colossal waste of time, no fun at all and murder on the self-confidence.

It reminds me of myself and legions of other former teenagers who sat by the phone and stared at it waiting for it to ring. (This was during pre–cell phone days when phones had cords and were actually attached to walls.) I learned the hard way that it did *not* work for the prom. Why would I expect it to work now? If it were not for the matchmakers, my mom, Lil, and Larry Katzen's mom, Marion, I'd still be waiting for my prom date to call!

People who wait for others to come to them can often be found in the corner of the room, holding up the walls while envying those who circulate around the reception or the cocktail party meeting people.

It's quite appropriate to approach someone in a pleasant, friendly way, smile, introduce yourself and say something like, "This is my first meeting. Is there always such a good turnout?"

Caution: People who fall victim to the Prom King/ Queen Complex and sit around waiting for the world to find them are often perceived as snobs, aloof, even arrogant, when they may be feeling uncomfortable or shy. They may or may not actually *be* shy, but that is how they've come to think of themselves.

LOSE THE LABELS

In one of my early jobs as an elementary school teacher, the lesson I learned is that these labels often became self-fulfilling prophecies. The class Troublemaker always found a way to maintain that dubious distinction. The Talker (today's conversationalist) always managed to get red checks next to "Keeps Profitably Busy." I'm afraid I fell into this category, but to this day I can't imagine anything more compelling about school than social intercourse with my classmates. Multiplication tables? Diagramming sentences? Give me note passing (the precursor to text messaging) and furtive whispering in the back row!

We need to stop labeling ourselves and other people.

"Most people experience 'situational shyness,'" says Dr. Philip Zimbardo, author of *Shyness: What It Is, What to Do About It*. Certain situations make all of us feel reticent. We may be as shy about an important sales meeting, a product review or a child's parent-teacher conference as we feel about walking into the grand ballroom of a major hotel and having a thousand people turn their heads in our direction. Different situations evoke different feelings and responses. But with training, practice and the refining of our communication skills, shyness can be reduced or eliminated altogether.

In fact, shyness is a highly adaptive trait, according to Dr. Bernardo J. Carducci, author of *Shyness: A Bold New Approach* and professor of psychology and director of Shyness Research Institute at Indiana University Southeast. "Unlike introverts, who feel energized being on their own, shy people want to be with others." This is more about shyness in chapter nine.

Leaders and other successful people have learned how to overcome their shyness. They don't wait; they reach out and extend themselves to people. In *The Magic of Thinking Big*, Dr. David J. Schwartz says, "It's a mark of real leadership to take the lead in getting to know people . . . It's always a big person who walks up to you and offers his/her hand and says hello."

For my book *What Do I Say Next?* I interviewed and surveyed one hundred people from around the country who I—or a friend—thought were *great* conversationalists. I coined the term to describe these *ConverSENsations*. Their responses to two of the survey questions were shocking. The first showed that 75 percent of these ConverSENsations still thought of themselves as shy. These were people who seemed to be gregarious, but they worked through their shyness for various reasons, including:

- It was their job.
- They wanted others to be comfortable with them.
- They wanted to be comfortable and successful.

The second revelation was also interesting. Of these one hundred ConverSENsations, not one denigrated small talk. They generally saw it as a way to get to know people and find common ground.

So there you go! People who are good at small talk may be shy, but they are also interested in people and don't wait to be introduced to them.

ROADBLOCK #4
"BETTER SAFE THAN SORRY"
(RISKING REJECTION)

You work up your nerve and approach a stranger. You smile, say hello and introduce yourself. The other person casts you a disinterested glance that screams, "WHO CARES?"

This hurts. None of us wants to be rebuffed or ignored to our face. Our egos are on the line when we extend ourselves to others, because there is always the possibility that they won't be interested in talking with us.

But Mother's Dire Warning that we're "better safe than sorry" puts a real damper on risk and risk is the name of the game when you are working a room.

I like to think of this risk as a challenge. If you don't have any skin in the game, you never win. If you don't take the risk and reach out to people, you never make new friends or new contacts. Most of us are strong enough to withstand a temporarily chipped ego. We risk our lives all the time on the freeway and some of the same people who participate in risky extreme sports (mountain climbing, kite surfing, sky diving, etc.) are those for whom a roomful of people is too much of a risk.

The truth is very few people will be openly hostile or rude when we approach them—if for no other reason than that it's bad business. The person who appears to be disinterested may not be judging or rejecting us, but may be distracted with another worry: Mother may have fallen and broken a hip and the family has to make a convalescent-care decision or the company may be merging and downsizing possibilities loom. Or that person who seems so distant may be one who is much shyer and less confident than you. And he or she could be your new client, employee or your business partner.

ROADBLOCK #5
"MANGLED AND MIXED MESSAGES
CONFUSE US"

We still run the risk that our warm, open, friendly manner will be misconstrued as an invitation to a liaison or a pass. Women are especially vulnerable to this misinterpretation. A touch on the arm that is intended as a simple gesture of understanding can be misconstrued as an indication of sexual interest or intrusion.

And then there is the person who "gets" no messages, mixed or otherwise, and misbehaves anyway. At a recent conference I experienced the inappropriate behavior of one of the attendees who, interestingly enough, was not one of the members with whom I had any conversation, let alone one that could be misconstrued. He came out of left field, draped his arm around me and asked if his "self-introduction [which he repeated] would work in a bar." Picture this. He was six feet two and weighed about 220 pounds (I'm four feet eleven). His arm was draped around me and he was leaning on me! I chose to honor professional boundaries. I told him, as I moved away, that I didn't have an answer because I didn't go to bars and that my book is a business book.

Although Mother's warning is a bit extreme, we have to go about our lives, be very clear with ourselves about our intent and exercise a bit of caution in this area. Over the past twenty-five years, sexual harassment has continued to be a topic and behavior of concern. It makes sense to be aware of the issues and still be open and friendly. But we need to keep our hands to ourselves and watch our language.

RISKING THE ROADBLOCKS

These five roadblocks are part of what stop us from mingling, circulating and working a room. In the next chapter, I'll discuss specific remedies for each roadblock.

But there is something else that can stop us from moving comfortably around a room, something subtler than the five particular roadblocks we've just discussed. It has to do with self-perception, self-confidence and self-esteem. People who register low in these areas can talk themselves out of meeting people and feeling at ease talking to them.

In the classic *Talking to Yourself,* Dr. Pamela Butler was one of the first to deal with the concept of self-talk, which has become more widely recognized in the last twenty-five years. These are the things we say to ourselves in our minds, sometimes without even being aware that we are saying them. Self-talk can be either positive or negative. Dr. Butler says that we can change negative self-talk to positive self-talk and that this transformation can have benefits in all areas of our lives.

Mary Orlin, of WineFashionista.com and a contributor to the *Huffington Post,* shared that she often hears the voice that says, "Who will want to talk to me? What will we have in common?" As executive producer of NBC's *In Wine Country,* Mary is used to being behind the camera. (We met when she was travel producer for CNN.) "I have to give myself a pep talk, remind myself why I'm attending the event and think, 'I'm going up to people, introduce myself and start a conversation.'"

Mary has built multiple networks in travel, the media, the wine industry and now her big passion—the perfume industry. "I went to New York to attend Sniffapalooza because it's an important event for perfumistas to meet perfumers,

Here is some negative self-talk that might come up when you think of working a room:

- I've always had trouble meeting people. It's just the way I am.

- I can't make—and don't like—small talk.

- I don't have anything important or interesting to say. I'll just embarrass myself. Better to keep quiet and be cool.

- Why would anyone want to listen to me? All these people have more important things to do.

Take a moment to write down any negative self-talk you may have and then rewrite those statements as positive ones. The above comments might be rewritten in this way:

- I'm having fun practicing meeting people and I'm getting better at it all the time. I'm enjoying mastering a new skill.

- Small talk is a great way to get to know new people.

- I want to extend myself to other people and know that the most valuable thing I have to offer is myself. If I'm open and honest, I'll feel good about myself and so will they.

- We're all busy, but everyone enjoys connecting with other people. I'm a valuable, likable person. Extending myself is a gift that others appreciate.

industry leaders and other fragrance lovers. There's a luncheon between sessions at a New York restaurant. By the time I arrived, the seats near my friend were taken, so I sat in an open seat not near anyone I knew.

"I took a very deep breath and introduced myself to the people around me. It was not comfortable. The fellow across the table was fascinated that I wrote my own wine blog. We talked during the lunch. Because he was also a wine enthusiast, he invited me to visit Sherry-Lehmann, a well-known wine shop down the street.

"We talked about joint venturing on an event pairing wines and perfumes. It's now in the planning stages. If I hadn't introduced myself to these 'strangers' and allowed my self-talk to inhibit me, I would not have had the conversation, been invited to Sherry-Lehmann or have a new venture in the works and I would not have made a great new friend."

It works! I attended a party and met a nice couple. The wife told me that before her marriage, her professional networking group used my book for their discussion forum. She committed to revising her self-talk and attended a party. She saw a nice man, whom she learned was single and struck up a conversation about their host, which led to other topics of interest. That nice man? You guessed it—now her husband! Yenta the Matchmaker takes her bow. I still wonder on what page I wrote that advice.

AN ELEVATING EXPERIENCE

One of the rooms that really confounds us is the elevator. Should we talk to the boss? The chairman of the board? A stranger? Have a pleasantry prepared and a smile for the times it appears to be appropriate. However, there are times when your courageous conversation may interrupt the boss lost in thought. Doing something outrageous, an antic or shtick, may backfire. What we want to be is outgoing, perceptive and pleasant. Being outrageous could make us appear foolish and that does not enhance our careers. Assess each situation on a case-by-case basis.

In business seminars you will hear people talk about preparing fifteen- or thirty-second elevator presentations and pitches. If you're looking for venture capital funding, a concise pitch is mandatory. When you attend a networking breakfast, where you are expected to give the thirty-second or even one-minute ad or introduction, have one prepared!

However, you must "read" that tiny moving room as you enter the elevator before you launch into a contrived, rehearsed, self-promotional pitch or introduction. Rather, try a spontaneous, off-the-cuff comment accompanied by a warm, friendly smile.

After giving an evening speech in New York, I returned to my hotel, where I realized that I was starving and that the famed Carnegie Deli was on the next block. Visions of corned beef began to dance in my head.

I stepped into the small elevator to find that I faced three strangers. It felt so odd because we were in such cramped quarters that I asked, "Are we all going to the Carnegie Deli for corned beef?" We all laughed and conversation started and moved from delis to food to the hotel, organically segueing as conversations do.

As we exchanged laughter and then cards, I glanced at each I was given. Aaron Rothman's card indicated that at that time he worked for Comedy Central, one of my favorite stations. I immediately confessed my devotion to *The Daily Show* and Jon Stewart. Aaron offered to get me tickets for the show when I returned to New York, which he did. What fun to watch Jon Stewart warm up his own audience first-hand! If I hadn't taken the risk to say something about the Carnegie Deli and corned beef to three strangers, I wouldn't have had that opportunity.

Allow yourself to make off-the-cuff, impromptu comments. You never know—it could contribute to a very elevating experience.

CHANGE/RISK/REWARD

Change of any kind is a risk and feels uncomfortable—even when the change is for the good. It's a little sad to leave the old house, even when we're moving into a much nicer one. We leave behind the old, familiar ways and step onto new ground. No matter how wonderful the change—getting married, expanding your business, moving to an exciting new city, switching careers—there is always a certain amount of discomfort.

For most of us, working a room is a change and challenge. *Extending ourselves to people is almost always worth the risk.* When we try and succeed, it makes us feel like a million dollars. But when we allow negative self-talk to prevail, we can become overwhelmed by the roadblocks and talk ourselves out of taking a risk.

If we don't seize the moment, it will be gone, along with the opportunity.

How many times have you seen someone who looked vaguely familiar but were afraid to go over because he might not be who you thought he was? I say, so what if I *am* wrong? The worst that can happen is that he says he's not that person and I've made a new acquaintance—possibly a new friend.

OLD LINES: NEW FRIENDS

Recently I sat in a hotel's outdoor restaurant overlooking the Capitol, enjoying dinner with Tracy Chiles McGhee, a Washington, DC, attorney. How we know each other began in 1981 when I attended my first meeting of a local professional association. One of the men there looked like a person I had met the previous June at a career-training conference. He was standing alone at the bar. Several questions raced through my mind when I saw him. What if he wasn't the man I had met, but just a look-alike? Would he think I was coming on to him? On the other hand, what if he really *was* the person I'd met and felt slighted because I didn't recognize him? Should I go up and say hello or wait for him to come to me?

Of all these possibilities, I decided that the worst result would be that he was the person I'd met and thought I was ignoring him. My value system, which includes more than a mild dose of guilt in my DNA, took over. I approached Farrell Chiles and mentioned the June conference. He was *not* the person I had met, but we had a pleasant conversation.

He had been following the original Careers series in the *San Francisco Examiner* and remembered several of my columns. It made me feel terrific. I was very glad that I'd overcome my reluctance to approach him. The benefits have been immeasurable. We play significant roles in each other's networks and we have been friends ever since—which is how and why I was having dinner with his daughter, Tracy, two decades later. Since that first encounter, Farrell, now an author and speaker, and I tell the story of our unique first meeting and always pay tribute to that great old overused line, "Don't I know you from someplace?"

CORRALLING YOUR COURAGE

No one can give you the courage to introduce yourself to a stranger. But some people are more supportive of this behavior than others. My advice: Stick with those who encourage you to take the initiative.

One way to muster up the courage to take a risk and talk to strangers is to ask yourself, "What's the worst that can happen?" Surprisingly enough, your worst fear is usually *not* a matter of life and death. And the odds are that disaster will not occur—and that even if it does, you will survive.

Taking the risk is almost always worth the discomfort. It's a cliché, but "nothing ventured, nothing gained" makes sense. With technology moving the world at warp speed, embracing real-time opportunities for face-to-face connections makes sense.

Pay no attention to people who restrain you from talking to strangers when you want to do so. After dinner at a local restaurant, I had asked a gentleman at the bar with his two friends to take a photo of my friend and me. He had a big smile on his face and was so nice and amenable. When my friend later said he thought it was Chris Robinson of the Black Crowes, I was ready to run back into the restaurant to apologize and hope he'd take a photo with me. My friend operates on a different system than I and said I shouldn't bother the musician on his night off. At the least, I owed Mr. Robinson an apology, but I erred twice. The second time was allowing myself to listen to the advice of someone who suggested what I ought not do—based on what he wouldn't have done. I still wish I had apologized to Chris Robinson (and had a photo taken with him).

I hope I get a chance to remedy that situation in the future.

CELEBRITY SIGHTINGS

One of the situations that confounds us occurs when we see well-known or famous people. It doesn't matter if they are local community celebrities or national ones. It happened to me when I was having my hair cut in San Anselmo. Angele Perez, my hairstylist, leaned in and whispered in my ear, "Don't look now, but three chairs over is Robin Williams." Of course, I almost snapped my neck to look immediately! There he was, in a quiet conversation with his stylist as she cut his hair strand by strand talking about his trip to France. What I did was immediately tweet a comment about the salon sighting to the effect that it was not the time nor the place for me to approach him. He was having a moment in his life in which he was entitled to his privacy.

At a public event, it's appropriate to acknowledge our appreciation of the work of a celebrity or community figure but not when they are with family as a parent, son or daughter or sibling. Again, we need to be respectful and assess each situation as it occurs.

PRACTICE MAKES PERFECT . . . CENTS

Practice talking to strangers in safe settings: in the supermarket, in line at the movie theater, out on the links. One Los Angeles real estate agent confided that she couldn't make cold calls if her life depended on it. Instead, she talks to strangers at the supermarket: about the weather, the parking, the price of organic vegetables, the movie she just saw. Her conversations have yielded her houses she has listed as well as those she has sold. Some people aren't open to her spontaneous comments, but others are. For those who can't make cold calls, a super resource is Joanne Black's book, *No More Cold Calling*, which is also the name of her business.

ROANE'S REMINDERS

Mother's Dire Warnings still lurk in our subconscious. These five roadblocks can prevent us from making the most of a party or a business event. When we know what they are, we can remedy them.

★ Don't talk to strangers.

★ Wait to be properly introduced (the Scarlett O'Hara Syndrome).

★ Good things come to those who wait (the Prom King/Queen Complex).

★ Better safe than sorry (risking rejection).

★ Untangle mangled and mixed messages.

Advisories:

★ Be aware of negative self-talk and change it into positive self-talk.

★ Extending yourself to people feels risky, but the benefits are well worth the discomfort.

★ Remember, what you think is the worst thing that could happen most often won't.

3

THE REMEDIES: REMOVING THE ROADBLOCKS

Now for the good news: For every roadblock, there is a remedy you can apply. Mother's Dire Warnings can stop us at any time unless we apply the appropriate remedy.

REMEDY 1
REDEFINE THE TERM *STRANGER*

From a very tender age we are told not to talk to strangers. The solution: Redefine the term. Obviously, we have to exercise some caution in today's society. Not every street corner in town is a suitable place to mix and mingle. And there will always be some people who, for some inexplicable reason, make you feel very uneasy. Go with your gut reaction; it's a great guide.

I promise you that talking to strangers yields great value, opportunities and experiences. If you are attending a meeting of professional colleagues, you're not really with strangers. If you go to a PTA meeting, you may not know anyone in the room, but you all have a common interest in quality education for your children. When you go to a new health club, a new church, a new synagogue, a new charitable or political organization, a professional trade show, you have a *common interest* with those people.

When you go to a party, you probably know the host or hostess. At a wedding, you and every other guest have some connection with the bride or groom. At a baseball game, notice how everyone talks to everyone else who is rooting for the same team.

Take five minutes to think about what you have in common with people at an event *before* you get there. This is the planning that helps you feel more comfortable and more prepared. You share interests, issues or government regulations with anyone who does the same kind of work you do, who is interested in your work or whose work interests you. People who sell respirators, perform surgery, repair medical equipment and process insurance claims have a common bond. They all deal with hospitals. If you volunteer for the local United Way, March of Dimes or public radio station, you have an interest in common with both the other volunteers and the people who volunteer for other organizations.

The best advice that I share with clients and audiences came from a gentleman farmer who called into an NPR radio station during an interview. He said that when he was growing up and went into town for dances, they had a saying: "The roof is the introduction." Think about it. It makes sense. You already have something in common with the other people in the same room, under the same roof: the purpose of the event, the traffic, the parking and the food, just to name a few.

People who have children have a common bond— whether they are construction engineers, musicians, used-car salesmen or company presidents. According to my brother

Ira, "My contemporaries who have parents in their late eighties seem to have the same concerns. It doesn't matter what religion, race or ethnicity, people who have senior parents have a common bond."

> *These common interests can be the basis for conversation.* Understanding what we have in common with others takes the edge off our reluctance to approach them as "strangers."

A PASSOVER PLOTZ

Being the stranger among people who all know each other is more than "not easy," it's difficult—whether there are thirty or three hundred people. Even for me. I was going to Atlanta two days before my speech. Both of these evenings were the first two nights of Passover, when I attend Seders. I was attending the second Seder at the home of a dear friend, author Connie Glaser and her family.

What to do for the very important (to me) first night? I finally asked my client for help. Who knew that Savannah College of Art and Design (SCAD), my client, was across the street from The Temple, a prominent Atlanta synagogue! The rabbi arranged for me to attend a Seder at the home of congregants Mia and Mitch Spolan. I didn't even think to do an Internet search on them because I was so happy to be included. Had I done that, I would have learned that Mitch was then a senior vice president at Yahoo! (now at LivingSocial).

Not being acquainted with the hosts, I knew I had to redefine *stranger* and focus on commonalities. I arrived with a hostess gift (from the SCAD store), introduced myself, thanked them and offered to help—just like mother taught me. What we had in common were the event (a Seder dinner is a traditional dinner and big undertaking), the Passover holiday and shared traditions and memories of prior Seders of our youth.

After the Seder, I helped clear the table and noticed Mia's open laptop in the kitchen. I saw her maiden name was the same as mine. Talk about a coincidence! "Mia, are we related? Do you have family in Chicago?" No, we weren't related, but we immediately exchanged emails and connected on Facebook. That observation changed and deepened our conversation. A wonderful friendship started because Mia and Mitch Spolan welcomed this stranger to their Seder table.

Business events can yield personal payoffs and social events can have professional ones. A friend of mine attended a formal fund-raiser for his son's school and, in talking with another father whom he knew from Little League, discovered that the other dad's work was executive search. A happy coincidence, since my friend was planning a career change!

A Rae of "Stranger" Sunshine

Rosemary and Rae Foxcroft, a mother and daughter from Durban, South Africa, were traveling in Israel. On a day tour, they noticed a young woman who was alone. Rae, a warm, friendly person, decided to talk to the lone traveler and learned she was a teacher from America on her first visit to Israel.

All they had in common was the tour they were on at that moment. But it was enough to start a conversation. Rae and Rosemary thoughtfully included their new American friend and they became the Three Musketeers of the tour.

What impact did their willingness to approach and include this "stranger" from the opposite side of the world have? Incalculable. How do I know? You guessed it; that lone traveler was yours truly. They were role models who have inspired me to talk to and be inclusive of strangers since then.

The conversation that Rae Foxcroft started has continued for decades and culminated in my recent visit to see them and the whole family in South Africa. How did a friendship grow and flourish before we had email? The old-fashioned way: We picked up pens and wrote letters and we called. After decades of that, email was created, but we still wrote letters and called. Both Rae and granddaughter Joanna have visited. And then Rosemary and I connected via Facebook and that has deepened our communication. Now Rae, at eighty-seven, has become a prolific texter, and we also stay in touch the "new-fashioned" way.

But nothing can surpass the bonds of friendship that were nurtured by our time together as we walked along the Golden Mile on the Indian Ocean in Durban, visited the Nelson Mandela Museum in Howick and the Durban Botanic Gardens and shared meals and laughter, all because of kind words to this stranger.

Recently, Rosemary and Hedley Adams took me on a safari to Kruger National Park, all planned and "self-catered" by Rosemary, the friend I met decades earlier. They pointed out a safari practice among strangers on the gravel roads: Drivers in passing cars and trucks will stop to tell each other where they spotted an animal. If it hadn't been for the kindness and good eyesight of these strangers, we would have missed seeing the majestic lion, two leopards and three cheetahs. I'm indebted to these thoughtful strangers.

Use common sense when approaching people you don't know, but loosen up the definition of *stranger* so that Mother's Dire Warnings don't keep you from establishing contacts and communication. Whether you're at a charity awards banquet, a spouse's company dinner dance or your child's soccer team play-offs, identifying the common ground helps you break the ice. You will feel more comfortable and that will be your reward for changing a behavior and breaking through a roadblock.

REMEDY 2
PRACTICE A SELF-INTRODUCTION

Scarlett O'Hara may have needed a "proper introduction," but we live in a different world. We may never meet another living soul if we wait for a fairy god person magically to appear and introduce us around. We'll just stand in the corner, watching the real Mingling Mavens who seem totally comfortable moving around the room, meeting strangers, conversing and circulating through the crowd to have a good time.

Every so often you actually get lucky and attend an event that has a greeting committee. The problem is that not everyone on the committee knows who you are, who you want to meet or how to introduce people properly—so they may not be able to give you much of an introduction, and they may not introduce you to the people you want to meet. Don't let yourself be limited by their lack of skills, their lack of information, their lack of contacts or all three.

The truth is that we are on our own. Before we leave for an event, we need to have a *planned* and *practiced* self-introduction that is clear, interesting and well delivered.

What you say about yourself will depend on the nature of the event. At a chamber of commerce reception, for example, you could say your name and what you do—with energy. But at a purely social function, your occupation may not be as important as how you know the host or hostess. Your self-introduction should be tailored to the event.

When I attended a wedding in Chicago, for instance, I didn't use my business introduction as a best-selling author and professional speaker—although I was prepared with business cards in my evening bag. Instead, I said warmly (and carefully, because it was a bit of a tongue twister), "I'm the first girlfriend of the father of the groom!" Trust me, conversations started!

A good self-introduction:

- Begins with your name
- Includes something about yourself that establishes what you have in common with the other people at the event
- Lasts about seven to nine seconds

But your self-introduction should give the essential information, and perhaps something interesting that may engage people in conversation. Patricia Fripp, professional speaker and executive speech coach, recommends that you give the benefit of what you do rather than your job title. "This allows the others to ask a question or make a comment that moves the conversation forward," she says. "And you have engaged them." They feel good because they started the exchange.

You can either begin with your name or end with it.

- "Hello. I'm Bo Brady. I help people 'take stock' of their lives." (Stockbroker)
- "Hello. I'm Judy Farley, former roommate of the bride."
- "Hello. I'm Shelly Berger. This is my first meeting, and I wish I knew a few people here."
- "Don't these desserts look decadent? Hi, I'm George Clooney, chocoholic."

Once you have planned how to introduce yourself, practice. You'll feel much more at ease with it and have a wonderfully effective remedy for the Scarlett O'Hara Syndrome.

REMEDY 3
MOVE FROM "GUEST" BEHAVIOR
TO "HOST" BEHAVIOR

Remember the Prom King/Queen Complex, and Mother's Dire Warnings? There is no need to get gray hair waiting for good things to come to you.

> *RoAne's Cliché Cure:*
> *Good things don't come to those who wait.*
> *Good things come to those who initiate!*

Whether it's talking to a stranger at an event, making an introductory phone call or posting your résumé on a job search website, actions create more actions and often positive interactions.

Dr. Adele Scheele, author of *Skills for Success*, says that people in a social or networking situation tend to behave either as "hosts" or as "guests." The hosts exhibit gracious manners—meeting people, starting conversations, introducing others and making sure that their needs are met. Hosts are concerned with the comfort of others and actively contribute to that comfort.

Guest behavior is just the opposite. Guests wait for someone to take their coats, offer them a drink and introduce them around the room. Often, the wait is interminable. If no one performs these services for them, guests move to the corners of the room and stand there until someone rescues them. They may be suffering the agonies of shyness, but other people interpret their behavior as standoffishness.

Dr. Scheele suggests that the key to success is moving from guest behavior to host behavior. This has been identified as the most valuable "tip" from my audiences and readers, whether they were CEOs, engineers, entrepreneurs or hedge-fund managers.

Michael Carroll, vice president of Alliance Management at UnitedHealth Group, personifies the good host. I've watched him in the hospitality suites at several different events. Michael graciously welcomes guests, their spouses and children. He keeps his eye on the room, pays attention to those on the periphery and approaches each person. He is not only a catalyst of conversation, but he also brings people into the group conversation and helps them connect with other guests.

One of the reasons I've been hired to speak and consult with companies is that they sponsor events, and their guests (who are often clients and potential clients) are not effectively welcomed or hosted by a selected or trained team. A banking executive who was once a guest in a luxury box at a Major League Baseball game told me he was made to feel unwelcomed!

Most of us were taught how to be a gracious host. We just need to transfer those skills to other events. In my experience—working with a bank hosting a preopening event at Disney Hall, a Fortune 20 company that hosts guests in hospitality suites at major sporting events and with law firms sponsoring events at professional conventions—I have found that some people have developed their hosting skills more than others, but all of us have some level of "innate host behavior" that we can build upon.

Guests and a "Host" of Behaviors

What exactly do hosts do? Basically, the host's job is to extend himself or herself to the guests and make them feel comfortable. If you are having company or throwing a party, you do the following:

- You plan a guest list and a menu.
- You clean out the hall closet.
- When the guests arrive, you welcome them at the door, take their coats and invite them in.

- You smile and greet them.
- You offer them food and get them something to drink.
- You provide conversation starters, perhaps an interesting story or piece of information about the guest. At the end of the evening, you retrieve their coats and thank each guest for coming.
- Most important, you introduce them around, mentioning the things they have in common with other people.

In myriad presentations, attendees have said the most memorable trait of a host is the person who introduces us to others—matchmakers of a sort.

The host responsibilities listed above are things that most of us have done. It may be time to dust off those social skills and start practicing them at public events. The only way to move from guest to host behavior at events is to *do it*. Try one behavior at a time. Shirley Davalos is a certified hypnotherapist who helps people who want to change the habits they no longer find beneficial in their lives, like smoking, overeating, compulsive worrying, as well as those behaviors they find daunting, like speaking in front of a group and meeting new people. She talks with all her clients about "Tiny Habits," Dr. B. J. Fogg's baby-steps process of changing, adding or deciding to drop a habit (for more information, see http://www.bjfogg.com/). Shirley says, "Tiny Habits are simple, easy and take *no* motivation to complete! You may be able to change your attitude about entering an event simply by seeing yourself as a host who makes connections and creates the opportunity for people to feel welcome at an event."

I may sound like a Pollyanna, but when we focus on someone else's comfort before our own, it takes the onus off us and we are more comfortable as well.

Volunteering to be on the greeting committee of your organization is one way to meet everyone who comes in the door; it's your *job* to meet people and make them feel comfortable. You have something specific to do, and it is just the thing you want to do anyway—meet and connect with people. You have an excuse to be as outgoing as you want to be. And the benefits are bountiful.

At a meeting of the Northern California National Speakers Association, I saw a woman who looked very nice and yet uncomfortable standing alone. I remembered how daunting my first meeting was, so I introduced myself and welcomed her. Lee Robert, singer, songwriter, storyteller and the Queen of Cowgirl Jazz, and I have been dear friends ever since. Our conversations over time have laid a foundation of a firm, heartfelt connection that has strengthened our loving friendship.

Caution: "Acting" as a host will not be successful if it is, indeed, an act. If you really don't care about the people you meet and greet, it will be very evident. "Acting warmly" is self-contradictory. Either you is or you isn't.

Moving from guest to host behavior is the perfect remedy for the Prom King/Queen Complex. It makes the meeting or the evening *your* event. You feel more comfortable extending yourself to others because it is your *job* and others are naturally drawn to you.

The good news is that you can act as the host even if you aren't the host or on the greeting committee.

THE GOOD GUEST GUIDELINES

Although we ought to act like a host at events, we need to be very mindful of what constitutes good guest behavior, whether the event is hosted by a company, an association, a client or a friend. There's no "one size fits all" set of rules. They vary for each event and/or sponsor because each has its own culture, practices, precepts and protocol.

What doesn't vary is that good guest behavior is based on respect, consideration and acknowledgment.

- The good guest attends every event, party or gathering with a self-introduction and some prepared conversation linked to the event or theme and focuses on making other guests comfortable.

- The good guest is an interested listener who makes introductions and exits conversations gracefully.

- The good guest notices guests who are standing alone, starts conversations and introduces them to other guests.

- The good guest pays attention and talks to spouses, significant others and children.

- The good guest doesn't judge other guests based on age, race, job title, religion, physical disability and so on.

- The good guest knows we are in the era of Facebook, YouTube and Vine and behaves accordingly.

- The good guest brings something (stories, news, anecdotes) to the Banquet of Banter (*What Do I Say Next?*).

- The good guest is mindful of the event, the purpose or theme, and is prepared to have a good time.

Some general, commonsense rules of thumb for guests at hosted events:

- Dress appropriately and for the occasion.
- If you're not sure, ask.
- Don't dress for a friend's wedding the way you'd dress for a barbecue unless, of course, the wedding reception is a barbecue.
- Arrive within fifteen minutes of the appointed hour unless it's an open house.
- Bring a host/hostess gift for a social event or dinner party. Avoid gifts that require work on the part of the host. (Forget flowers; they have to be cut and arranged in vases.)
- Greet the hosts, whether it's an office, business or purely social event.
- Introduce yourself to other guests. The hosts and/or greeting committee are busy and can't be relied on to do all the introducing of guests.
- Circulate. Excuse yourself graciously and move on. Or bring people with you to meet other guests and help expand their circles of conversation.
- Converse with as many guests as possible. To prepare conversation tidbits, read the newspaper or content curators like the *Daily Beast* and the *Week*. (More on conversation in chapter twelve).
- Avoid controversial topics with people you don't know (politics, religion and any offshoots of either area).
- Know the difference between a lively discussion and a heated one. A good guest avoids the latter.

Worth repeating: If someone makes a statement you find objectionable you can either say "That's another way to look at it" or "That's not the way I see it." Or the cagiest of them all: "Hmmm!" a noncommittal response. Or the universal placeholder: "Interesting."

- Offer to help out at small, hosted gatherings with set up, passing hors d'oeuvres, clearing the table—just like Mother taught us.

Side Benefit: If you help clear the dishes, you get to meet and talk to people you may not have met yet and have a pleasant exchange.

- Curb your enthusiastic use of naughty words.
- Don't curb your enthusiasm.
- Avoid overindulging in food or drink. The good guest behaves according to the "everything in moderation" mantra.
- Snack before you go. This one is from my mother who always gave my dad a small sandwich (by today's standards) before they left for an awards banquet, family celebration or wedding.
- Arrive in a celebratory mood if the event is a celebration, whether it's a wedding, graduation, retirement or anniversary.
- Remember, you already have something in common with the other guests.
- Keep your antennae up at all times. There is an abundance of good conversation topics to be found everywhere.

- Listen with ears, eyes and heart.
- Turn off cell phones unless you are waiting for—or performing—heart surgery.
- Corollary: Do *not* text at a party and *never* while talking to another person. Excuse yourself and go out of earshot if you receive an urgent call, make it brief and then return to the gathering.
- The good guest does not spend the evening on his or her smartphone. That is dumb and rude.
- *Thank* the host before leaving.
- The good guest goes everywhere to have a good time and to share that good time with other guests.
- The good guest sends a "thank you/lovely party" email followed by a handwritten note, stamped and delivered by the US mail.

Houseguests have additional thoughtful behaviors to embrace, and although it isn't the purview of this book, there is one warning I couldn't help but share: *Never* color your hair at someone else's home! I didn't make this up. Two friends had that happen, and one ended up with rust dye in her towels and the other had golden chestnut dye in hers. That's one way to get on the "Do Not Invite Ever Again" list.

REMEDY 4
EJECT THE "REJECTER" AND MOVE ON

Fear of rejection is sometimes a self-fulfilling prophecy. When we're afraid people will reject us, we often avoid them so that it doesn't happen. Even when it comes at us from out of the blue, it's hard to take. It's no fun to put ourselves out, extend a hand and a smile, introduce ourselves and get a withering stare in return. Remember, give people a second chance because their thoughts may be elsewhere.

The only advice I can offer in response to this kind of rude behavior is to *move on*. If there is no chemistry or interest, we should not waste our time trying to convince anyone to converse with us. There are other nice people in the room who would be open to meeting us.

The other person's behavior probably has nothing to do with you. The shy person may not know what to say. The preoccupied person is just that. The next time you see this person, all could be well and they will be engaging.

But, for now, excuse yourself and move on.

REMEDY 5
UNMIX THE MIXED MESSAGE

With so many men and women working together today, we have to watch our behavior so that those not intended as sexual will not be misinterpreted as such. However, there are several things you can do to prevent your words, gestures, clothing and manner from being perceived as improper.

The first is to ask yourself if your behavior really *is* being misinterpreted or whether you actually do have an interest in this person. If your interest really is romantic, face the truth yourself and proceed in a way that won't jeopardize your professional relationship.

We can't control others' thoughts and actions, but we can be aware of the signals we send—and of whether or not we want to send them. Let's not contribute to the confusion.

Unmixing the Signals We Send

- Be clear about your purpose. Stick to business.
- Stay away from double entendres and off-color jokes and comments.
- Be conscious of body language—yours and theirs.
- Don't dress for misperception. For women: Avoid low-cut, bare midriff blouses and postage-stamp-size short skirts and other suggestive clothing in any business situation.
- Lose your "touch," at least in situations where it is apt to be misinterpreted.
- Don't send inappropriate or off-color emails or texts. (A lesson learned by a number of politicians in the limelight.)

AVOID MISINTERPRETING SIGNALS

The other side of the coin is to be very cautious about acting on a "perceived" interest. It may be just friendly conversation and nothing more. Take your time and thoroughly assess the situation so that you preserve the business relationship or friendship.

Continue to be friendly and outgoing but not flirty. Be aware.

The differences between male and female behavior patterns, motivations and conversation are well documented in research. Dr. Deborah Tannen's body of work reflects these issues. In the last twenty-five years, popular literature has addressed these gender differences ad nauseam.

How to Work a Room is about communicating with many people of myriad differences while building rapport, trust and friendships. Each of these remedies represents a change in behavior, but you will reap the benefits a hundredfold. We'll talk about some of those benefits in the next chapter.

ROANE'S REMINDERS

The good news about the five roadblocks to working a room is that there is a remedy for each one. With a little practice, a little risk-taking and some old-fashioned social graces, Mother's Dire Warnings will never again stop you from moving through a room with ease and grace. The added benefits are making good contacts and, most important, having a *great* time!

ROADBLOCK	REMEDY
Don't talk to strangers.	Redefine the term *stranger*.
Wait to be properly introduced (the Scarlett O'Hara syndrome).	Practice a seven- to nine-second self-introduction tied to the event.
Good things come to those who wait (the Prom King/ Queen Complex).	Move from "guest" behavior to "host" behavior.
Better safe than sorry (risking rejection).	Eject the rejector and move on, graciously.
Mangled and mixed messages (the intercepted pass).	Unmix the mixed messages. Watch words, dress, and body language.

BENEFITS:
THE BONUSES
OF BEING THERE

Have you ever been invited to a dinner, reception or meeting that you couldn't avoid but that didn't sound very exciting? You write down the event in your calendar, drag yourself there, put in your time and come home feeling as if you've wasted three hours.

With a little planning, that need never happen again. An event doesn't exist that can't be made productive or at least fun, if we give it a little thought before we go. It doesn't take much time or effort to turn those "chore" events into "choices" when we approach them as adventures into the unknown, our private Discovery Channel.

TURNING CHORES INTO CHOICES

To work a room effectively, we need to know why we are doing it. If there is nothing in it for us or for other people, if there is no goal, reason or purpose, many people wonder, why bother? The reason may be as simple as your boss invited you or your client is sponsoring a fund-raiser for the local Leukemia & Lymphoma Society or March of Dimes or your nephew is graduating or the local team is having a pancake breakfast.

There are two questions to ask yourself:

1. How will it look (to the boss, your nephew or the team's coach) if you were to choose not to attend?
2. How will you feel the next day if you decide not to attend?

This is long-term or big-picture, thinking. In some cases, choosing *not* to attend is the right choice. More often than not, once we are at the event and see people we know and meet some new colleagues, neighbors or clients, we are glad we said yes.

If you have decided to attend, you should know *why*. The benefits will vary from room to room, depending on the nature of the event, but you should have a focus for attending. Why have you chosen to spend your time there instead of surfing the Net to do research, watching *South Park*, practicing your golf swing, playing Words with Friends, helping the kids with their homework, going for a run or visiting your relatives?

Only one person can answer these questions: *you*.

PLANNING PAYOFFS

Before you attend an event, ask yourself what you would like to accomplish—both on a professional level and on a personal level.

It's important to identify these benefits *before* the event.

Remember that "business" events can have personal benefits as well and that purely "social" events can do wonders for your business. Think about what you want as rewards or compensation. I use the term *compensation* because deriving a benefit is a payment—or payoff—for expending the energy and investing the time. And *work* is defined as the exertion of energy!

In my presentations and consulting, I give people time to jot down what they feel are the most important personal and professional benefits of working a room. These are the points they make most often:

Professional Payoffs

1. Perceived as powerful and in control
2. Established communication/connections/rapport
3. Increased resource base/potential clients
4. Gained insight; learned new information
5. Increased business opportunities
6. Enhanced career options
7. Created face-to-face visibility
8. Had fun!

Yes, fun is a professional benefit. *In fact, the best business minglers often have the most fun,* because they have learned the joys of working a room and are a joy to talk to in any room. What's not to like about getting new business, learning about a new restaurant or software, feeling good about yourself and enjoying other people?

Personal Payoffs

1. Comfort
2. Self-confidence
3. New contacts/friends
4. Newly acquired knowledge
5. New experience
6. Created face-to-face visibility
7. Fun!

THE FUN FACTOR

It's no accident that *fun* appears on both the personal and professional payoff lists. In these 24/7/365 times, who would want to spend time commuting, parking, circulating and chatting—just to have a lousy time?

Identifying the potential benefits of a meeting, party, convention or any other event is one of the best ways to motivate, tantalize or prod ourselves into making the most of each event. It builds purpose and confidence, and that leads to even more confidence.

And we're not just there to "get ours." It works both ways. *Those who attend events to push forward their own agendas are obvious and, more often than not, annoying.* Each of us has something to offer other people, and we should focus on our potential contributions as well. We can benefit the other attendees by offering information, advice, an ear, leads, ideas and whatever else seems appropriate or useful to them.

However, if, like many people who think they are networking, you "give" for the sake of "getting back," you missed the point.

The fun comes in the form of doing a kindness. According to psychologist Dr. Sonja Lyubomirsky's *Myths of Happiness*, "Doing good deeds is actually the direct cause of an increase of well-being." That is a great benefit. Starting a conversation with the person standing alone is an act of kindness.

BELIEVING IN THE BENEFITS

It's important to believe in the benefits, to make them real and vital, so that they give us energy and spur us on. As with everything else about working a room, identifying the benefits gets easier with practice. I often ask people to think about the last event that they attended. I then ask them to identify, with twenty/twenty hindsight, the benefits to them if they had worked the room effectively. Think of an event you attended recently and try it yourself.

The important question to ask yourself is, "What would I have done differently?" Jot down your thoughts. When we take time to think, assess and involve our muscles, hand-eye coordination and brain, we tend to remember what we write. That helps us the next time we go to an event.

At the end of my presentations I ask attendees to jot down what they learned and will do differently as a result of attending my program. Putting pen to paper provides a visual plan. Try it. What works for grocery lists works for our goals lists as well. In other words, "The hand remembers!"

The personal benefits can be at least as important as the professional. Even if you never discuss business, the people you meet while working a room can become lasting friends who enrich your life.

Benefits

Event _____

Sponsor _____

Purpose _____

Location _____

Attendees _____

Reason for Your Participation _____

_____

Potential Professional Benefits:

1.

2.

3.

4.

5.

Potential Personal Benefits:

1.

2.

3.

4.

5.

The *San Francisco Business Times* cosponsored a women entrepreneur's award evening. While I met several business contacts by hanging out at the dessert table, the evening was a success for another reason. Three times that night I bumped into the same woman. The third time we laughed, and Allison Fortini-Crawford, a San Francisco– and Marin-based real estate agent said, "Geez, third time's a charm. It must be that we are supposed to be friends!" She and I have been friends ever since! Will we do business with each other? As my grandmother always said, "You never know!" But I spend time and holidays with Allison and Brent and am now Auntie Susan to Liam and Lauren.

You may have similar stories of chance meetings and your network of colleagues and friends. If you stop to think about it, many of them probably came from working a room.

ACCUMULATING CONTACTS: THE MILLIONAIRE'S ROLODEX

Being able to work a room effectively has one benefit that is extraordinary and unique: You can build an enormous network. You're on your way to having something in common with millionaires.

Before he wrote *The Millionaire Next Door*, Thomas Stanley studied two thousand millionaires. (This occurred when having a million dollars was a lot of money. I'm kidding, it's still a lot of money.) He found that the most important trait they had in common was a huge Rolodex!® Before you roll your eyes, thinking that Rolodexes are no longer used, think again. Several years ago the *Wall Street Journal* had a feature article stating that some CEOs still have them at the tip of their fingers. Why? So they can pick up the

phone to call directly. In fact, April 23, 2013, a post by Gen
Y author Dan Schawbel on *Businessweek*'s management blog
featured a Rolodex and the advice "Your Rolodex is more
important than your knowledge base."

Today your contacts can be online, imported into VIP-
orbit, a mobile contact management program designed by
Mike Muhney (who also cocreated the contact management
database program ACT!). But the fact remains, the list of
names we have in our Rolodex (or database) are those with
whom we have had *personal* contact! No more *cold* calls or
blind, mass emails.

Stanley also says that these millionaires have an "un-
canny ability to distinguish quality contacts." They don't
just collect business cards; they can identify the people who
are able and *willing* to help them, the people with whom
they can share support, information and, possibly, business.
A huge Rolodex is useless unless, like the millionaires Stanley studied, we see it as a resource pool of people, ideas and
advice.

TAKING UP A (CARD) COLLECTION

Founder of BNI, Dr. Ivan Misner, author of *Networking Like
a Pro*, produced a series of podcasts on networking faux pas
based on the errors people commit in the name of networking.

At a business mixer he met a woman, who upon hearing
that he founded BNI, told him that she was quite good at
networking. Intrigued, Dr. Misner asked, "Really . . . what's
your secret?"

She told him that she attends business events with a
friend. They draw an imaginary line in the middle of the

room and see who collects the most cards. "The loser then has to treat for lunch," she told him. Dr. Misner then asked her what she does with the cards. "We add them to a distribution list and send an email out to the list that let them know about my services. They're all prospects, right?"

Wrong. "That's not networking, that's direct sales. Networking is more about fishing than hunting and it's about building relationships," said Misner.

Working a room is one sure way to expand your contacts and build relationships. According to Stanley, these millionaires showed the same guts and courage in talking to people at events as they did in conducting their businesses.

TWO-WAY STREETS

Remember: We sometimes forget that each of us has something to offer. We can benefit the other attendees by offering information, advice, an ear, leads, ideas and so on.

I may not be able to answer a technical or a tax problem, but I can offer ideas on the world of publishing, the world of speaking and promotion. And although nobody ever asks me for a recipe, I can suggest a great restaurant. If we make a list of what we know, do, like and have some experience in, we will know what we bring to the banquet and will feel more confident in our ability to contribute.

ROANE'S REMINDERS

★ Learn to approach any event with purpose, energy and enthusiasm.

★ Identify the potential benefits *before you go*. These benefits can be personal or professional or both.

★ Having fun and meeting new friends can be just as valuable as striking deals. (Striking deals can lead to new friends and be a lot of fun!)

★ Being a resource to others, not just focused on your agenda, is preferable.

★ We all have something to contribute. If we list our preferences, interests and experience, we know what we can offer others!

★ As far as results, in the long run . . . "You never know!"

THE DYNAMIC DUO: CHARM AND CHUTZPAH

Working a room successfully depends on seeing the roadblocks, responding with the appropriate remedies and identifying the potential benefits. But in the end, what gets us through the night is the dynamic duo of *charm* and *chutzpah*.

I can hear it now: "Charm and chutzpah in the same breath? They're a contradiction in terms—and behaviors." Not true!

CHUTZPAH: THE COURAGE TO CONVERSE

When I first wrote about chutzpah, I had to define it (according to *Joys of Yiddish*) and quote a psychologist who used the term. Talk about reaching a tipping point! Now chutzpah has become part of the vernacular. The old, negative connotation was that of gall or nerve. I use the term to mean "boldness" or "courage to take risks."

And walking into a room of strangers is a real risk—our egos are on the line. I know there are several extreme athletes and adventurers who would rather be rappelling, kite surfing or skydiving than risk the possible rejection a room can proffer.

That's why a dose of chutzpah is perfectly paired with a dollop of charm.

CHARM: THE SECRET INGREDIENT

Here is what *Webster's* has to say about charm:
Verb: to captivate, delight, attract, please
Noun: a power to gain affection

These definitions make most people shout, "Where do I sign up?"

In "charm" school I was taught how to dress, walk, apply makeup, smile, behave and be well mannered. These things are important, but charm includes something more, an elusive quality that draws us to people and makes us believe they care about us. When we charm people, they become comfortable and at ease.

THE CHARMERS

- Katie Couric
- George Clooney
- Robin Roberts
- Tom Hanks
- Dr. Shaquille O'Neal (whom I follow on Twitter)

Who Do You Find Charming? Why?
1. _____
2. _____
3. _____
4. _____
5. _____
What do they do that makes you think so?

Once we identify charming behaviors, we can emulate them. Pick one. Practice it. Then pick another. Take the baby steps suggested by Dr. B. J. Fogg. Even more helpful is to make a list of those lacking in charm and what they do that makes them so. Then avoid those misbehaviors like the plague in any room.

Charm is a combination of warmth, good nature, positive attitude, a good sense of humor, charisma, spirit, energy and an interest in others. My friend Diane Parente, a founder of the Leadership Style Center, has it. She is a consultant and speaker who helps clients define their image, and she has a wonderful sense of humor and laughter. People *want* to be around her. Charm is the ability to convey a type of caring that comes from the heart and soul—and she has it.

An advice columnist once defined *class* as the "ability to

make people of all walks of life feel comfortable." To me, that definition also applies to charm.

Several years ago, the Mill Valley Film Festival honored actress Felicity Huffman, then a star on the television hit show *Desperate Housewives.* At the reception in her honor, Felicity greeted each of us with great warmth and made us feel as if she had waited all day to meet us. When she saw people who were looking unsure if they should approach her, she went over and introduced herself. We, too, should treat people as if we "waited all day to meet them."

NAME TAG TITLE WAVE

Ignoring someone because the title on her name tag doesn't impress us is a cardinal sin. During a question-and-answer session after one of my presentations, an executive asked how, if she could only "invest time with decision makers, could she easily identify them?" This is a question sales-people often ask after being trained in the old-school of selling mentioned in Daniel Pink's book, *To Sell Is Human.* I looked at this busy executive, paused and said, "I think there is a commandment against thinking like that. If not, there should be!" So I wrote it in *The Secrets of Savvy Networking.* How uncharming of her! And foolish. It ignores those who influence "decision makers"—and the fact that they could be the decision maker next year. You never know!

ONE AND ONE IS THREE

When chutzpah and charm come together, it's synergistic. The whole is greater than the sum of its parts. You don't just have chutzpah and charm, you have *magic*!

You care about people, and you have the courage to walk up to them and let them know it. That's a powerful combination, and one that enriches everyone concerned. But there has to be a balance between the two.

The dynamic duo of chutzpah and charm isn't a "to do" or a technique. It is something that we all have and that we've developed to a greater or lesser extent. Now is the time to let it out and spread it around.

There is no more effective way to work a room than to . . . *be nice* in a room! People remember the people who make them feel special, comfortable and conversant and whose demeanors make them smile. You'll never have to bring, do or wear attention-getting gimmicks at any business or social event again! Nice is good—and memorable. Like Tom Hanks, that should be our goal.

Some of the new rooms we are now working are virtual ones and have virtually expanded over the last decade. Being a savvy online mixer and mingler is vitally important.

ROANE'S REMINDERS

★ Chutzpah and charm are the dynamic duo at the heart of working a room successfully. We all have the potential for these qualities.

★ Practice makes them stronger. They let us work a room with style and grace—and, ultimately, are what attract people to us.

★ Identify who is charming and why. What do they do and say? Don't do and don't say?

★ Emulate them.

6

HOW TO WORK THE VIRTUAL ROOM

The volume of traffic in the virtual room continues to increase exponentially. We now have several generations of people whose virtual socializing, conversing and social networking has exceeded the real time they spend on each of those activities. With that, they've lost a lot of the personal touch.

Yet the online world not only gives us new types of rooms to work, we also get thousands of possible rooms in which to communicate about anything, anywhere, anytime.

The room has morphed into a mansion where myriad activities take place. The virtual room is now a shopping mall, a banking center, a rotisserie league in fantasy baseball land, a medical library, a classroom, a poker table, a convention, a fashion runway, a business forum, a matchmaking service, a photography studio and the therapist's couch. We get information and advice on any topic, any hour of the day or night.

There are stories of people finding long-lost relatives, friends, even romance (one of my friends married an online writers' group chat room friend!); of seniors whose frailties keep them homebound but who have now found a new way of socializing; of those who stay in touch with a grandchild or find a community online; of those suffering from similar symptoms or those who find an online support group or those who locate the perfect previously owned car. There are apps that help you find where you parked your own car! And they are so helpful. These new rooms can and do create a community—a virtual one without the boundaries of walls or time. Yet there are still boundaries of better behavior to observe.

A word of caution worth repeating: Employers conduct online searches as part of potential employees' background checks. Postings on Facebook, videos on YouTube, photos and videos on Instagram and even your own personal website are open to scrutiny. Checking Twitter feeds is part of the process. Search yourself with Google, Bing and Yahoo! to see what comes up. Be savvy about sending emails: They can be shared. If you're uncomfortable with the photos or verbiage, make a change. Scrub your Facebook page. You can find out how at CBSNews.com. Doing so could determine whether you're hired for a great job or promoted to the next one.

THE MYSTIQUE

Anonymity is a feature of the online world, where people hide behind a handle; a pseudonym. That runs counter to the concept of heartfelt conversation. It's difficult enough that we hear no tone or inflections, that we see no facial expressions, but we now have no idea with whom we are really chatting. But once we discover other Trekkies, classical-jazz fans, fellow meeting planners, mountain bikers, grandparents concerned about education, salespeople interested in best practices, moms of twins, people who are caring for elderly parents, the shared support and information is nirvana.

To work a cyber room, we must be both technically and socially adept to manage our professional and personal success.

ONLINE ALL THE TIME

There are several methods of conversing online: forums, instant messaging, webinars and email. While email is the "least sexy" usage, according to the *Wall Street Journal's* Walter Mossberg, it is the "most compelling, addictive and practical activity available online."

We are using online tools to converse face-to-face, like Skype or Apple's FaceTime. Parents who travel for business can help check homework, companies can hold visual conference calls and friends can see as well as hear each other. From babies to bubbas to boomers and bubbies, everybody's doin' it! We are connecting in cyberspace in astronomical numbers in myriad ways. It leaves a lot of opportunity for errors in judgment and behavior.

Virtual communication has a history. Four decades ago it was mostly used by the military, the government and academia. Now it is de rigueur. Most businesses and companies understand that customer service includes cyber communication options.

LIVE CHATS

Online banking has adopted "live" chats as a way to "internetwork" with customers. Banks and companies are also using live chats to sell their products and services. I saw this when I was online buying travel insurance for my trip to South Africa. All I had to do was click on an icon.

Call me old-fashioned, but that is a circuitous route to get to a live phone conversation, one that could have begun by just picking up the phone in the first place.

While some days I feel like sending a text or even a hand-written note (by this, I mean a note written by hand, on paper, not a computer-generated facsimile) or picking up the phone to hear the person's voice (these days, that is mostly to leave a message), the option of writing an email at 11:30 p.m. is great. Whether it's to my best friend in Mobile or my cousin in Chicago or my agent in Los Angeles, in the morning (when I am still asleep), they log on, and presto! There I am . . . or at least my message is. Managing our actions and behaviors in the virtual room is as important as how we behave in the "real" rooms we visit.

Research from Stanford University found that time spent on the Internet is causing Americans to "spend less time with friends and family," according to Norman Nie, a political scientist. Yet we still have to know *how* to work virtual rooms as well as how often.

INSTANT MESSAGE MADNESS

When we "work" the virtual room or are logged on, we can learn if our buddies are online, too. We can say hello and have an instant message sidebar chat that resembles a real conversation (except there is nothing visual or auditory to act as clues).

However, sometimes the instant message is an interference and brings another line of behaviors into question. Susan Sikora, a San Francisco talk-show host, wondered, "What if I am working on a project? Or have a deadline? Do I answer or ignore? How do I 'bow out' graciously if it's an inconvenient time for me to chat? And the 'handle'—what if I don't recognize the cleverly masked name?"

Let common sense be the guide. If you have the time for an instant conversation, you'll know. If you want to respond and then go back to work, say so. "So glad to hear from you. Working on a deadline. Hope all is well. Take care (or Good-bye)." Or do what many people do—just ignore the instant message. That may be rude to some, but others find that being engaged in a side conversation while online is annoying and disruptive.

MULTITALENTED MULTITASKERS

The generation that grew up with computers, now called Digital Natives—the term coined by Marc Prensky in his book by that title—are technically adept and seem to thrive on multitasking. The father of a teenager told me that he marvels at how his son can instant-message a couple of friends simultaneously while doing his homework. I asked Dad if his son does it all well. "Yes . . . except for the homework!"

Make no mistake, the younger generation in the workforce is used to speed. Instant messaging and texting provide it, and in many cases, that's their preferred mode of communication.

Caution: The research on multitasking indicates that, yes, we can do several things at once. But, unfortunately, none will be done very well.

DISTRACTION MAKES US DUMBER

The *New York Times* recently reported on research at Carnegie Mellon University's Human-Computer Interaction Institute that indicates that "the distraction of an interruption (cell call, instant message, text) made test participants 20 percent dumber."

Bob Sullivan and Hugh Thompson, authors of the book *The Plateau Effect: Getting from Stuck to Success*, propose that "multi-tasking is a misnomer, and what we're really doing is 'rapid toggling between tasks.'" And that toggling requires switch time, which can be costly.

THE INSTANT MESSAGE MEETING

What was once used for social chats has become a communication option for businesses. In the global workplace, people around the world can all attend the online virtual meeting and instant-message one another as they deal with company business. Many companies use in-house instant messaging clients, such as Yammer, to support communication and collaboration.

Instant messaging allows for a "conversational" exchange that includes brainstorming, meeting, strategic planning and scheduling appointments.

#HASHTAG 4U

Hash now has its own tag! Today meetings, campaigns, product launches and people have a hashtag, and conferences have Twitter hashtag feeds that are part of the Twitterverse and provide a source of information. I even read about a wedding in Napa Valley of two very tech-savvy people that had its own hashtag.

BREVITY? THE SOUL OF WIT OR WITLESS!

I have read a number of lists of email dos and don'ts in the last decade since I wrote one that was published in 1993 in *The Secrets of Savvy Networking.* Flipping through my own book and finding this list totally surprised and pleased me. I had forgotten that I had written about it!

So many lists admonish emailers to "keep it brief." That can be good advice, *some of the time.* If, by brief, we are thinking telegram-like staccato word use, as if we paid by the letter, let's rethink that.

Including a pleasantry, a greeting, an appropriate "please" or "thank you" or a personable PS adds the high touch to our high-tech touching base.

Warning: When we count our words, we may be discounting our message. Strike a balance between long and terse. As a former English major and teacher, I would summarize by saying that *we can have short sentences, just not sound "short" in our sentences. We want them to be declarative (statements) not imperative (orders).*

Example:

A. "Joe, it would help if you could get us the figures by today. Thanks."

B. "Get us the figures by today."

To which one would you be inclined to respond? If you read these samples and think B is correct because it's to the point and doesn't waste words and time, please visit my website (www.susanroane.com) and take my "Schmooze Quotient Quiz."

THE LEVEL PLAYING FIELD

One of the advantages and a great beauty of virtual communication is that our physical attributes have no bearing on what we "say" and no effect on others. I can remember an email exchange with someone who had read *What Do I Say Next?*, where I reveled in the equality of the virtual room. She was hearing-impaired and shared with me just how email chat rooms and online groups and their variations have allowed her to be more effective, successful and confident. And she was not judged or embarrassed by the comment, joke or directive she could not fully and accurately hear! For me, as someone who taught hearing-impaired students mainstreamed in our school and learned some sign language, that email touched my heart.

EMAILSTROM

Some of us work the virtual room all the time! I first read about Dr. Kimberly Young's online addiction research in 1995, and now almost two decades later, I am convinced that over 90 percent of the wired and wireless would answer yes to most of her questions.

Signs You May Be Hooked: A Quick Quiz

- Do you compulsively check your email, Facebook page, Twitter feed and Instagram (ten to twenty times a day)?

- Do you lose track of time when you are online?

- Are you experiencing a problem in personal relations that can be blamed on the time you spend online?

- Have you gained weight or suffered eye, neck, thumb or back strain?

If you answered yes to any of these questions, log off— go to a movie, take a walk, meet a friend for latte or read a book, either on paper or on an e-reader. In other words, stop and smell the roses. Now that's a thought . . .

Technology is supposed to support communication, not supplant it.

FAMILY INTER(NET)VENTION

Although it's hard to believe that people are still doing this, I was shocked when a colleague complained bitterly about a cousin who had used cyberspace for her own (mis)conception of the informal "Cousins Club," comprising her extended family that stays in touch online. "She sends ten 'FWD' emails, a week of jokes, poignant poetry (to her) and other drivel. There is never a 'Hello. How are you?' just her forwarded emails with the six screens of recipients. If she was so adept at using her computer, she could at least cut and paste and send just the message, with a one-sentence note. If there were techno-torture chambers, we'd put her in one!" My friend said that it did bring the cousins closer together and increased communication about how to stop this very "FWD" person.

Rule of thumb: Send the email to yourself and place the recipients in the "bcc" (blind carbon copy) section.

DELETE-ISM

We can delete or use our spam filters or we can say something to the sender. I had to take the direct approach with a friend/colleague and talked to her in a real-time conversation so that my tone, my pacing, my sincerity and my caring could be heard: "I don't read forwarded online jokes, especially if there is more than one screen of names, but I enjoy hearing from you and how you are and am so glad you stay in touch."

We are still friends, and do business by phone, in person and online. If I had written the same words and sent them in an email or text, she could have read a different tone into my comments.

CYBER-SAVVY

The cyber room is unstructured, and yet, as there has always been throughout history, there is a codification of the laws. While Moses did not bring the cyber laws down from the Mount Sinai of Messaging ("Take two tablets and text me in the morning"), they rule!

Sending and receiving emails on company time can be used against us. Period. End of story. The venerable *New York Times* fired employees for forwarding an inappropriate email. Before we hit the send button, we need to reread our emails to be sure they *should* be sent and that we are sending them only to those intended to read them.

We need to be as savvy about tweets and posts and photos on Instagram. Careers have been crushed, friendships have faltered and relationships have been ruined because of online communication. A good rule of thumb: Do not send any email, tweet or post you wouldn't want read in court, in front of your grandmother, your boss, your clients or your significant other.

Companies now have sophisticated software programs to monitor employee use and abuse of company time for employees' computer use. Be very cautious about the types of sites you visit on company time.

Be aware: There are programs that can reconstruct emails, keystroke by keystroke. So can most IT security people and hackers.

VIRTUAL NETWORKS

Several entrepreneurs had the idea of combining the concept of networking with the power of the Internet. According to Konstantin Guericke, one of the cofounders of online
business network behemoth LinkedIn, which has over 225
million members worldwide at this writing, helps members
locate information, leads and jobs among the people their
contacts know, "When you find that one of your former coworkers knows someone you want to meet, you can request
an introduction through LinkedIn to maximize the chance
the person is going to respond, based on the reference from
your mutual connection." As a member, I have found this to
be quite true. Recruiters search LinkedIn as a source for candidates. The importance and impact of LinkedIn in business
are without parallel.

THE UNBEARABLE "LITE"NESS
OF BEING SELF-ABSORBED

When Seth Godin wrote *Permission Marketing*, it all made
sense. Before he did, people with (cyber) sense (or simply
those with common sense) knew not to send stuff without
permission.

An author who wanted my feedback on his book really
broke these rules on several counts when he emailed me a
119-page document (281 kilobytes)! I was appalled because
he never asked me:

- If I were interested in seeing it
- If I had time to sit in front of a screen to read, assess and
  edit it

- If I would mind using my computer time and paper printing it
- If this fell under the guidelines for Pick My Brain Consulting, where I coach would-be authors and Mingling Mavens.

Instead, he expected I would do this for him in my "spare" time—when I am not writing books, giving presentations, running my business, working out, going to the movies, hanging out with my friends and family, going to Stanford football games to cheer on grandsons Shayne and Patrick Skov or doing the ironing! (Notice what is last on my list.)

Getting permission is important and can enhance business success. Not everyone who gives you a business card at an event wants to receive weekly emailed missives, sales pitches or recirculated jokes. How to get permission to stay in touch? Ask.

CAN WE *NOT* TALK?

There is a difference between those who prefer not talking to others and those who don't prefer it. There are times when it's appropriate and expedient to send the email or text that confirms the meeting location or time. If it's important, we just have to be sure the email is received.

Carl La Mell, president and CEO of Clearbrook, a nonprofit organization that assists people with disabilities in the Chicago suburbs, called an urgent meeting of his senior staff via email. By coincidence, one of his directors called him about another issue. "We talked briefly and I closed with 'I'll see you later today at the meeting.' She sounded confused and asked me what I was talking about. She never received the email. Now we make sure there are voice mail confirmations as well."

The social or personal email can also get lost in cyberspace. Before we get upset at the lack of response, resend it. Or at least ask if the email arrived. Better yet, when emailing an important document, call or text to let the person know it's on its way. Never assume, always confirm.

YOU'RE SUCH AN E-CARD—A CYBER "HALLMARK OF DISTINCTION"

While Facebook gives us the option to send birthday wishes to our friends and even reminds us of their birthdays, some people use greeting-card sites. They are fast, convenient, acknowledging—or are they? What they are is free. But not free from some issues and annoyances.

They often come with pop-up ads. And, according to Letitia Baldrige, etiquette expert, if the recipient must stop work to download the greeting, "It's unpardonable." If I have to click on a link, a greeting, a dancing bear . . . you get the drift. It's a way for the person who forgot—until that day—to show they were thinking of us. For those living in other parts of the world, it is the perfect option to stay in touch on important occasions without the global postal issues.

THE E-NOTE OR TEXT OF THANKS

The perils of losing the personal touch are huge. It is perfectly sensible to dash off a thank-you email for a speedy acknowledgment. Some people now send a thank-you text, *which is then followed by the formal thank-you note.* Are you cringing at the thought, because you are too busy to pick up a pen? Miss Manners (and I) have said that if we have the time to unwrap, deposit, ingest, enjoy, wear and utilize "gifts," we certainly have the time to show our appreciation, manners and character by picking up a pen and writing a sentence or two. But if we are so busy that we cannot send a note, in the case of gifts, then "send them back *unopened.*"

The Hard Truth: People whose generosity is not acknowledged may not be motivated to send the next gift.

If you forget a birthday until it's too late to mail a card, just send an easy-to-open, no-extra-work email of good wishes. Real birthday, Valentine's Day and holiday cards that I receive, read and display on my parson's table are now even more special. When it was time to change from Hanukkah to the next occasion, I reread my cards and saved them. Then up went the birthday cards. When it was time to display Christmas cards, I reread the lovely thoughts, fun greetings and birthday wishes of my friends, who "cared enough to send the very best." I, for one, will continue to buy, save and send real-time cards. I add a personal message in my own handwriting. It's a touch that cannot be replaced by cyber sentiments.

THE GIFT OF TIME, LEADS, INFORMATION, SUPPORT

The savvy networker also acknowledges the gifts we receive that are not wrapped and beribboned. We may shoot a quick email, LinkedIn or Facebook message to thank a colleague for a lead or a bit of helpful information. But then a note (handwritten, of course) is to follow. If the lead we get turns into a major client or a new job, the acknowledgment card should accompany a gift of thanks. The growth of the gift card business has skyrocketed because it's the perfect way to say thank you without having to buy wrapping paper and people get to buy what they want. Our behaviors by distinguish ourselves from the crowd and make us memorable. Let it be for the right reasons.

BREAKING UP IS HARD TO DO . . . IN PERSON

For the person who has bad news to deliver, be it a downsizing, the loss of a loved one, a catastrophe or a breakup, take heed. *Do not fire, quit or dump via email, text message or Facebook.*

A friend's daughter found out her beau had flown the coop when she checked his Facebook page and saw he had changed his relationship status. Not nice!

Three C's to Seize the Moment

When it involves another person, have the *courage, consideration* and *character* to do what is difficult.
Face the music, face the person.

Because email and texts are easy to use, it does not mean that they should be! Our behaviors are judged and remembered. Some things merit a real-time conversation.

A CONDOLENCE E-CARD?

If someone experiences the loss of a loved one, an email of support, sympathy and caring may be okay if it fits the schematic of the online relationship. And then a sympathy card or note is to follow.

Like other cards, they can be reread, held, displayed, reread again, saved. Yes, an email or e-card can be saved, but there is no comparison to a handwritten one. In this instance, a sympathy note and/or card sustains the person in mourning. On the printed card we send, a note in our own writing gives comfort during a time of loss and grief.

Since I wrote this section for the 2007 edition, my mother has passed away as has Mumsy (Joyce Siegel). I've saved both sets of cards and have reread them. The handwritten expressions of condolences on the sympathy cards are a great source of comfort. Moreover, I feel a deeper degree of connection to those who sent them.

A very tech-savvy friend mentioned that when his mother died he received over eighty condolence texts. He wasn't bragging because he added wistfully, "But I only received twelve cards. Some of my longtime friends who knew my mother only sent text messages." It doesn't have to be a formal sympathy card; a handwritten heartfelt note that can be saved and savored will suffice.

And, by the way, expressing sympathy is best done in person or, if distance is an issue, on the phone. In the case of it being an online-only pal who suffered a personal loss, online support and expressions of condolence are okay.

There are different rituals observed by people of different faiths. Whether it is a wake, a funeral mass, a life celebration or the tradition of sitting shivah, we want to be sure that we know the customs of that "room." For some, a flower wreath at the church service is appropriate. Other families prefer a donation to a nonprofit or charity.

In this virtual room and world, there are still some situations that are not best served by anonymity and speed. We are judged by our behaviors in virtual and real rooms and want to avoid being characterized as sleazes.

ROANE'S REMINDERS

Do

★ Proofread for punctuation, spelling and flow (but keep in mind, grammar-check and spell-check are not always accurate).

★ Check your email regularly, and if you do so more than eight times a day, take the addiction quiz (see page 79).

★ Remember the "magic" words and pleasantries.

★ Assess the situations that require real-time communication, even if email is easier.

★ Pause and reread emails before you hit send.

Don't

★ Use obscenities. They read worse than they sound.

★ Send more than one screen of information without permission.

★ Fire, dump or reprimand via digital options.

★ Use all uppercase letters—it is the equivalent of shouting.

★ Send any emails, texts, tweets or posts you would not want to be read by others.

★ Use your office computer for shopping, searching or relaying jokes/messages that could cost you your job.

★ Forward screens of email sayings, jokes, warnings or questionable sites.

★ Waste people's e-time.

★ Send an email written in anger (wait a day, reread, reassess).

7

MR. (OR MS.) SLEAZE WORKS A ROOM: OR HOW *NOT* TO DO IT

I would have thought that after twenty-five years of addressing the sleazes in the rooms we enter the problem would have been resolved. Not by a long shot! *The people who are ultimately the most successful at working a room are those who genuinely like, respect and trust other people. When we don't really care about other people, they sense the insincerity and rarely take kindly to it.* Both my readers and audience members, from CPAs to CEOs, have shared horrifying stories about the smarmy and ill-behaved bulldozers who may even think they are creating rapport! You'll still find these violators of savvy socializing in all facets of your personal and professional life.

BEING "SLIMED"

At a benefit, Richard approached me and told me that he "*really* knew how to work a room" and "had a great deal of experience at it." He appeared to be knowledgeable, charming and smooth—on the surface. But as we spoke, *his eyes moved around the room to see who else was there*, and I sensed he wasn't about to waste time with people he didn't consider important. To me, he had no idea how to manage his mingling!

Richard personified the results of research from Dr. David Dunning of Cornell University, that the "incompetent are often supremely confident of their abilities. They are blissfully ignorant, because the skills required for competent assessment are also the ones they are missing."

Everything Richard did seemed calculated. He heard my words and responded, but he didn't really listen. When *he* spoke—mostly about himself, his past, his ideas, his successes, his goals—he locked me in with eyes that felt like lasers.

Like Bill Murray in *Ghostbusters*, I felt like I'd been "slimed"! Mr. Sleaze was a user and a loser. And, unfortunately, he's still on the loose. We see sleazes at networking events, professional association gatherings, even at church and synagogue functions. They overwork a room and are to be avoided and never emulated.

> *Top Tip: If you can tell someone is working a room, that person is doing it wrong!*

SCAN-DALOUS ADVICE

An article in a national magazine aimed at a younger business audience caught my eye because the title was "How to Work a Room." As I read the article, I was appalled. It advocated that while talking to someone, you should be "scanning the room for better options." The article offered tips on the best way to be a successful scanner. I shudder to think that young businesspeople who are building their careers and reading this magazine might be foolish enough to follow the advice. Most people know when the person they are talking to is glancing around the room to find someone more important and better connected, and they find it to be off-putting behavior.

Bottom line: No scanning, roving eyes; pay attention. Forget checking your phone for emails, texts and tweets while speaking with someone. Be in the moment and avoid this most insulting behavior. Ignoring this caution will make an indelible impression in any room and makes you memorable—for the wrong reason.

MR. OR MS. SLEAZE'S DISGUISES

We've all met sleazes at parties, meetings and conferences. They may wear two-thousand-dollar Armani or Prada suits or expensive jeans instead of the proverbial "sharkskin." They may look perfectly conservative, stylish and even prosperous or cool. They may even appear to be the prince or princess of our personal or professional dreams. And they may say all the right things.

But you just *know* they don't really care about you, your latest microchip design, your newly minted app, your prospective IPO, your interests or issues, your career or anything that isn't about them. They almost never follow through with what they promise.

Their behaviors do not support their words. If our behavior does not support our words, it subverts them. And then we are remembered for bad behavior. Words are important. But the adage is true: Actions speak so much louder.

The sleazes of the world come in many forms. They are male and female; techies or Trekkies; Millennials, boomers and Gen-Xers; wealthy and struggling. They can be anyone. The common denominator: They have no respect for anyone who can't "do something for them." If they are in sales, they are just trying to make their contact quota, and it shows. They might as well carry a sign that says, "It's all about me!" That is *not* how we make contacts that create connections with colleagues, coworkers, clients and cronies. They think networking and mingling are sciences that can be quantified. But they aren't. They are an art—the art of communication.

© Chronicle Features, 1988

Mr. Lapham is going to be our sleaze factor.

LEARNING FROM SLEAZE

Is there a lesson in Mr. or Ms. Sleaze's behavior? You bet. The technical skills of working a room are not enough. Interest, warmth and the desire to connect with others must be genuine and sincere.

I hate to sound like your grandma or mine, but when in doubt, apply the Golden Rule. Treat other people as you would want to be treated. It's old-fashioned, but it's easy, true and almost fail-safe. Dr. Tony Alessandra, author of *The Platinum Rule*, recommends we go a step further and observe people's behavior and treat them the way they want to be treated.

I say "almost" fail-safe because there are some people—only a few, I hope—who don't care how we treat them, because they don't care about *us*. They treat everyone with a chilling combination of disregard and disdain and don't expect anything different from others. They are the Roadblock #4 people who tempt us not to Risk Rejection. All you can do is apply Remedy #4 and move on.

NO JOKING MATTER—HUMOR THAT HURTS

The jokester who works a room with inappropriate humor isn't funny. We need to be sure we do not comment on something that could embarrass another person. The best guideline I've heard is: Never tease or make comments about something that cannot be changed in a minute.

The Schmulowitz Collection of Wit and Humor in the San Francisco Public Library contains most of the research studies on humor. That is where my suspicions of gender differences in humor were confirmed when I was writing the first edition of this book. Males generally found the teasing/poking-fun humor to be funny, while women preferred situational humor. Think twice before saying "that funny thing" if it is at someone else's expense. "Can't you take a joke?" is a tired excuse and shifts responsibility to the person being ridiculed. My mother's warning applies: "Listen to what people say when they are joking; much truth is said in jest." More on humor later.

FATAL FLAWS

There is good news and bad news for Mr. and Ms. Sleaze. The good news is that if being remembered is the goal, they achieve it. People do remember. And it can get you discussed . . . with disgust.

The bad news is that they are remembered for all the wrong reasons. The sleazes leave a negative impression, and that rarely enhances one's social life or business network. They are the proverbial glad-handers, backslappers and business card dealers who give networking a bad name.

In addition to being remembered as an insincere user and an unfeeling manipulator, Mr. or Ms. Sleaze often brings to the meeting or party a whole bag of unpleasant social tricks and shticks.

Avoid all of these behaviors and the people who exhibit them!

HOW TO HANDLE A SLEAZE

Extricate yourself . . . quickly. There is no reason for you to put up with bad behavior or to waste your time being gracious to someone who doesn't even know or care that you are being gracious. Try to be polite, especially if the comment was made by a boss or client. Remember that a sleaze isn't terribly sensitive to the difference between polite and impolite. Dr. Dunning's research about the incompetent rings true here. The most important thing is to get away. Excuse yourself and get away by saying, "Oh, I hope you enjoy the rest of the event." Then move at least one quarter of the room away. If the person committed an unpardonable act, just excuse yourself and move on.

THE SELF-PROMOTER

When she was a senior editor for a national magazine based in New York City, Laura Gilbert, now a web editor for a sports league, attended many events and witnessed a variety of behaviors. "At one event, a guest was discussing the annual running of the bulls in Spain and added that he could never do it. 'Fran' responded by saying that she's an athlete—in fact, that she dances professionally, though she's currently supporting herself by consulting because of a hip surgery, which was supposed to be minor but wound up having complications. After going off on ten random tangents, Fran finally returned to the topic by adding, 'But still I would never run with the bulls, even before my operation.' " To Laura, it was a nonstop self-promotional commercial.

"Mentioning what you do so that others can ask questions and have a conversation with you is good. But giving your résumé in a sentence is over the top, especially if you aren't in a job interview," said Laura. "Also, complaining about your medical problems is a huge no-no when you're making professional contacts—really, nobody wants to hear it."

Upon hearing this story, Sherwood Cummins, a Presbyterian minister and my personal trainer, described people like Fran perfectly: "She used his information [running with the bulls] as a springboard to dive into her own agenda." This is a behavior to avoid. It is not only obvious but also mildly offensive.

Caveat: Amazing as it may seem, people do not attend events, meetings and conferences to make our agenda dreams come true, no matter what room we are in.

ROANE'S REMINDERS

Sleazes come in a variety of disguises and tend to:

★ Make others uncomfortable

★ Be self-absorbed

★ Look past you to see who else is in the room

★ Try to push their agenda, products or services

★ Drink too much

★ Tell off-color, inappropriate jokes

★ Have no interest in those who can't help them

★ Try to make their contact and sale quota

★ Make fun of others as a "conversation ploy"

★ Size up people based on "titles"

★ Use their introduction as a commercial

If you have met a sleaze, the voice in your stomach will signal you clearly. Pay attention and *move on*!

8

NEW ROOMS
TO WORK:
THE SOCIAL
MEDIA MÉLANGE

Technology, new sites and apps have opened doors to new rooms to work and join as well as new ways to be part of that room. By the time this book is published, more new rooms will be available that didn't exist when I was writing this sentence. For those more experienced (older) people in the workforce seeking new careers, it behooves us to know where and what these rooms are and how to participate and be visible in them in order to plan and prepare for second and third careers.

Although I wrote about LinkedIn and Facebook in this book's 2007 edition, their growth has been explosive and increased exponentially since then. Other sites have flourished. We may not want or need to let our contacts know our current location on Facebook, but what about Foursquare, which is another vast room that is focused on locations. The Foursquare community has over ten million members, people who want: (1) to let people know where they are, (2) to see if any of their "pals" are in the same area and (3) to possibly meet up.

The reason I was persuaded to join was a bit different. A senior executive at one of my presentations shared how he was convinced to join: "My twenty-five-year-old son told me I had to be on Foursquare because, if I checked into Foursquare as I was checking into a hotel, I could possibly be upgraded." That sounded good to me. Some hotels and venues check Klout.com, an online site that ranks social media impact, to determine who gets upgraded. On the other hand, ignoring those with real-world clout would be a mistake. We are balancing the online with the offline and some days it feels like sitting on a seesaw!

WORKING NEW ROOMS

Each site, app or online venue has its own process, format and focus and its own set of rules, regulations and etiquette. This chapter is by no means a complete how-to guide on using each, but it will give you an overview of what rooms and resources are available. Again, by the time the book is in your hands, there will be new sites to set our sights on.

Some of the more prominent (as in eight-hundred-pound gorillas) new rooms in this chapter are:

- Twitter
- Facebook
- Foursquare
- LinkedIn
- Instagram
- Pinterest
- Google+

My favorite new room to work is Twitter, which launched as I wrote the last edition. I find Twitter to be educational and interesting and the challenge of writing in 140 characters has made me a better reader, editor and writer. Twitter has also brought new colleagues into my life as well as new friends.

TWITTER VERSE-ATILE

The Twitter-verse is a vast room that's crowded with people, companies and chatter. But it is also a forum for sharing information, learning and conversing with other Tweeters. I follow smart people who have expertise in areas of my interest, people who retweet informative URLs, some colleagues and friends and family. When I told @ShayneSkov11, currently a linebacker for Stanford, that his Grandma Susan was following him on Twitter, his immediate response was "Oh, I better watch what I say!"

No kidding! That's a policy we all should follow, not only on Twitter but everywhere in our lives.

I now have some wonderful new friends and colleagues I met through Twitter. Though I'd never spoken to writer and consultant Dorie Clark in person, @DorieClark is now a friend. It happened because I follow author Daniel Pink, one of my favorite smart people; when he retweeted Dorie's supportive tweet about his book *To Sell Is Human*, I, in turn, retweeted Dan's tweet retweeting Dorie. It may sound confusing, but because she is topnotch when it comes to working the Twitterdom, Dorie Clark sent me a thank-you tweet and our Tweetversation began!

Dorie writes for Forbes.com and the *Huffington Post* and is a reinvention and branding consultant. When her book

Reinventing You came out, I was able to help support the launch through social media and introduce her to another Twitter friend, @DanSchawbel. Since they both live in Boston, they've connected in person and are now developing a strong professional relationship.

Dorie, with whom I had never spoken, is a friend. I know we'll continue to support each other and eventually meet face-to-face. But if it weren't for Twitter, we wouldn't have connected. @DorieClark is someone you may want to follow, too.

FROM ONLINE TWEET TO FACE-TO-FACE MEET

Early on, Christian Fea (@ChristianFea) followed me so I followed him back. His tweets were so informative and he often retweeted Jeremiah Owyang (@Jowyang), whom I then followed. Jeremiah is a social media thought leader; he is smart, funny and so engaging. In his picture, he had a big smile. When he changed his photo to the more professional (serious) one, I had to protest. Jeremiah, though followed by 127,000 people, allows for direct messages, a feature of Twitter. So I sent him one saying that I missed his former smiling photo. That started the dialogue.

When his former firm, Altimeter Group, was holding an event in San Francisco, I was invited. Although he was one of the hosts and had many people with whom he had to connect, Jeremiah took the time to talk with me. That exchange proved to me that nothing replaces the benefits of face-to-face interaction.

You may think Twitter won't serve you, but if your colleagues, coworkers and customers are on it, you may want to reconsider. It can even be used for job search purposes. To learn more about the humongous room called Twitter, I recommend the *Ultimate Guide to Twitter for Business* by Ted Prodromou.

A TWEET CONNECTION

When Laura Gilbert lived in New York and worked at a women's website, she did a feature on a niche sport and became Twitter-aware of a young woman named Rachel who covered the sport for her own site. They started tweeting back and forth, spoke on the phone about a project Rachel was doing that Laura's website might support, became friendly and met in person at one of the events.

Laura says, "Our friendship grew as we began to talk about houses, relationships, dogs and industry gossip. In fact, I'm helping her pick out her wedding dress. We did nothing other than reach out to someone with a common interest!"

Laura's advice:

- Be genuine.
- Find something in common.
- Establish trust. Laura and Rachel never asked each other for a business favor, although they would now gladly do them for each other.

Something that began online with tweets, followed by face-to-face time, blossomed into a lasting friendship. Will they ever do business together? You never know!

TWITTER TIPS FOR THE PROSPECTIVE TWEETER

- Sign up. It's easy.

- Search the site to see which pundits, news organizations, journalists, colleagues, teams and talents are on Twitter. (I follow @DailyBeast, @DailyShow, @CBSNews, @StanfordFball, @NewYorkTimes, @TomFriedman, @scobleizer, @VIPOrbit, @DanielPink, @FightingIlliniBuzz, @UFC, @CNN, @Mashable, @IvanMisner, @DorieClark, @SethMeyers, @USAToday, @SFBallet to name just a few.)

- Click "Follow" to get tweets in your stream. See who they follow and follow those you prefer. Some people will follow you back!

- Add interesting thoughts and links to valuable articles, videos and information. Retweet those of others.

- Add your Twitter handle to your email signature, stationery and business cards.

- Tell people you're on Twitter.

- Follow #Hashtag conversations in your profession or hobbies.

- To get a quick lesson on Twitter's "rules" of etiquette, search Google or your favorite search engine.

- Buy Ted's book.

Again, be mindful of what you say on Twitter. You never know who may be hanging on every one of those 140 characters!

LINKING UP AND LINKEDIN

Anyone who is working, has a practice or a career or is looking for a job should be on LinkedIn. It's an important room to be in. LinkedIn added an algorithm to the offline, analog, face-to-face networking, which has exponentially increased our capability to connect and reconnect with first-, second- and third-degree contacts.

When I met cofounder Konstantin Guericke at an event where we were both presenters, it took eight months before he nudged me into the fold in 2005. Konstantin continues to coach and coax me in my LinkedIn presence.

Because there's still so much more to learn, I took a social selling workshop from Kurt Shaver of @SalesFoundry. He offered phone-coaching sessions I wanted and needed. Kurt went to my LinkedIn page and checked it out prior to our call. He asked me about the Lioness group I had joined. He was curious because he had just returned from a safari in South Africa and wondered if there was a connection. Yes and no.

No connection to the Lioness Group but a huge one to South Africa—where I would be visiting in spring. Kurt and I shifted gears and he became my "trip to South Africa adviser." Thanks to Kurt, I added Cape Town's wine country, a breathtaking historic area, to my itinerary. It was wonderful advice.

What started as a LinkedIn coaching call turned into a lively conversation that helped shape my visit to Cape Town. It all started because Kurt "worked" the LinkedIn groups, he asked me about one group and the rest is history. An unplanned result: our friendship.

This may seem like a long, tangential story. But the rooms we work can have many cubbyholes and, like a river, many tributaries. We, too, need to be open and follow those nonlinear paths of LinkedIn. For many more expert ideas, information and suggestions, check out Kurt Shaver at TheSalesFoundry.com, recently selected as one of only five LinkedIn Sales Solutions Certified Partners in the United States.

There are also smaller, "boutique" rooms to work and join on LinkedIn in the form of over 1.3 million different special interest groups (as of this writing). These groups allow LinkedIn members in various professions to connect, share ideas, informative solutions and best practices.

Some LinkedIn groups arrange for face-to-face mixers to meet each other in person. The fact that I had joined the Lionesses proved to be beneficial beyond my imagination. Each group has its own format that the host will share so that we know how to participate.

THINK *BEFORE* YOU LINK

It's a mystery to me how LinkedIn seems to know who we know, used to know and ought to know by some magical method. It was more than a mystery to Bonnie Hughes, an independent studio teacher. Like most of us on Linked-In, she receives invitations to "link" from total strangers. (LinkedIn advises not to accept invitations from people you don't know.) "But one invitation that baffled me, and gave me a good laugh," Bonnie recounted, "was from the client who didn't pay me. I had taken him to small claims court and won! When I saw his invitation, I couldn't help but think, 'You really want to connect with me? I sued you and you lost!' Needless to say, I ignored his invitation the three times it was sent."

There are multiple benefits to having a presence in the

new social networking rooms, as well as the face-to-face rooms. But we do need to think before we send an invitation to link.

FACEBOOK FOR BIZ AND "FRIENDS"

If you have a business, you may want to explore creating a Facebook Business Page. Kim Bosse of KB Media designs and manages her clients' Facebook pages as part of their social media marketing strategy.

Kim recommends that we "pick one platform to build a presence and do it well! I recommend focusing on Facebook because it's business-friendly and has the largest population."

Some additional suggestions from Kim Bosse:

- Don't just talk about yourself (this applies to a personal Facebook page, too!).

- Facebook content can include holidays, news events, local happenings, funny photos and within those posts, you can incorporate your important business content (e.g., for a restaurant: "Spring is here! Our sidewalk patio is ready for you to enjoy!"). Hint: By including a word in your post that people are talking about—*spring*, for example, your post will reach more people.

- The cover image for your Facebook page should be emotional, evocative, a photo or group of photos that are visually stimulating.

Facebook personal pages are another wonderful way to keep in touch, to be apprised of what's going on in that room and to see what's prominent in the lives of your "friends."

You can let them know you are in that room with them with a little "poke," a comment or a private message. I know many young couples who keep their families posted via Facebook. One new grandmother told me that she asked her daughter for photos of the baby. "My daughter told me that they were posted to a special friends and family Facebook page. When I said that I didn't have one, she told me to get one. So I did!" A colleague's ninety-two-year-old mother joined Facebook to see her great-grandchildren's photos because they live on the other coast. Necessity is now the great-grandmother of invention!

Caution: Because we communicate via Facebook, we often feel like we are in contact and even connected. The problem is that we forget that we really haven't been in actual real-time contact. To keep the high touch in this high-tech room, I post many items, both business and personal, including a variety of photos from places I've been, such as each of the South Africa's Big Five I saw while on safari, Chicago-style deep dish pizza (my favorite) and a candid shot of me writing this book in my local outdoor mall. But in addition to these general updates, to maintain real connection with friends I send individual "How are you?" emails and (shocking as this may be) I use my phone to call people, to hear their voices, and have a two-way conversation. We need to stay in real-time as well as online touch.

We should distinguish between our Facebook pals and our dearest friends, the ones we can call in a time of need. We need to remind ourselves to pick up the phone and set a time to meet with our close friends and family, when geographically possible.

Caution: Never add or post anything to these new "rooms" that you wouldn't want your favorite grandparent, your boss or your children or parents to see and read. Be mindful of posting photos, and watch your language and comments, as these rooms are being watched not just by our friends but by current and potential employers and the courts, too. In fact, checking out homepages, Facebook and Twitter is now considered a mandatory part of a lawyer's due diligence. Make sure you're diligent about not doing anything that's incriminating or cringe-worthy in this era of YouTube.

It's very difficult to scrub (erase) photos, tweets, comments and videos because they are cached somewhere in this "cloud-storaged" sky.

COMMENTS LEAD TO CONVERSATION AND CONNECTION

I subscribe to the site CBSNews.com because it's a wonderful source of ideas, information and news. Michael Hess, a small-business person and owner of Skooba Design, is one of the contributors. One of his columns mentioned face-to-face communication and was so spot-on I wrote a comment offering kudos to Michael, who wrote me back and said he'd like to have a real conversation on the phone.

We felt like we were talking not just as kindred business spirits but as fast friends as well. Michael runs a "new school" business that is web-based, but he calls himself "old school" when it comes to manners, customer service and quality communication in general.

The online world can be smaller than it might seem, and there are often fewer than six degrees of separation. I'm a big believer in checking to see if people are related to or know people I know. It's what I advise clients to do, because that's been such a regular source of "you never know" conversations for me. I asked where Michael was located. "Rochester, New York," he said.

"Michael, this has nothing to do with business—I only know one family in Rochester, my sorority sister from the University of Illinois and her husband." I mentioned their names and asked if he happened to know them. It was a long shot to be sure, but after a surprised pause, Michael said, "Susan, you aren't going to believe this, but they are two of my in-laws' closest friends!" Walt Disney was right—it's a small world after all! Our conversation changed and became even more connected because we had people in common. It made me very happy that I listened to my former assistant, Mary Haring, when she said, "Susan, you can't just blog. You have to read other posts and write a comment. Blogs are a conversation."

Mike Hess is a thoughtful, savvy writer and speaker who shares his business model and message with readers of CBSNews.com and audiences around the country. He is a great guy, whom I now know because he responded to my comment on his post. Mike really knows how to work the website room; he has a lot to teach the rest of us. We look forward to eventually meeting face-to-face but are pleased we are pals.

Because of my comments on a blog post by Douglas Rushkoff, a media theorist and author of *Present Shock*, I e-met him. His quick and engaging response prompted me to follow him on Twitter and recommend his book. When I received the link to his Bookspan interview, I watched it and then posted it on social media. Listening to this smart, thoughtful man was "ear" opening.

Thanks to Mary's wise advice, I also wrote a comment on a blog post by Tamar Weinberg on Techipedia.com in which she mentioned face-to-face communication. She wrote me back immediately and we started a late-night online conversation because she was writing a book: *The New Community*

Rules: Marketing on the Social Web, a superb resource. We stayed in touch. The following year we met when I was in New York to guest lecture at NYU.

ALERTED BY GOOGLE

I receive links to blogs and features about face-to-face, working a room, creating luck and savvy networking by setting up Google alerts for each. If there's a subject you find interesting and want immediate notification on the latest news, events or research concerning it, a Google alert is the twenty-first-century equivalent of "press clippings."

INSTAGRAMIFICATION

Our age may make a difference in our choice of social media. We are fickle, ready to switch to the next flavor of the month. Friendster, Napster and MySpace do not have the cachet they used to have. Today eighteen- to twenty-nine-year-olds are sharing photos via Instagram. In fact, according to the Pew Research Center, "Gen Z, the post 9-11 generation, prefers Instagram to Facebook." I learned that during the inauguration, where Olivia Skov, my thirteen-year-old granddaughter, had been working/playing on my iPhone. When I decided to post an Instagram photo off the TV of the inauguration, about twenty responses of people I didn't know caught me by surprise. They thought I was Olivia, as she had logged into her account on my phone. The good news: They thought the photos were cool.

I had to text Olivia so she could teach me how to log out of her account! She is now my go-to techie.

NEW MEANING TO THE TERM *GETTING PINNED*

Pinterest is one of the fastest-growing websites to date. The site has more than four million unique visitors. I've been one of them since March 2012. People share and connect over photos and videos of their favorite food, furniture, jewelry, clothing, accessories, bedding, DIY products and projects, books, other sites—you name it. This room is focused on visual images and very little commentary. It's a vast room that continues to grow because we like seeing what other people like and recommend, and we want to share what we find interesting and useful with our like-minded communities. Sharon Harris, a CPA and my Chicago host, told me, "It seems like every thirty- to forty-year-old woman on the North Shore pins everything they like and buys things other people pin and like."

I "pinned" a T-shirt because it cracked me up and added my comment. It's been pinned and "liked" 280 times. I even met someone who repinned my pin! The T-shirt said, "If ballet were easy, it would be called football." My comment: "Doubt that football players would agree, but they don't scrimmage en pointe!"

To learn more about effectively using Pinterest, look for resources like Karen Leland's e-book the *Ultimate Guide to Pinterest for Business*.

GOOGLE+ GROWING CIRCLES

Google+ is another site many people and businesses have embraced. According to Guy Kawasaki, author of *What the Plus!*, Google+ is about our passions and finding a like-minded "circle" of people who share those passions whether it's a sport, a hobby, a profession or an activity. The focus is on shared thoughts, ideas and comments rather than photos or videos. The people in a Google+ circle may not be "friends" you know or used to know, like on Facebook, but there is a shared interest that creates new connections and bonds.

You can set up different circles specific to interests, professions, relationships, and so on. Unlike Facebook, only the people in the designated circle see your posts. It's a room in which to have a presence. To help you manage the mingling in that great room, I recommend Guy's book.

Another "room" that has grown is Tumblr, a microblogging and social networking site that has—to date—over 108 million blogs. In this room, acquired by Yahoo! for $1.1 billion in 2013, its users—in the demographic twenty- to forty-five-year-old age bracket—can post and share a text blog, photos, links, music and videos—all from a browser. In fact, the Tumblr microblogging is generally visual, consisting of photos and videos rather then text like Twitter. It's another room that stands to grow in size and that you may be interested in joining.

There are tutorials on how to join, enter and enjoy being on each of these sites and apps. Pick the ones you think might work for you. Give them a try. These rooms are a part of the "McMansion" of mingling and connecting. I mention them because that's where people are meeting, connecting and hanging out.

Online rooms that we'll have the opportunity to work will continue to be created around the world.

ROANE'S REMINDERS

★ Technology has provided new rooms we can enter.

★ Each room and site has its own process, format, guidelines and protocol.

★ There are tutorials, websites and online forums to provide information on Twitter, Facebook, Foursquare and LinkedIn.

★ These new rooms help us to connect or reconnect with, stay in touch with and be apprised of professional and personal events of people in our lives.

★ Never write or upload anything to a site or app that you wouldn't want revealed in front of your favorite grandparent.

★ Postings on Facebook, LinkedIn and Twitter are checked by potential employers and others. Be aware!

★ Social media sites are a place for conversations, shared information and connection.

9

DON'T SHY AWAY FROM THIS CHAPTER

Shyness is a huge issue for over 90 percent of American adults who self-identify as such. While some, according to Dr. Philip Zimbardo, professor emeritus at Stanford University, are situationally shy, others feel they are generally shy: They claim to have worked through it but admit to the occasional relapse. About 8 to 9 percent of us are phobically shy and require individual treatment, but for the other 92 percent, the strategies in this book will help push you through your social discomfort.

THE POINT TO REMEMBER

In every "room" you enter, the majority of people feel equally uncomfortable or shy. Some may be introverts and/or shy or not. They could be colleagues, coworkers, clients, cousins or even your CEO. We may think that they are disinterested or disengaged, snobbish and aloof. A client for a Big Four firm told me, "If you're wearing a running suit or jeans, people will give you the benefit of the doubt and think of you as shy, but in a fancy suit and expensive tie, they think you're a snob."

The reality is they are just uncomfortable. Remember, Dr. Carducci, director of the Shyness Research Institute at Indiana University Southeast and author of *Shyness: A Bold New Approach,* indicates that shy people want to be part of the group. Susan Cain, author of *Quiet: The Power of Introverts in a World That Can't Stop Talking* and an admitted introvert, claims that introverts often have valuable social skills, though they may prefer listening to speaking. To her, "introversion is a preference for environments that are not over-stimulating." Based on her assessment, rooms full of people at a conference, meeting or party are not a comfortable place to the introvert, even if the people could be professional or personal contacts.

EMBRACE OUR INNER SHY PERSON

While many rooms are easily worked by the bon vivant, the bombastic and the braggarts, the shy are none of the above. They are the people who focus on their conversation partners, listen, share ideas and offer leads. Their eyes don't dart over our shoulders and around the room.

"We don't need less shyness in the world, we need more. Shy people are wonderful. Imagine if everyone were like Howard Stern or Madonna," said Dr. Carducci at the annual meeting of the American Psychological Association.

For those who are shy and want to feel more confident in any room, I've adapted the "Seven Quick-Step Shyness Recovery Program List," which originally appeared in my book *What Do I Say Next?*

THE SEVEN QUICK-STEP SHYNESS
RECOVERY PROGRAM

1. **Decide to recover.** The ability to communicate and converse is part of business. Bosses expect it. And bosses are expected to do it.

2. **Observe those who are Mingling Mavens and Conver-SENsations.** They are role models. Note what they do and say and replicate.

3. **Be approachable.** Smile. Make eye contact. This is natural for shy people, who tend to focus on their conversation partners rather than scanning the room while engaged in conversation.

4. **Have three to five interesting news stories to discuss.** Stay abreast of what's going on by reading newspapers, books and movie reviews or by joining a book club or discussion group.

5. **Practice recounting three to five incidents or stories that happened to you or others.** It might be something funny, provocative or "ear catching." Feel free to borrow from other people's lives—and remember to save the punch line for last.

6. **Take an acting, improvisation or conversation class.** You'll meet other people who may be shy, and you'll learn to take risks in a safe setting.

7. **Practice.** Smile. Say hello and talk to people along all the paths of life: the bridle path, the bike path, the track and in the elevator. Bite the bullet, take the risk and say something. You'll be pleasantly surprised. People respond in kind 90 percent of the time.

ROANE'S REMINDERS

★ Over 90 percent of American adults self-identify as shy.

★ Shy people generally listen and pay attention to their conversation partners.

★ Be approachable. Make eye contact and smile.

★ Have three to five interesting stories to share.

★ Take an acting or improvisation class.

★ Practice, practice, practice.

☺ GET SET! ☺

10

EIGHT STEPS
TO PERFECTLY
PLAN YOUR PRESENCE

You're set to go! You've identified the roadblocks, applied the remedies, identified the specific benefits of working a room, polished your chutzpah and your charm and learned to avoid either resembling or spending time with Mr. or Ms. Sleaze.

What's next? Before you rush out into the night or the afternoon or the morning—take some time to *prepare* yourself. The old army saw about the five Ps also holds true for business and social events: *Prior planning prevents poor performance.*

Whether the event is a trade show, cocktail party, a political fund-raiser, a dinner meeting, a conference or a reunion, *be prepared.*

One of the best preparation strategies I've heard comes from Tony Soprano's psychiatrist, Dr. Melfi. "Act as if . . . ," she told him in one of their always interesting sessions. It's sound advice even if you aren't a Soprano. *Act as if* you're comfortable at events. *Act as if* you are the host. *Act as if* you own the room. And you will.

You still have to do your homework. It's easier today because you can do an Internet search to learn about the company, the organization and the other attendees. You can check out event and company websites, Facebook and LinkedIn. You have to know what the event is, who is sponsoring it, who will attend. Then you can think of what *you* have in common with the other attendees. Before you leave for any event, be sure to take stock of your supply of business cards, be attentive to your grooming and mind the following eight steps.

I. ADOPT A POSITIVE ATTITUDE

Your attitude can make the difference between an event that is pleasant and successful—and one that ranks with the sinking of the *Titanic* (not the movie!). Unless you've been blessed (or cursed) with a poker face, it is extremely difficult to mask a negative attitude.

If you go to an event thinking, "Well, I have to be here, but I just know it's a waste of time," trust me, it will be! If you don't want to be there, people will know it. Jolie Pollard of JPJazz said that a fun and productive event at her local chamber of commerce helped change her attitude. "Now I prepare for events by saying, 'I wonder who I'll *get* to meet,' and that creates positive anticipation."

If, for some reason, you really don't want to go to an event, then *don't*. Better not to go than to create a lasting, lousy impression. Remember, no one looks around the room, sees a "sourpuss" (think Frau Farbissina in the Austin Powers films) and says, "Great, there's an unhappy person . . . I want to meet." Why waste a new shirt or a freshly cleaned silk dress or tie or the *time* it takes to attend an event if you don't plan to enjoy yourself?

You owe it to yourself to satisfy your own needs first, and the fact that you don't want or need to be somewhere will show on your face. Even if you plaster on a smile, *it will show in your eyes.*

Lemon Sucker Syndrome

The only people who consistently go to events intending to have a bad time are those who suffer from what I call the Lemon Sucker syndrome.

You can identify these people by the look on their faces—*excruciating pain*, for no apparent reason. Lemon Suckers are miserable, and they *love* their misery! If you try to cheer them up, they'll hate you for it. You may have a Lemon Sucker in your office or in your family.

Even those of us who are not Lemon Suckers can occasionally *look* that way unless we prepare a positive attitude before the event. And most people have enough experience with the Lemon Sucker syndrome that they will give us a wide berth if they see that uninviting look.

We check our makeup and straighten our ties before going out. A positive attitude is even more important and deserves at least as much attention. A little bit of enthusiasm and a smile go a long way.

2. DRESS FOR THE OCCASION

An easy way to make yourself feel comfortable at an event is to dress appropriately for the occasion. How we dress makes a statement before we open our mouths. According to Diane Parente of the Leadership Style Center, "The manner in which we present ourselves can enhance or destroy our credibility."

Many conventions end with a formal dinner where gowns and tuxedos are recommended attire. One year, at the National Speakers Association convention banquet, three of the members were not wearing tuxes. They looked different. One of my colleagues was fine with wearing his suit, but "Joe" told me that it was his first convention and he felt out of place. It wasn't intentional, but he had glanced over the brochure too quickly and missed the sentence on recommended attire. Joe said he wouldn't do that again. Sure enough, the following year, he wore a tux. He looked quite dashing, I might add. Because he felt much more comfortable, he felt more confident, met more people and had a better time.

Doing what we need to do to make ourselves comfortable is important. Dressing appropriately is easy enough to do in order to prepare ourselves for every occasion. If you're not sure of the attire there is a surefire way to find out: Ask.

3. FOCUS ON THE BENEFITS OF THE EVENT

We've discussed the importance of knowing why you are attending a meeting, party, dinner or reception. The twenty-first century finds us with many tugs for our time, so you must know what you stand to gain from leaving your home or office and working the room. Your focus, which will vary from event to event, will keep you on track.

As odd as it may sound, feeling happier may be a benefit of going to an event with strangers. According to a 2006 issue of *Psychology Today*, Tayyab Rashid, then a University of Pennsylvania psychologist, randomly assigned college students to bowl by themselves, with close friends or with strangers. To his surprise, Rashid found that the people who bowled with strangers were happier. The sense of well-being we gain from making new acquaintances adds a dimension to our day or evening.

This stranger/well-being research started a trip for me down "memory bowling lane." It was my PE requirement one semester at University of Illinois, Champaign-Urbana. While I did meet a lot of "strangers" and had a great time, I received a D for the course. Guess who doesn't go bowling . . .

What's Your Purpose?

Is your purpose in attending this event to be visible among your peers? To show the boss that you support her favorite community project? To be a role model for your employees and demonstrate the importance of participating in the trade association?

Mandatory Mingling

Whether you are in Generation X, Y, Z or "Me," the purpose of going to an event may be that "duty calls." Just as on Mother's Day and Thanksgiving, there are certain events where our presence is expected, and the goal may be to fulfill this obligation because staying visible is crucial to careers.

That doesn't mean you have to have a bad time. Even if you "have to" attend a certain cocktail party, you can also focus on the benefits of meeting new people, exchanging conversation and bringing back some business cards or adding into your phone the contact information of people with whom you connected to expand your network. And having fun!

Before the event, take some time to fill out an index card like this one or on your note-taking app. If you find that your list of benefits continues on the back of the card, so much the better!

| EVENT: | LOCATION: |
| SPONSOR: | ATTENDEES: |

Benefits of Participation	
PROFESSIONAL	PERSONAL

You might even slip the card into your purse or wallet, re-create it on your phone and sneak a look at it *before* you enter the room. It will remind you of your focus and of how you are being compensated for your time—in nonmonetary and perhaps even monetary terms.

> A WORD OF CAUTION: *Be* guided
> *by your goals, not* blinded *by them.*

We all know people who are on their way to their goals, and watch out for anyone who gets in their way! These people don't usually attract others to them or work a room with much success. Their charm level is nonexistent.

Focusing on the benefits of an event helps generate enthusiasm and keeps us on track, but genuine warmth and interest in other people are what make us succeed.

4. PLAN YOUR SELF-INTRODUCTION

The best self-introductions are energetic and pithy—no more than seven to nine seconds long. They include your name (obviously) and a tag line that tells other people who you are and gives them a way to remember you. Giving a benefit of what you do gives other people the opportunity to relate, ask a question or share an observation.

Tailor your self-introduction to each event. John Doe, the new director of development for Memorial Hospital, might use these variations:

- At his first meeting of the Development Directors' Association, where everyone in attendance is a director of development, he might say, "I'm the money-raiser for Memorial." It's alliterative and memorable.

- At a cocktail party to introduce administrators to new board members, he would say, "I'm John Doe, your director of development."

- At his daughter's wedding, "I'm John Doe, father of the bride." Or more lightly, "I'm providing the dough for this party."

These introductions are pleasantries. It helps to include a little humor.

Your self-introduction has three purposes: to tell people who you are, to give them a pleasant experience of you and to give them a way to engage.

Speak clearly and *look people in the eye.* Although different cultures have different customs about eye contact, this is an American custom and practice. Your introduction can be laced with humor and perhaps even some information that will stimulate conversation. But in the final analysis, *what people will remember are the warmth, interest and enthusiasm they feel from you.*

5. CHECK YOUR BUSINESS CARDS

Before there were business cards, there were calling cards, and their function was similar. Handing out business cards tells people your name, company and position and gives them a way to contact you in the future.

Ignore the buzz that business cards are dead. Most of us benefit by having a card to offer. The purpose of business cards is to give people a tangible, physical way to remember you and something they can slip directly into their card files or scan into their contact-management programs or use the CardMunch app to snap a photo that automatically converts to a LinkedIn contact. This is also how you should use *other* people's cards.

GUIDELINES FOR BUSINESS CARDS

- *Make sure that your name, your company name and your numbers are readable.* Select a typeface that is big enough and clear enough so that no one needs a magnifying glass or four-foot arms to read your card. Fold-over cards still don't work in a card file holder/Rolodex. Neither do vertical cards or the undersized mini-model cards. Forget the fancy designs that obscure the numbers. Place your phone number last, after your fax number, if you have one. Email addresses should be easy to read. Website addresses should be in a bold typeface to stand out. You may want to include your Skype name/number and your Twitter name. Some executives write their cell numbers on the card as they give it out, adding a personal touch.

- *Devise a system for carrying your own cards and for collecting cards from others.* I keep a clear plastic card case in my purse with a baseball card as a divider between mine and the ones I collect.

- *Add a person to your database or file a card only if you can retrieve it by remembering the person's name and why you wanted to contact that particular person.* Many people just snap a photo and add the person to the mobile address book. The next tip will help you remember.

- *Write a mnemonic device on the cards you collect—as soon as possible—to help you remember who they are.* If they said something interesting, ask permission to write it down. If you plan on scanning the card, do not write on the front of it.

- *Bring enough cards.* I learned from my "femtor," the late Sally Livingston, that no one wanted to take home a used napkin—even if it had my name and number on it. Napkins don't fit into anyone's Rolodex. The excuse that "I just gave out my last card" reflects poor planning. No one is impressed by how many people you met moving down the buffet from the bagels to the Brie.

- *Never leave home without them!* As Mom says, "You never know who you'll run into." (Mom did occasionally end a sentence with a preposition.)

- *Do* not *pass out brochures.* Brochures are expensive. They are meant for people who are genuinely interested in doing business with you. They are also bulky. People at a reception have no place to put them, and nobody wants to leave looking like they should have brought a shopping cart. Brochures are also a great way to follow up, so don't waste that opportunity by giving them away at the first meeting. You can always send your online brochure later or mail a hard copy.

- *If you want to give your card to someone who has not asked for it, ask for that person's first.* "May I have your card?" Most people will respond in kind, especially if you hold your own card conspicuously, as if you are ready to trade. "May I offer you my card?" is clear and polite.

- *Avoid "sticky" situations.* Don't reach for the buffet with one hand and your card with the other. No one wants to take home a card caked with sweet-and-sour sauce.

- *Pass out your cards selectively.* If your gut gives you a warning, heed it. Don't use business cards to play power games. Although some industries don't provide business cards, favoring instead mobile contact databases, most professions and companies still provide them. *The exchange of cards should follow a conversation in which rapport has been established.* Above all, be protective and polite.

Let's borrow from the Japanese tradition: When you receive a card, *honor* it by looking at it, looking at the person. Honoring a card helps you remember people . . . Perhaps you can make a comment about the card.

If your company does not provide you with a card, there are sites that sell and help you design your own business cards. So will your local print shop. A card is the best way to exchange information, but if you don't follow up, the card is meaningless.

6. PREPARE YOUR SMALL TALK

Some people cringe at this idea. They don't like the notion of preparing conversation, and they say that small talk is trivial. I say, "How do you start a conversation with a stranger or colleague? With war? Famine? Floods?" Hardly.

Whether the event is social or professional, there may be no special host to ease you into the room and help begin conversations. You may be on your own.

Small talk allows you to learn about other people. If you think about what has been said and respond to that, you're communicating. Small talk is absolutely essential; it is a way of finding mutual areas of interest. In *What Do I Say Next?* I wrote that small talk leads to big business, and it does. More on small talk and conversation in chapter twelve.

CANE CONVERSATION

Small talk can lead to an unanticipated once-in-a-lifetime experience, as it did for Jim Hughes. Because of an old football injury, Jim had to use a cane when he was taking a walk along Sausalito's waterfront.

"I felt the pain increasing so I planned to sit down on a bench I could see in the distance. There was an older gentleman seated there who also must have been resting. Normally, I never notice canes, but once you use one, you tend to see them. I saw that his was beautifully carved, mentioned that to him and asked where he got it. When he said he got it in Israel, I asked if he was there visiting family.

"You can imagine my surprise when he said he was in Israel to help negotiate a peace settlement! I looked at him much more carefully and realized—oh my goodness—I was talking to President Jimmy Carter! He later said he was here for his book signing. I mentioned I had been mayor of Calistoga and we talked a bit about politics and being an elected official. He was so down-to-earth and charming.

"It wasn't until I got up to leave and amble my way home that I noticed the two Secret Service men-in-black watching the president and keeping their eyes on me."

If Jim Hughes had a negative attitude toward small talk, had not noticed the cane or had not asked this stranger about it, Jim would have missed out on the once-in-a-lifetime experience of having a private, relaxed conversation with a former president of the United States.

SILENCE IS NOT GOLDEN

In *The Art of Conversation*, James Morris points out that although we "realize that it is bad manners to monopolize a conversation, it's equally bad manners not to talk enough."

In *What Do I Say Next?* I wrote that the "banquet of banter is a potluck." We wouldn't go empty-handed to a dinner where people are bringing appetizers, salads, desserts, beverages and entrées. By the same token, we must prepare morsels and the meat of conversation to bring to every room.

One of my favorite authors, Michael Korda, author of *Success*, *Power*, and former editor-in-chief of Simon & Schuster, is the nephew of movie magnate Sir Alexander Korda. Korda says that one of the things his uncle had going for him was that he never let things get *too serious*. In an article on small talk, Korda writes, "A bore is someone who has no small talk . . . Silence is not golden—it is the kiss of death." Korda was spot-on.

In this same article, Korda discusses the difference between small talk and large talk: "Large talk is for business negotiations, medical matters, things that involve money, health, life, the law . . . *Small talk should intrigue, delight, amuse, and fill up time pleasantly.* Given that, anything will do, from dogs to delicatessens. The aim of small talk is to make people comfortable—to put them at their ease—not to teach, preach or impress. It's a game, like tennis, in which the object is to keep the ball in the air for as long as possible." Small talk is how we connect with others and learn who and what we have in common.

You will walk into a room with more confidence if you have at least three pieces of small talk prepared—light conversations that you can have with anyone you meet. Whether it's motherboards, mother ships or motherhood, an exchange of pleasantries makes everyone feel more comfortable before you begin to think on your feet.

Bring your OAR: *O*bserve, *a*sk, *r*eveal. The topics might include a local sports team, the organization for which you are meeting or even the weather! You will have *something* in common with these people, simply because you are attending the same event. Remember, the "roof is the introduction." It's best to avoid controversial subjects like politics and religion, but you'll probably find several areas of common interest if you look. Dan Maddux, executive director of the American Payroll Association, recommends that his staff read the Lifestyle section of *USA Today* and *People* magazine or even a favorite homepage like Yahoo!. "They are great sources of conversational tidbits, fill you in on what's going on, and are generally *not* controversial!"

> *Being a good conversationalist includes being a good listener. When people talk about themselves, listen with your ears, with your face and with your heart.*

Serious discussions have their place, and you may enjoy deep, intimate talk with your friends. Probing conversations are off-putting. Small talk is a good way to break the ice and *begin* friendships.

7. MAKE EYE CONTACT AND SMILE

"It's good to meet you" is believable only if your voice, tone and warm, sincere smile match your words. This line doesn't play very well through a frown or even through a look of indifference.

"It's good to meet you" is the best greeting only if you are certain that you haven't met before. An appropriate substitute for "It's good to meet you" is "Nice to see you." I learned that the hard way.

At a San Francisco business mixer, Patricia Fripp introduced me to a woman, and I told her that it was nice to meet her. She glared at me, and in a tone that was like nails on a chalkboard, in front of several people, said, "Susan, we've already met." My response, "I'm sorry, please excuse my memory glitch." Unfortunately I can't write what I really wanted to say to this woman, but I tell this story in many of my presentations to illustrate that what she did was foolish. She made her point but lost sight of the big picture. Unless we have met someone a number of times and have had substantial conversations, we need to cut people some slack, in these 24/7 information-overload times.

There is no reason to put people on the spot. It's bad behavior and bad business practice. Savvy networkers don't do that.

Engaging in eye contact, being in the moment and having a smile are critical in building rapport. A colleague and his wife attended a birthday party for one of her associates. My friend told me later that the "birthday boy," a middle manager for a bank, never looked him in the eye as he shook his hand. "He all but said, 'I'm looking for someone more important to talk to,' " my colleague said. "I was ticked off. How did he know I wasn't more important—or would be someday?"

A roving eye gives the impression of an insincere, hand-pumping Mr. Sleaze. People always remember the room surfer. Equally off-putting is the untimely texter, who's all thumbs on their keyboards.

But a word of caution . . . eye contact does not mean *glaring* or *staring*, which can be rude. Glaring rarely builds rapport or enhances communication. Author David Givens suggests that we alternate between looking at the person and looking away in order to display just enough interest and also just enough vulnerability to be approached. "Cultural standards vary, but in the United States a comfortable range is looking for seven to nine seconds, and then looking away for only a few seconds." Beyond that, the "looking" may become a glare or the "looking away" may suggest that we're scanning the room for better opportunities.

8. PRACTICE YOUR HANDSHAKE

A handshake is the business greeting in America. It's the only appropriate area of touch and must be well done. Jellyfish need not apply here. A firm clasp is the handshake of prefer-ence for *greeting* people, *agreeing* to a deal and *departing* as friends. It's a web-to-web handshake that is neither weak nor forceful. In my presentations, my audiences practice their handshakes. In this global economy and diverse workplace the custom of handshaking can differ based on culture and national origin. We also want to be mindful of arthritis, and the rise of carpal tunnel syndrome.

These are some handshakes to *avoid*:

- *The Jellyfish.* A hand moves your way. You grasp it and it turns to mush. Do you want to do business with this person? People with jellyfish handshakes create the impression that they are spineless—an unsavory perception, to be sure. Remember: Jellyfish sting.

- *The Knuckle Breaker.* Your hand disappears into a vise and comes back the worse for wear. This kind of power play is best left to members of the Mafia. In recent years, some women have adopted the Knuckle Breaker in an effort not to be perceived as pushovers. Women do need to have firm handshakes, but I recently met a young attorney who was five feet one, no more than 103 pounds, who shook my hand with such strength that it came back feeling like chopped meat. At a seminar in Toronto, a fellow about six feet three responded to my handshake with such a Knuckle Breaker that I screamed, "Ouch!" Was he trying to show me his strength or power? He showed me that he had no clue about shaking hands with a woman.

- *The Finger Squeeze.* This person doesn't clasp your hand; he or she grabs your *fingers only*. When done with a light touch, this gesture appears prissy and/or suggests that the person isn't sure he wants to touch your *whole* hand. With a heavy touch, the Finger Squeeze can become the Ring Squeeze. Marks from your ring are clearly etched in at least two other fingers, and you wonder if you should leave the reception to get an X-ray.

- *The Covered Handshake.* In this handshake, one of the
  parties puts his or her left hand over the hands clasped
  in the handshake. This may be perceived as a show of
  warmth by those of us who are "touchers," but others
  may see it as a power play or feel that they are being pa-
  tronized. There may be times when a covered handshake
  is perfectly appropriate. Be sensitive to other people's responses, and let your intuition be your guide.

We don't want to become overly analytical. A Ford
Fellow and I were doing some consulting on the same project. He pointed out that I touched people as I spoke and very
seriously told me that this was "a schematic organizational
power play." That was what he did—planned power plays.

"How interesting," I replied as I laughed aloud. "And all
this time I thought it was because I was from a long line of
huggers and touchers!"

Since it's not always easy to read people or to assess their
reaction to a covered handshake, play it safe and stick with
the traditional firm clasp, with no left hand playing around
the edges.

MEN, WOMEN AND HANDSHAKES

Men have been trained from childhood to shake hands.
Women must also master the art. It's up to the woman to
extend her hand first whether she is meeting a man or another
woman. Men are taught to wait and see if the woman initi-
ates a handshake. A woman never conveys a mixed message
by extending her hand to a man when she is appropriately
and professionally dressed.

THE BUSINESS KISS CONUNDRUM

To Miss Manners' horror, kissing has also become a business greeting in certain industries. "Bussing for business" is common in the entertainment, hospitality and human resource fields. People involved in banking, manufacturing, accounting and the law are less likely to be seen blowing one another little "air kisses." In the days of sexual harassment grievances and lawsuits, just be careful: never in the office and never on the mouth. A kiss is a feature of a relationship, a friendship, and it is never to be presumed. It is safest to make do with a handshake—the only "kosher" contact!

THE SHAQ SOLUTION

If *you* are uncomfortable and want to avoid the kiss as a business greeting, simply stand as far away from the other person as the length of your arm. Extend your hand, *smile* and lock your elbow. If Shaq (whom I follow on Twitter) did this, he would keep people about five feet away from him. It's a good way to give yourself some "breathing space" and still make others feel welcome.

ANOTHER TOUCHY SUBJECT

Being a "breath of fresh air" at every meeting, interview and party is the optimum behavior. To that end, avoid garlic and onions before and during any event.

One of the rules for White House dinners during George W. Bush's administration was no garlic. It makes sense to avoid that which would make us self-conscious and which makes talking to us an olfactory challenge.

A tip for event planners and hosts: Have the caterers stuff the mushroom caps with something other than the "stinking rose."

STRIKE A POSE

A word to the wise: Observe people's behaviors—their facial expressions, gestures and body language. While it is *not* a quantifiable science, there is a great deal of information—books and websites—on the subject of body language that is useful. In fact, there's been a marked increase in the amount of social science research on the positive impact of expansive posture and poses. According to social psychologist and Harvard professor Dr. Amy Cuddy, interviewed for a *New York Times* article on stance, "Posture-induced feelings of power and competence make you feel more at ease." Dr. Cuddy's TED talk about her research, "Poses Are Powerful," is available online.

COMMON SCENTS

The perfume industry spends millions of dollars to persuade people to buy their products. Because we want to smell good, we use soap, toothpaste, deodorant, perfume and aftershave. Consequently, offices, elevators, concerts and cubicles can reek of conflicting scents. The best advice for both men and women is to go lightly on the scent. According to Lana Teplick, a CPA who has had to work in client offices, "Some people are sensitive to scents. Rather than add my perfume to their workplace, I just don't use it." Makes perfect scents to me.

ROANE'S REMINDERS

Take the time to "be prepared." Remember the eight steps for planning your presence:

★ Adopt a positive attitude.
★ Dress appropriately.
★ Focus on the benefits of the event.
★ Plan your self-introduction.
★ Check your business cards.
★ Prepare your small talk. Bring your OAR (observe, ask, reveal).
★ Make eye contact and smile.
★ Practice your handshake.
★ Strike a pose.

Advisories:
★ Kiss off the kissing.
★ Be conscious of body language.
★ Avoid garlic and onions!
★ Have fun and the room will work you!

11

SEVEN STRATEGIES: FROM JUMP-START TO SMOOTH STOP

You've done your preparation, but what if your internal engine starts to stall at the thought of actually walking in the door? These seven strategies will give you a quick jump-start and bring you through the event to a smooth stop.

I. THE ENTRANCE: GRAND OR OTHERWISE

What time should you arrive? Arrival time is usually based on the starting time of the event—not on making a conspicuous entrance. There is no such thing as being "fashionably late" to a meeting. Take a tip from shy people: They arrive on time or within fifteen minutes of the appointed hour. That's how they avoid the discomfort of walking into a crowded room.

When you arrive at the event, take a deep breath, stand tall and walk *into* the room. Hanging out in the doorway creates a fire hazard, a traffic problem and the impression that you're either timid about coming in or are standoffish.

There may or may not be an official greeter. Anticipate

that there will *not* be one and enjoy the pleasant surprise if there is.

Publishing expert Judith Briles, "the Book Shepherd" and CEO of Author U, recommends volunteering to be on the greeting committee yourself. That way "you get to meet everyone because it's your job." If you are shy, this gives you something to say to people right away.

Give the room a quick once-over. Where's the bar? Where's the food? Where are people congregating? Where can you position yourself to meet the most people?

A professional speaker who addresses audiences of thousands told me he is shy and has great difficulty attending cocktail parties and talking to people one-on-one. His solution is to position himself between the entry and the buffet table so that everyone has to walk by him to get to the food. He is always surrounded by people, albeit hungry ones.

Once you are in the room, look around for people you know. If you see someone who looks vaguely familiar, go up and introduce yourself. Find out if that person is who you thought he or she was. There is no point in wondering, "What would happen if . . ." One of two things will happen: You'll be right and renew the acquaintance or you'll meet a new person. Chat for a while and move on.

2. THE BUDDY SYSTEM

If the thought of entering a room is daunting, try the buddy system. Make a deal with a friend who must also attend these events, and go together. But don't limit your arrangement to "having someone with whom to walk in the door." The buddy system can be a great way to work a room—if you do some prior planning and strategizing.

BUDDY STRATEGIES

- *Introduce each other around.* This is one of the main advantages of going to an event with a buddy. You may know people your buddy doesn't know, and vice versa. Even if neither of you knows *anyone*, you'll both meet people in the course of the event and can introduce each other to your *new* acquaintances.

- *Brush up on your introduction skills.* Present your buddy as a pleasant, interesting person who has something in common with the other attendees. This means *listening* to people to find out what their interests are.

- *Give people enough information about your buddy to begin a conversation.* Use a positive tone of voice.

- *Make sure your buddy does the same.* Patricia Fripp and I do this at many events. She says, "It's like being with your own PR person. We say about each other that which we would *not* say about ourselves. 'Have you met Susan RoAne, best-selling author with over a million books in print and a great speaker?'" I introduce Patricia similarly. "Have you met Patricia Fripp, one of the best speakers and executive speech coaches in the country, and an author as well?" Believe me, conversations happen!

- A Seattle-based business consultant once said that some people are "legitimizers" simply by virtue of who they are and *how* they introduce other people. They are individuals with a certain amount of status, and they *know how to present other people* in the *best light*. That is something we all can do. People want to be around and do business with "legitimizers," the people Malcolm Gladwell refers to as "connectors" in *The Tipping Point*.

- *You and your buddy should split up as soon as possible.* If you act like you are Velcroed together, your ability to work the room and meet people is limited. (Most people admit that it's tough to approach two people, as it feels invasive.) You'll meet only half the number of people, and those you do meet will think you are joined at the hip. This also applies to significant others who can be buddies. This is a terrific strategy for spouses. Meet and mingle separately and then reconnect. Another is to stand side by side rather than face-to-face in a room to indicate approachability.

- *Develop a "rescue" signal.* You and your buddy will want to periodically regroup to assess and restrategize and to help extricate each other from conversations that have gone on too long.

3. THE WHITE-KNUCKLED DRINKER— AND OTHER ACCESSIBLE FOLK

You're inside the room, and you and your buddy have decided it's time to split up. Where do you turn? Who do you talk to? You don't recognize a soul and feel conspicuous standing alone.

Initiating conversation can be challenging. Remember, our mothers taught us *not* to talk to strangers. But we've remedied that. We also fear rejection and perhaps suspect that we're not interesting, witty or attractive enough. But we've remedied those things, too. And because we are attending this reception in order to meet others, *we can't afford to be wallflowers.* It's time to step out there on our own, work up our courage and *do something.*

What I do in this situation is *look for the person standing alone.* If you want to manage the mingling at any event, look for people who are clutching their glass of wine or water or cup of coffee so tightly that their knuckles are taut. They are more uncomfortable than we are, probably shyer and just as interesting.

These people usually welcome your conversation because you save them from anonymity. They may be shy or just uncomfortable. No one else is talking to them. If you walk up and start a conversation, you're doing a good deed, being kind and earning a few "Planet Points," and also moving *yourself* away from the wall. (Planet Points are what we get for earning our right on the planet by doing good deeds that are supportive and thoughtful of others.)

SEIZE THE MOMENT

Make eye contact, smile and say something. According to research, a simple "Hi!" or "Hello" is the best icebreaker. Maybe the other person is just shy or anxious. Make your conversation so fascinating that other people are drawn into your little group and expand the circle to include them. When you see someone who wants to join in, step back and reset the circle. To the person you included in your group, you'll be memorable.

> *When you focus on other people's comfort more than your own, your self-consciousness disappears.*

Remember, the white-knuckled drinker is more uncomfortable than you are and will welcome your conversation.

4. NAME TAGS THAT PULL

While people still have mixed feelings about name tags, they are very important for business and social events. Name tags have the following obvious benefits:

- You can address a person by name, which is always preferable.

- They provide information you can use to begin conversation (company, job title, location, area of specialty).

- If you see "that familiar face" but aren't sure if the person is who you think he or she is, you can sneak a peek at the name tag, especially if it's worn on the right-hand side.

At many trade shows, cocktail parties and other events, name tags are provided. The person's name should be large and bold enough in type to be visible even if you are standing a few feet away. The company name is often a bit smaller, and you have to get closer to read it.

"The badges on lanyards ('leashes') all fall around someone's *pupik* [navel] and that's not where you want to look—either clip them on the right side or tie or raise the lanyard up so your badge is above your bosom or 'pecs' if you are a guy!" advises Joan Eisenstodt, a Washington, DC–based meetings consultant, trainer and facilitator extraordinaire.

Many civic organizations and churches use name tags to encourage mingling. Sometimes the name tags are color-coded to distinguish members from guests or new members. An unwritten rule is that members seek out guests and new members and make them feel welcome.

You might take a cue from this rule, and make yourself an unofficial greeter of guests and new members.

Name "Tag": You're It!

If you are asked to fill out your *own* name tag, you have some leeway in describing your position or specialty. This is a chance to identify yourself in an interesting way. The best example remains financial planner Fritz Brauner. He told me that when he put the designation "Financial Planner" on his name tag at a business mixer, no one looked twice. But when he wrote "Money" beneath his name, he was approached by many interesting people who wanted to know what he did.

A sense of humor does help! At a chamber of commerce business social, one member had a name tag that caught my eye and made me laugh. Instead of writing his name he had written "Name Tag." Corny, but we began a conversation quickly and easily.

If you are planning an event and use computer-generated name tags, be sure the names are big and bold. If people are to fill in their own name tags, provide thick markers.

Technology allows us to "zap" name tags right into our smartphones and mobile contact programs. There is a skill and an etiquette for this microchip mingling that has affected business card exchanges at professional trade shows. Some conventions provide name badges/cards with chips that contain basic data about the attendee including name and address. An exhibitor simply "swipes" an attendee's card as you would do with a credit card, resulting in a mailing list. The CardMunch app will snap a photo of a business card and add it to your database.

While zapping cards is an efficient way to exchange pertinent information for follow-up, what's at stake is the conversational exchange that helps to build rapport and determine the attendee's needs. Zapping a card is quick, but be sure it doesn't supplant the time to talk face-to-face.

PLACEMENT OF YOUR NAME TAG

Always, always place the *name tag on your right-hand side*. This has not changed in twenty-five years. When you extend your right hand for a handshake, the line of sight is to the other person's right side. If the name tag is placed on the left side and you sneak a peek away from the line of sight—you'll get caught! The idea is to make the name tag as visible as possible so that others can read it easily.

NO–NAME TAG EVENTS

Name tags are not used at some business and many social events. At these events, you're on your own to introduce yourself to people and engage them in conversation. Most people, especially those who are standing alone, will welcome your greeting and conversation. Remember: The "roof is the introduction." You already have something in common if you're at the same event.

Several years ago I attended a wedding in northern California where we were given name tags. It seemed odd at the time, but now it doesn't seem such a bad idea.

THE (FORGOTTEN) NAME GAME

We all forget names from time to time, even the names of people who are important to us. People who must attend parties, benefits, conventions, fund-raisers and reunions with humongous numbers of other people can go into what I call nomenclature overload. Name tags will often prompt that "Bill Smith" that's just on the tip of your tongue.

We're all inclined to be hard on ourselves if we forget a name, but as one man said in my El Paso presentation, "I think we have unrealistic expectations of ourselves. We meet hundreds of people each week. Our parents may have met only ten new people in a week, and our grandparents perhaps only one! How can we expect to remember all those names?"

We often can't remember proper names easily or quickly and for good reasons, according to Dr. Lori Samps, psychology professor at the University of Colorado, in a 2005 article in *Psychology Today*. They are more difficult to remember than a person's occupation. Her reason is that the brain makes more memory links to livelihood. Perhaps it would be helpful to associate the name of people we meet with the face *and* occupation.

If you have forgotten a name or two:

- Say so—with humor.
- *Always* state your own name when greeting other people. (They may have forgotten your name as well.)
- Most people will reply in kind. (Embarrassment of the forgotten name will be averted.)
- Repeat their names. And don't make people struggle to remember your name.
- If you always state your name, you will relieve the other person from nomenclature overload and will be remembered kindly.

And if we do forget a name: "Oh, it's been one of those days. I must have run out of RAM" or "So sorry, this is one of those days. I even forgot my own name!"

Never, ever ask, "Do you remember me?" It puts people on the spot and can make for an uncomfortable scene. Mingling Mavens don't do that to others.

5. GREAT OPENING LINES

The quest for the perfect opening line may be as old as humankind. Too often we lose an opportunity to meet someone because we spend precious time trying to think of the perfect opening line—and there is no such thing.

The good news is that there are a million perfect openers. What you say will depend on who you are, the person to whom you are talking, the circumstances, the response you want to get and what pops into your mind. It is far better to say *something* than to wait for the perfect clever remark. Even if what you say isn't going to change the world, don't miss the opportunity to begin a conversation. Just make one off-the-cuff comment about the venue or event.

Research now supports what expert minglers have always known: The best opening line of all may be a smile and a friendly "Hi" or "Hello." "Hey" may be more commonly preferred by Generations X, Y and Z; while its use will increase, you might want to assess when it's most appropriate. As far as using "dude" and "bro" in a greeting, use with caution.

"Miranda" was at a party in northern California when she was introduced to a Harvard-educated musician. "He turned to me, smiled and said, 'Hey, dude.' I looked him in the eye and said, 'That would have been the perfect greeting if I were a dude. Look again!' "

Conversation Starters

Common experience is always a good conversation starter. Try:

- Talking about the organization or cause
- Discussing the venue
- Mentioning the view
- Discussing the food (presentation, calories, taste or lack thereof—but no whining)
- Offering a comment such as "I had a great lunch last week at the convention and visitors bureau event."
- Responding with a question like "Oh? Where was it held?"

Bring your OAR and it will rescue you from any conversational quandary. Observe. Ask. Reveal. The magic is in the mix.

OBSERVE

Look around the room. Observe the situation. What is happening? Does there seem to be a good crowd? Where are people positioned? Do they seem to be enjoying themselves? Was the traffic or the parking difficult? What do these people have in common?

Observations about any of these things might be good conversation starters. Saying something humorous or unexpected is even better.

It's best to avoid negative comments. We don't want to give the impression of being kvetches or whiners.

Avoid statements like:

- "The food looks pathetic."
- "This hotel is far more run-down than I had expected."

Go for upbeat, unusual observations that will pique people's interest about the theme, the setting or the decor.

ASK A QUESTION

The questions you ask should be relevant. Visit your favorite search engine or Facebook or LinkedIn to do your homework to find out about the group and the people who will be attending the event. Even if you don't know much about the organization, you can ask questions such as the following:

- "What's been the best benefit of joining this group?"
- "How would you suggest I become involved?"
- "How do you know the bride [honoree, groom, birthday boy, anniversary couple, politician, etc.]?"

Questions should be open-ended enough to encourage a response but not invasive. Here are some sample questions for various events:

Political Fund-Raiser:
- "What made you decide to support this candidate?"
- "How have you been involved in the campaign?"

Charity Benefit:
- "How did you get involved with the March of Dimes [MS Society, etc.]?"
- "Have you visited their new website? Their mobile app?"

Professional Association Banquet:
- "Are you a member of this association?"
- "How have you been active in the organization?"

Neighbor's Daughter's Wedding:
- "How do you know the bride or groom?"
- "How did you meet him [or her]?"

Jogging Track:
- "How often do you run here?"
- "How does this compare to the other tracks you've run?"

FOR YOUR CONSIDERATION

You may want to mix open-ended questions with those that require only short answers. Otherwise, you could exhaust your conversational partner, whom you don't want to feel you've put on the spot by your curiosity.

QUALIFYING QUESTIONS

There are those who advise us to ask a lot of smart, open-ended questions and just let the other person talk. *Wrong.* If all you do is ask questions and contribute nothing about yourself, your comments or interests, that is *not* conversation. It is an interrogation. There are those of us who are suspicious of the grilling. No matter how charming or interested you may be, conversation is a "duologue."

Caveat: Besides sounding like the Grand Inquisitor, there is another downside to asking a barrage of questions. A 1998 *Fortune* article on leadership featured the findings of researchers at Harvard who surveyed and studied leaders. They found that strong leaders maintained the floor while those who asked many questions yielded it, according to Sarah McGinty, formerly of Harvard's School of Education. She further noted, "A person who feels confident . . . is more inclined to make statements than ask questions." We need to do both. The savvy socializer strikes a balance among the trifecta of conversation techniques.

REVEAL

Disclosing something about yourself is a good way to establish your vulnerability and approachability. However, there is a risk involved. Be careful not to reveal anything so personal that it burdens the listener.

Good Openers

- "I don't believe it took me forty-five minutes to get here, and I was only three miles away!"

- "It never fails. I always manage to get teriyaki sauce on my tie. At least it highlights the design."

- "This food looks so good, I'm glad I forgot to eat lunch."

GETTING TO KNOW YOU

People do business with people they *know*, *like* and *trust*. When we bring who we are (in appropriate amounts) to what we do, we allow others to feel more comfortable and to relate to us on a personal level.

Self-disclosures should be generally positive. In his book *Trust Agents*, Chris Brogan, social media maven and blogger, writes that digitally savvy influencers or "trust agents," tend to "reveal stuff about themselves because it makes them more approachable."

But we need to be thoughtful about our revelations. Some time ago, I attended a luncheon meeting for a professional association and said hello to one of the officers. When I asked how he was, he mentioned his separation. Then he elaborated on his teenage children's questions about his love life *and* his sex life. I realized he needed to talk to someone, but that meeting was neither the right time nor the right place—and I was not the right person. I knew we wouldn't do business together because he said too much.

The winner of my client's major Pinnacle Award told me she does not "sell" to her customers. "I just get to know them, their circumstances, and only suggest which bank products fit their needs and lifestyles. But the key is that *I let them get to know me* so my calls are always returned, because they are from a *person they know*, not from a banking institution."

Everything in moderation. We want to make sure that we don't burden clients, customers and even friends with too much personal information.

Food is almost always a wonderful basis for communication. Grandma knew that food was a great conversation starter—that's one reason she made lots of it. It's no accident that meetings, get-togethers, social engagements and family affairs are often centered on a meal. When people come together over food, a certain amount of nurturing takes place—at least on the physical level but often at the mental and professional levels as well. And we have a built-in commonality for conversation.

"FLIRTING"—WITH DISASTER

And while we're on the subject of great lines . . . what about flirting? What about the words, body language, facial expressions and glances that can find their way from a purely social situation to a business setting, or vice versa?

To some, flirting is a way of exchanging friendly banter, very much like small talk. Good-natured, friendly banter is fine and can be appropriate even in the office.

To others, flirting is a "come-on." It all depends on the flirter, the flirtee and what is actually being said and done. Flirting is appropriate and even necessary at a singles event. It is a way we signal our interest in others.

Use caution when flirting in a business setting, especially in front of coworkers, clients, colleagues or the boss. One person's small talk is another person's come-on. Ask yourself if you want that deal or that promotion riding on what someone thinks of you as a business associate or as a flirt. Of course, there are long-standing business relationships where people hug hello. But those hugs are earned over time, never presumed. To avoid misinterpretation: No double entendres, no off-color comments, no touching beyond the handshake.

6. MOVING IN: BREAKING AND ENTERING

Over the years, my audiences, readers and clients continue to say how difficult it is to break into already formed groups. To reiterate the tip for the shy: *Never go to an event more than fifteen minutes after the designated time.* The small groups that appear closed will not yet have formed.

There is a difference between *including* yourself in other people's conversations and *intruding* on them. Getting into a conversation that is already under way requires confidence and a dose of chutzpah, but also some sensitivity. *Watch people's body language and listen to the tone of their conversation for clues.*

As I drove along Highway 80, I read a billboard and laughed out loud. "Breaking In Is Hard to Do." I thought it referred to a mingling moment. In smaller letters the billboard's sponsor was revealed, Bay Area Alarm Company, and the slogan made sense. But the slogan rings true for 93 percent of us who are shy at events. Breaking in *is* hard to do.

When Laura Gilbert was a senior magazine editor standing with a friend at a cocktail party, they were approached by a woman in her early twenties, probably in her first publishing job out of college. "Instead of introducing herself, she looked at us and said, 'So, who do you write for?' She never even asked our names. On the way out, she and her friend said, 'Nice to meet you!' and I wanted to say, 'But you *didn't*!'"

We want to be included, continue with the ongoing conversation, and be memorable for the right reason.

Over the years my audiences have offered wise advice for including without intruding:

- Avoid approaching two people who look as though they are having an intense conversation. If they seem totally preoccupied, you can assume that they are flirting with some profound ideas or with each other.

- Approach groups of three or more who look like they are having fun. Position yourself close to the group. Give only facial feedback to the comments being made. When you feel yourself included, either by verbal acknowledgment or eye contact, you are free to join the conversation. This is *not* the time for you to switch the conversation to you, your product or your agenda. You are the new guest in the group.

"Carmen" has a big smile and a most charming manner. She lives in New York but is originally from Canada and believes that getting permission from a group to join them is wise and polite. During my presentation in New York, Carmen told us what she does when everyone is already in their small groups: "I go up to a very animated group, wait until people have stopped talking and ask, 'Do you mind if I join you?' No one has ever said, 'Yes, I mind.' Instead, people open up their circle and I am included." Carmen's manners and thoughtful, polite verbiage work well.

- Be open to others who "want in." When you see someone on the periphery of your conversation group, step back. You will have included someone who had been excluded. That's a thoughtful behavior that will make you memorable!

According to Demetrius Greer, who was the director of attorney recruiting at Paul, Hastings, Janofsky, and Walker, LLP, "Being polite is imperative. If you merely want to extend a greeting to someone in a conversation, you might say, 'Excuse me for interrupting, but I wanted to be sure to say hello.' Then move away." You may find that your interruption is a welcome relief and that you are invited to join the conversation.

CONVERSATION INTERRUPTERS

What if someone interrupts *your* intense or important conversation? According to Dr. Geraldine Alpert, a psychologist in Marin County, north of San Francisco, you can be both firm and gracious. "Acknowledge the person politely and thank him or her for saying hello. Indicate that you need to finish this conversation but will catch up with the person later. *Then do so.*"

On the other hand, if you observe someone's back is facing the room, the message is clear: Don't interrupt.

7. MOVING ON: EXTRICATING YOURSELF

"I'd love to chat longer, but I'm working the room."

Many of us feel uncomfortable with ending a conversation. Someone, somewhere, told us it was rude. And we don't want to make people feel as if we don't want to talk to them.

Actually, the etiquette of social events is that we are *supposed to circulate.* No less an authority than Miss Manners suggests that we spend no more than eight to ten minutes with any one person. We've been invited so that we can mingle and meet the other attendees. It's an opportunity to circulate among peers, colleagues and potential clients and to meet as many people as possible. The idea is *not* to engage in conversation with one person for the duration, although we sometimes do that because it can be easier.

However, in spite of advice to the contrary, we cannot assess business contacts in less than one minute. Don't believe anyone who makes such claims. Conversations take longer, and you never know who or what people know in a minute. The One-Minute Mingler? No way.

GRACEFUL EXIT

How to make a graceful exit? I once found myself talking for twenty minutes to someone whose company I didn't find particularly pleasant or stimulating. When the colleague I was with asked why I had done that, I hemmed and hawed and said I hadn't wanted to be rude. "Susan," he said, "why didn't you just say 'Excuse me' and leave?" Now there's a concept! The following are three ways you can make a gracious exit.

Exit One

To make your exit easier, wait until *you* have just finished a comment. Then smile, extend your hand for a closing handshake and say, "Nice meeting you. It's interesting that you heard all the great comedians because you bartended in the Catskills." When you summarize the conversation in a short sentence, it shows you have been listening. The old "I need to freshen my drink" line has its drawbacks, first among which is that politeness dictates you should ask others if they would like *their* drinks freshened, too. Then you not only have to return, but you've bought a round of drinks.

Diane Parente, who is full of energy and charm, often will say before she exits a conversation, "I could monopolize you all evening, but I know other people will want to meet you."

Once you extricate yourself, visibly move one quarter of the room away. It underscores the fact that you really did have someone to see or something to do and that you didn't leave that person simply because you were bored. Approach another group or someone else standing alone.

Exit Two

If you spoke to someone who was neither open nor enjoyable, pleasantly say, "I hope you enjoy the rest of the . . ." (conference, meeting, party). No need to be rude because he or she may be preoccupied with other worries. Again, move a quarter of the room away.

Exit Three

Take 'em along. Introduce your new pal to other people. When we help people meet others at an event, they remember our kindness. (And we get another Planet Point, and maybe a new client or referral or friend.)

Before you leave the event, *be sure to thank the host or hostess.* Even if it's a trade-association luncheon rather than a social dinner party, someone is in charge and has spent time planning the food, the program and all the details of the event. Seek that person out and thank him or her. Most people don't, and you'll be remembered and make the right impression.

Beware of the time-consuming, draining thirty-minute departure, in which you say good-bye over and over again, begin short conversations, say good-bye again and slowly, painfully inch yourself toward the door. Ronn Owens, a San Francisco radio talk-show host, suggests that when you are ready to leave, *leave!*

ROANE'S REMINDERS

The following seven strategies will help you work any room.

★ Enter the room with confidence, orient yourself and look for people you either know or *want* to know. And *be nice to everyone!*

★ Go alone or use the buddy system. Go with a friend, a colleague or a significant other and work the room separately. Most people will not intrude on a conversational pas de deux.

★ Seek out other shy people who will appreciate your interest and conversation. Introduce yourself to people who are standing alone.

★ Make the most of name tags. Use the information as a conversation starter, and place the name tag on your right-hand side.

★ Great opening lines come in a million forms. Just about anything will work if it's delivered with a smile and honest interest. Try "Hi!" or "Hello" or, in some cases, "Hey, how are you doing?"

★ Don't be afraid to move in and join conversations already in progress and include those people who want to join your conversation.

★ Moving out of conversations is part of circulating through the room and meeting a variety of new people. Thank the host before you leave.

Advisories:

★ Beware of the consumption assumption. Just because there is an open bar, and we can drink freely, does not mean that we *should* freely drink! It's still business!

★ Treat everyone nicely: You never know!

★ Always introduce yourself by your full name to those whose names you can't retrieve. Ninety percent of the time they will respond in kind, and no one will have to struggle with the name game.

12

WORKING THE WORDS: SEVEN KEYS TO LIVELY CONVERSATION

You've prepared your presence and worked out your strategies for the event. You're in the room now and mingling with ease. You've even chosen someone you want to meet and introduced yourself with charm . . . and maybe a little chutzpah.

SO WHAT DO YOU SAY NEXT?

Even people who make wonderful self-introductions can be stymied by the next step—*making conversation*.

Initial impressions, be they at events or job interviews, are based on our ability to communicate and converse. The trick is to do so with ease, interest and energy. "Nothing is so contagious as enthusiasm; it moves stones, it charms brutes." This statement is attributed to Edward Bulwer-Lytton in the book *637 of the Best Things Anybody Ever Said*.

A sincere interest in people is the most important part of being a good conversationalist. If we're just waiting our turn to speak or manipulating others into talking so we can get information, they will know it. We can listen to others not only with our ears but also with our eyes and our whole face to let them know *we care* about their responses, feelings and thoughts.

Be in the moment. Make those two minutes with each person memorable—by giving them your undivided attention. Do not survey the room for the more important, well-known or attractive people. Leave the scanning to your scanner.

Your first topic of conversation with a new person probably will *not* be nuclear disarmament, famine or the possibility of world economic collapse—unless you are at an event organized around these issues.

As interesting and spirited as those conversations may be, they are *not* the discussions to have at events. According to Miss Manners, "Parties [events] are not the proper venue for holding serious discussions."

THE PREPOSITIONAL AND OTHER PHRASES

Dawne Bernhardt, my speech coach extraordinaire and friend, recommends use of the prepositional phrase to add conversation-sparking details to your stories For example: "I walked along the Embarcadero, past the gourmet chocolate factory, taking photos of the sights and scenery." Within the context of the sentence, these details may spark a comment or question, and you may find a common area of interest to pursue. In that sentence, "past the gourmet chocolate factory" is an added phrase that could invite comments. And it has! Chocolate is one of my favorite conversation starters.

Known as a terrific conversationalist with both clients and colleagues, Ravi Inthiran, now the director of global compliance at McKesson, has a knack for connecting. "I'm a car and motorcycle buff. A few minutes after I meet someone, I'll add a phrase or two about cars or motorcycles to see if there'll be a reaction. Most often there is. We established a common interest, and conversation flows."

What if you're not interested in cars or motorcycles? You could introduce Ravi to someone who is or you can be grateful to learn about his interests and ask questions. Or you "borrow" a relevant story from a friend who shares the car/motorcycle mania.

You will start with small talk. Again, there is nothing small, phony or unimportant about verbal exchanges that work toward establishing common interests or allow people to get to know one another better. I'm with Michael Korda: "There is nothing small about small talk."

Weather is a big topic of interest and that makes it a good topic to pick because it's what we have in common! It's either raining or snowing or sunny on all of us at the same time, and we get to watch the weather 24/7 on its own channel.

The following "Seven Keys to Lively Conversation" will help with both the initial small talk and with the more in-depth business exchanges that may follow. The Seven Keys are designed to make conversation easier, to give you something to say that is interesting and to identify the interests you have in common with the other person.

In the workplace, the common threads are obvious, but what builds rapport and relationships and makes the workplace a good setting are the ties and bonds we create with colleagues and coworkers. It's the sense of community that we build by sharing ideas, thoughts, interests and support. Bob Beck, president and founder of Robert Beck Consulting, LLC, helps people create "neighborhoods" of special interests so they have a common ground for discussions. "Conversation builds these relationships and ultimately the teams . . . which may be very fluid."

Like everything else, good conversation requires planning! To expand on this topic, I wrote *What Do I Say Next?* because so many people have told me that that is what stymied them the most!

I. READ ONE NEWSPAPER A DAY

To have something to talk about, reading a newspaper each day is a must! Even Bill Gates recommended it in a column he wrote several years ago. That's how we glean topics of conversation. Some people balk at this suggestion—until they try it. This is not only the best way I know of to build the "knowledge bank" from which to draw conversation, it can also be fun, entertaining and even addictive! Once you start, it's hard to stop. Whether it's online, an app or on paper, the newspaper is full of conversation topics.

Now we have news aggregates and curators like the *Daily Beast* and you can customize the news topics you prefer to see (e.g., the *Week* and *Flipboard*). We can program our preferences into Yahoo! and Google and wake up to what we want to read. "Newstalk" is no substitute for reading the paper. Television and radio news programs can condense a war into fifteen seconds and replay it every thirty minutes, a presidential election into thirty seconds. You simply can't get much insight into the issues in that amount of time.

People magazine provides great summaries but is also no substitute, and neither are other special-interest magazines. Fascinating as these publications may be, they rarely deal in hard news and don't come out daily.

Why should a busy person with a multitude of demands on his or her time read a daily newspaper? *Because a good conversationalist is well read, well versed and well rounded.* He or she knows what is going on in the world and can talk about the issues. Reading the paper makes working any room infinitely more manageable.

Information is power. Building that "knowledge bank" lets us contribute to conversations with more ease and interest.

It allows us to be aware of "pop cultcha." One does *not* have to be a Dead Head to know about the legacy of Jerry Garcia or a Trekkie to know about Mr. Spock or a teenager to be aware of One Direction.

Do you have to be an expert on everything? Absolutely not. But you must be well read enough to initiate or contribute to conversations. You need enough knowledge of general topics to pose intelligent questions. *Top Tip*: We must listen to the answers to our questions and comment on them—*not* on the price of Porsches or prickly pears.

Intelligent questions allow others to speak about their own areas of expertise and interest. They also give us the chance to *learn* from what other people say. Every event, meeting or party becomes an educational opportunity that provides us with additional information and resources to "bring to the next banquet."

Tips for Perusing the Paper

Whether it's online, in your hand or an app:

- *Start with your favorite section first*—even if it is the comics. I start with Leah Garchik's column in the *San Francisco Chronicle*. There is usually at least one item that begins my day with a laugh.

- *Scan the headlines and first paragraphs* if you're pressed for time and won't have a chance to read the whole paper until later. Fortunately, newspapers are written for busy people and so the major elements of any story—who, what, where, when and how—are almost always covered in the first paragraph.

- *Read the business section*—whether or not you find it particularly appealing at first. If you have a job or are self-employed, you are in business and you need to know what is going on in the business world. You'll be dealing with *other* people who are in business, and you need to know about their concerns.

- The business section isn't nearly as technical or intimidating as some people suspect. You don't have to be a venture capitalist to understand it. The business of newspapers is to *sell newspapers*, and they can't do this if they don't write things that regular people can comprehend and find interesting. Reading the business section gives you information that you can use to connect with people.

- *Read the sports pages!* Even if you aren't an avid fan, you're sure to run into avid fans, and this is a tremendous way to build rapport. Our goal in working a room is to make people feel comfortable with us and to create conversation. If other people are interested in the 49ers or the Cubs or the Maple Leafs, then you are ahead of the game if you know *something* about the sport.

- You don't have to memorize batting averages for the last thirty years, but if the World Series is being played in the city where you are doing business, you should at least know what teams are involved and what is happening. (Shameless plug: The San Francisco Giants, my local team, won the World Series in 2010 and 2012. It was a *huge* topic of conversation.) It shows that you are well-rounded and that *you care about other people's interests.*

- This is a global economy, and soccer is the number one sport in the world. Even if you're not a soccer fan, you know people who are: coworkers, clients and colleagues!

- In one of my presentations to CEOs, one CEO told me he was at a disadvantage because he did not "follow nor have any interest in sports." He further said, "About ninety percent of my employees, clients, colleagues and associates all talk about sports." I wanted to respond with my brother Ira's favorite refrain for the self-absorbed: "Get over yourself!" But I didn't.

- If this CEO already knows that sports are a topic of interest to 90 percent of the people in his work life, he is fortunate. It makes conversation easy to start and allows others to be comfortable. This CEO looked the "gift of gab" horse in the mouth. All he had to do was glance over the headlines and stop being so self-absorbed.

- *Don't forget the comics.* When a particular comic makes me think of someone I know, I often send it to that person. It's a good way to stay in touch, and humor is a wonderful way to connect. My favorite is Hilary Price's

Rhymes with Orange (and most cartoons in *The New Yorker*).

- *Read the lifestyle section.* Here you'll find features, book excerpts and reviews, humor, commentary, fashion news and articles on health, social issues and, well, lifestyles. The lifestyle section provides a wealth of information for your "knowledge bank," and much of it is perfect for starting and continuing conversations—statistics about stress, careers, divorce, back injuries, diets, commuting and so on.

2. CLIP AND COLLECT

Twenty-five years ago I wrote that the CSG (clipping service gene) was originally discovered at the University of Illinois, Champaign-Urbana, when I was a student there. Almost every letter from home contained a clipping. The "relevant article" was usually a letter to Ann Landers or Dear Abby from a brokenhearted mother whose offspring was at college and (choose one): (1) did not write; (2) did not call—unless there was a shortage of funds; (3) did not plan to come home for a holiday; (4) was not lavaliered or pinned; (5) turned down dates with lovely, eligible fellows or gals who were potential candidates for (6) the future potential of grandchildren.

Imagine my dismay when I discovered that CSG, which I identified in *What Do I Say Next?*, is an *inherited genetic* trait! The only consolation was that many of my colleagues had also inherited this chromosomal quirk, and it's a great conversation starter.

Now when I read about clients, colleagues and business

associates in online articles from *Fast Company* to the *San Francisco Chronicle*, I send the link with an email note of congratulations. I then send "an extra hard copy for the relatives." It's something that I appreciate receiving as well.

I mailed copies of every article from the *San Francisco Chronicle* Sporting Green about our outstanding Stanford linebacker, Shayne Skov (#11), to his other grandmother, Victoria GG Kellman, when she lived in New Mexico. "I enjoyed reading the articles online," she said, "but I loved receiving the actual article. In fact, I had several of them framed!" That made me happy I sent her the articles.

It's scary when we turn into our parents and do the things that used to drive us nuts! Sending articles (and even URLs) is appreciated. But trust me, turning into our parents is unavoidable!

3. READ NEWSLETTERS, PROFESSIONAL JOURNALS AND E-ZINES

Sometimes we're invited to events sponsored by organizations with which we're not entirely familiar. Such events as charity fund-raisers, political dinners or clients' Christmas/holiday parties may require some special preparation. The best way to get a handle on the organization is to visit the website and read its newsletter, professional journal or e-zine.

These sources can be invaluable. If you invest the time to read them, you'll be well compensated. You won't be an "outsider"; you'll be familiar with the group and its people and will have all the information you need to ask questions and start conversations.

Should you recognize a member from a photo you saw in

the organization's newsletter or blog, you can bet that person will appreciate and welcome you.

The same is true of reading minutes of the organization's meetings. If you are attending a meeting of a new division or group, ask for the minutes of the past three months. They may even be on the website. You'll impress people with your interest, get a better feel for what's been going on in the group and be prepared to contribute interesting and pertinent information to conversations.

Reading a company's print or online newsletter and visiting its website prepares me for events, parties and presentations I am hired to give.

4. TAKE NOTE AND TAKE NOTES

Other people's clever remarks and stories can be interesting, humorous or poignant conversation starters.

People connect to stories, not necessarily to facts and figures. These statements or situations come from friends, associates, children and people on the street—practically anyone. They happen in the home, at the office, at the health club or at the hairstylist's—anywhere you have your ears open.

What if we feel we don't have something in common with the person we just met? They have different interests that don't mesh with ours. It happens. If that person is the potential client we're supposed to meet, my suggestion is to "borrow other people's lives" and use the stories they tell us. I have no gardening skills or stories, but I borrow Sherwood Cummins' rose garden and talk about his fragrant Mr. Lincoln red roses or his Sterling Silver roses. I have no children, but I borrow the stories my friends tell me that I've written down in order to connect with people who do.

Lana Teplick, my friend and Mobile-based CPA, also provided a terrific tip for parents that I continue to share: "Always be the parent who drives. After a while, the kids think you're part of the steering wheel and continue their conversations as if you're not there. You will always know what is going on!" Parents appreciate her insight and recommendation.

Another friend with whom I taught elementary school, Sylvia Cherezian, is mother to two wonderful young men. One day when her son Charles was two, she cried in exasperation, "Oh dear, I've given birth to a child whom I would *never* have allowed in my classroom!" I share that comment with colleagues who mention that they have children and the conversation flows. I don't have children, so remembering these stories allows me to "borrow their lives."

HIP-HOP HAPPENING

Being Grandma Susan to the Skovs has provided me with volumes of great stories over the years. When Patrick Skov was ten years old, I noticed that he was wearing a pair of black side-snap pants. I mentioned his were similar to the ones I wore to hip-hop class. He looked a bit startled and said, "You really take hip-hop classes? Show me." I spent a minute trying to remember a routine and then tried to "bust a move."

Patrick rolled his eyes, looked at me and asked (a rhetorical question), "You actually paid for *that*?" I then realized I'd never be a backup dancer for Beyoncé. Patrick, now a fullback at Stanford, proved, once again, that kids still say the darndest and funniest things.

MY COLLECTION OF CLEVER QUIPS

Whether it's from a conversation with a friend, a client, a relation, the barista or a line from *Downton Abbey, The Daily Show* or *The Big Bang Theory*, I capture these great lines on paper and attribute my sources. You could say I'm never at a loss, thanks to other people's words.

In order to use these comments and situations as conversation starters, we have to *remember* them. Some people write them down in a journal each evening; others carry a small spiral notebook to jot them down or they may add them to their smartphones or use an app like Evernote or create a voice memo. Even the most unforgettable line or story can get lost if we don't take the time to record it somewhere. To rewrite this book, I had to read and reread a file full of stories I had jotted down. The miracle: that I could read them!

I often share the best piece of advice I received from my personal mentor, Mumsy (Joyce Siegel): "Do not spend your time with anyone whom, after you leave, you waste one minute thinking about what they meant by what was said."

People say great things that we can quote, and that contributes to our conversations.

Caveat: Always, always attribute, quote and cite your sources. If not, your "retelling" without proper acknowledgment could incite your sources. Get permission to use names. Some stories are funny but might be embarrassing. You'll notice that in this book my sources are quoted, and they have given me permission to use their stories.

QUIPS, QUOTES AND COMMENTS COLLECTION

"Only dull women live in immaculate homes."
>   —A guest on a TV talk show

"Sometimes the thing that comes around the corner is better than what's planned."
>   —Actor Robert Duvall on *Sunday Morning*

"There's no room in my head for poetry because it's full of . . . passwords."
>   —Stephen Colbert on *The Colbert Report*

"They say my show is being 're-purposed.' If that's true, I want to be re-paid!"
>   —Ellen DeGeneres at a National Association of
>   Television Program Executives convention

"If I take ginkgo, I can remember to take my Viagra."
>   —Harrison Ford, the Actors Studio

"The parts that didn't put me to sleep . . . bored me to death."
>   —Ira Rosenberg, assessment of *Chariots of Fire*

"When we forget, we open the door for repetition."
>   —Simon Wiesenthal

"I'm not a magician. It's a comb, not a wand!"
>   —Tracy Mazza, hairstylist, upon being informed by
>   a hairstyling client that she now wanted to have curly
>   hair

"Any play that can be described in one sentence should be one sentence long."
                    —Edward Albee

"The thing about a moral compass—if you take it out and look at it from time to time, you don't have to wait for history to tell you you were going in the wrong direction."
                    —Jon Stewart, *The Daily Show*

"When I was your age, television was called . . . books."
                    —"Grandfather" Peter Falk to grandson in *The Princess Bride*

"If you're not appearing, you're disappearing."
                    —Art Blakely of Jazz Messengers

"I rarely got in trouble for what I did—but always for what I said."
                    —Will Smith, the Actors Studio

"Caution is a virtue; self-interest is not."
                    —Countess Crawley (Dame Maggie Smith), *Downton Abbey*

"If you're going to have peer pressure, pick better peers."
                    —Comedian Lewis Black at a book signing

"She knows how to engage people in a few split seconds from meeting them."
                    —Prince William about his grandmother, Queen Elizabeth

"No one I know reads what I write. Thank heavens for you strangers."

—NPR's Sarah Vowell, at a book signing, aired on Bookspan TV

5. USE HUMOR (SURELY YOU JEST)

Humor has a special way of bringing people together. It can establish rapport and warmth among people. It's an unique and magical elixir that can even heal the body.

Both management and medical research support the value of humor. Laughter is good for your health. "Laughter works by stimulating the brain to produce hormones that help ease pain. It also stimulates the endocrine system, which may relieve symptoms of disease. Laughter can also help feelings of depression," said Dr. William Fry of Stanford Medical School. Since Dr. Fry's original research, we have read volumes about humor as a tonic. (We need to remember it's not a medical cure.)

You don't have to be a stand-up comic to use humor. Humor can be defined in two ways. First, it is the quality of being funny, and second, it's the ability to perceive, enjoy or express something that is funny.

The right sentence or phrase at the right moment can save a negotiation or a board meeting. But humor should be used judiciously, because it can offend as well as delight. I'm usually wary when I hear the phrase, "Did you hear the one about the . . . ?" Usually we just read it on a forwarded email or heard it on a late-night television monologue.

Humor Dos and Don'ts

- Practice your stories and punch lines. I once practiced my opening story for a presentation seventeen times before the timing was right.

- Watch comedies, both on television and at the movies, and read books about humor. I watch *The Daily Show* with a paper and a pencil by my side (and always attribute the funny lines).

- Use the "AT&T rule" to check any story or joke: Is it appropriate? Tasteful? Timely?

- Laugh at yourself: It is a trait of people who take risks. Some of the best stories are those you tell on yourself.

- Observe for irony. One day I saw a fellow in the lotus position outside Mollie Stone's supermarket. His eyes were closed in a meditative state. And . . . he was smoking a cigarette! Meditative or menthol? Talk about ironic.

- "Don't tell jokes if you don't tell them well," advises David Glickman, corporate comedian, professional speaker and author of *Punchline Your Bottom Line*.

- Don't put people down. "Roasting" can create a slow burn—one that can backfire.

- Don't use humor that is racist, sexist or homophobic or "humor" that slurs religion, ethnic origin or disability. (San Francisco cantor Rita Glassman shared a version of a nursery rhyme: "Sticks and stones can break my bones and names can only hurt me!")

- Don't be afraid to let go and laugh. It's good for you and makes working the room a lot more enjoyable.

6. LISTEN ACTIVELY, NOT PASSIVELY

As a raconteur and "talker," I have always been sensitive to the criticism about talkers. Research shows that just because a person is a good "talker" doesn't mean he or she is not also a good "listener."

All of us need to be good listeners, and that means more than staring into someone's eyes while he or she talks—while you're planning tomorrow's meeting or rethinking the movie you saw last night.

Active listening means *hearing* what people say, concentrating on them and their words and responding. When we really pay attention, concentrate on that one person and are in the moment, we improve our chances of remembering both the person and the conversation.

In my How to Work a Room program, people practice role-playing as "talkers" and "listeners." Thousands of "talkers" have said that the most important behaviors of active listeners, the things that most encouraged them to talk, were what I call the Magnificent Seven:

The Magnificent Seven of Listening

1. Making eye contact/nodding
2. Smiling and/or laughing
3. Asking relevant questions that indicate interest
4. Making statements that reflect similar situations
5. Having body language that is open and receptive
6. Hearing what is *not* said
7. Bringing the conversation full circle

If we are conscious of listening actively, our conversational skills will improve. Working a room will be less work and more fun. Conversation may be a dying art, but with preparation and interest, we can revive it.

7. JUST SAY YES TO NEW OPPORTUNITIES

One way to make interesting conversation is to say "yes" to opportunities that are out of your realm of expertise or area of interest. I often do that to expand my horizons and "conversation content." It's one of the eight traits of the successful people I featured in my book *How to Create Your Own Luck*.

That's why I went rappelling with a friend. It was an exhilarating experience and gave me fuel for conversation! I often say that rappelling is a sport aptly named.

There are some things I do only once; just to know I can. Like baking bread. Once I made an egg bread (challah) and, to my amazement, it was delicious. I've never done it since. There are bakers who make a living baking challah and they need my support.

When we say yes to new experiences that are out of our ordinary realm, we have more to contribute to the conversation of life!

I'M SORRY

There are some people who just can't admit they were wrong or that they said or did something that was egregious. The person who sincerely apologizes accepts responsibility and owns the mistake. That can clear the air, repair those fences that need mending and allow discussion, projects, meetings or conversations to move forward.

FAMOUS APOLOGIES

Some famous apologies are sincere, others contrite, others are nothing more than public self-service announcements. Still others, and the deeds that prompted them, give our professional comedians grist for their mills. We've been "entertained" by behaviors and apologies of governors, representatives, senators and several mayors.

"MY BAD" IS REALLY BAD

The new kid on the apology block, "my bad," is a trendy expression that is insincere. It's merely an admission without contrition. It discounts the mistake made and any feelings that were hurt. When you have messed up, don't make a bigger mess. Avoid the really bad "my bad."

Here are some examples of apologies that could work when we have erred:

★ "I'm sorry. I didn't mean to . . ."
★ "What was I thinking?"
★ "This looks like my doing."
★ "Let's see how we can rectify my error."
★ "Please accept my apology."
★ "I'll be more aware in the future."

Another apology to avoid is "I'm sorry, *but* . . ." That's considered a nonapology and doesn't show acceptance of responsibility or contrition. Save the spinning for your favorite dreidl or exercise class.

The person who never apologizes, never thinks he or she is wrong and never accepts responsibility for a possible mistake is difficult to be around. It's hard for the rest of us to interact with such a self-absorbed, self-focused and self-righteous person. The person who is never wrong comes off as the know-it-all, leaving the rest of us feeling like the "know very little or nothing" crowd. That gets old very fast.

FIVE FUNDAMENTAL LAWS OF CASUAL CONVERSATION

Here are the five basic laws that govern easygoing, casual conversation:

- *Be a conversational chameleon.* Adapt conversation to the individual by age, interest and/or profession. We don't talk to five-year-olds the same way we talk to ten-year-olds or thirty-five-year-olds.

- *Borrow other people's lives.* Share the stories, comments and quips of your friends who have kids or who are taking tae kwon do or who have season tickets to the opera—even if you don't.

- *Be a two-timer.* Give people a second chance.

- *Be nice to everyone.* Don't judge tomorrow's book by to-day's cover.

- *Be a name-dropper.* Always mention the names of people or places you could have in common to establish a connection.

An Emergency Name-Dropping

Name-dropping is not to be done in an officious and offensive manner. It's simply a way to find out if people are related to or know the people that you know or know of.

Sometimes that "room" can be a specialized one. Dr. Jaime Cintado is an emergency room doctor in San Francisco. He arrived early one morning to find a patient with a very deep cut on her finger. He looked at her cut and her chart. Because it was early and the waiting room wasn't full yet, he had time. He took a deep breath and said, "I don't suppose you're related to Robert Fripp of King Crimson." Dr. Cintado said he was thinking that she'd have no clue who King Crimson was.

Imagine his surprise when Patricia Fripp assured him that, in fact, the renowned guitarist and a founder of King Crimson was her brother! As he "glued" her finger, Dr. Cintado told her that he had heard Robert play in Nashville, where he went to medical school. And in fact, "Robert answered my question during audience Q and A."

When he finished treating her wound, Patricia suggested they find a place with better cell phone coverage, "I'm sure Brother would want to thank you for saving his sister's life." Dr. Jaime Cintado, fan of Robert Fripp, had quite a nice conversation with him. Now they have someone special in common.

Postscript: When Robert Fripp came to San Francisco and joined Patricia for a morning fireside chat/presentation at a local breakfast club, Dr. Jaime Cintado was there. Because he spoke up, he met the man whose musicianship he had admired.

What if she weren't related to Robert Fripp and Dr. Cintado mentioned him? She might have said, "No, but I get that question a lot." Their conversation would have segued to another topic. Maybe even Fripp Island in South Carolina? Who knows.

What we do know is that if Jaime Cintado did not ask the question about Robert Fripp, he would have missed the opportunity to meet him and become a hero and friend to both Fripp kids.

This cannot be overstated: You never know who people know or what their career move will be. Take a chance. Bring your OAR: Observe, ask, reveal.

FATAL FLAWS OF CASUAL CONVERSATION

These behaviors are to be avoided at all costs:

- Being unprepared by not reading newspapers, trade journals, websites and other information sources
- Controlling conversations; asking a barrage of questions, no matter how open-ended; or telling a nonstop series of jokes
- Complaining (kvetching) and bragging
- One-upping/competing, interrupting, not listening and slinging put-downs
- Offering unsolicited feedback (my pet peeve)

ECHOING THE SOUNDS OF SILENCE

Silence has its place in conversation. As the late Professor Morrie Schwartz of Brandeis University asked rhetorically in *Tuesdays with Morrie*: "What is it about silence that makes us so uncomfortable?" It allows us to consider what we have heard.

A late retired school executive secretary and my dear friend Gert Gurd gave me some sage advice, "Sometimes the unspoken word is the best thing you can say."

However, when we are asked to speak to an audience, conversing with them before our presentation is engaging and easier when we employ the Seven Keys.

ROANE'S REMINDERS

Remember the Seven Keys to Lively Conversation:

★ Read one local or national newspaper, either online or in print, or an online content curator a day. Local, national and international conversation starters fill the pages.

★ Clip and collect cartoons, announcements or articles of interest to you and your network. Send them (via URL and/or USPS).

★ Read magazines, professional and local business journals, e-zines and minutes for up-to-the-minute topics of conversation.

★ Take note and take notes when you hear something interesting or witty or observe the odd or absurd.

★ Use humor carefully. Be lighthearted and don't take yourself so seriously. No "dissing" of others.

★ Listen actively—with ears, eyes and heart. Truly pay attention.

★ Say yes to new opportunities. Doing, seeing or visiting something new and out of our everyday interests gives us something to talk about.

13

HOW TO WORK
AN AUDIENCE

You've been invited to give a presentation to a client's sales force or your local chamber of commerce, rotary club, college alumni or professional association or at a local high school's career day. You get a queasy feeling in your stomach and dry mouth!

It's been said that the number one fear is public speaking. Not true. The most uncomfortable situation that creates fear is walking into a room full of strangers, which most people will have to do at one time or another. But public speaking is also daunting and ranks as our number two fear.

Giving a speech to strangers! Talk about a double-whammy stomach churner. Remember, if you were invited to speak to a group, it's because of your knowledge, experience and success. People think you have something to contribute. Congratulations! That is a huge compliment.

One of the most effective skills we can develop is our ability to speak in front of an audience. CEOs do it all the time. When I was a teacher, it was a skill that I taught my students. It was *not* easy to get the self-conscious kids to take this "risk." But I knew they would have to present team projects in high school and that their oral presentation skills would serve them well in their futures. It was my job as their teacher to prepare them.

As you can imagine, I was *not* the most popular teacher. Because I also taught grammar, punctuation and research skills, my rep as the tough teacher of the boring subjects was already sealed. But I had/have a good sense of humor, and if a student wrote something that was funny, I laughed. None was funnier than Matthew Weinhold, one of my favorite students. He went on to win the Seattle Comedy Competition and has been a writer and voice artist and doing stand-up for over twenty years. I tell people I gave him his start in fifth grade!

Truth be told, I also taught my students to listen, and I made them behave. It was *not* enough for my students to write a grand paper or deliver it as an oral presentation. The students had to have good audience behavior for the other students' presentations, as they were graded on that, too. It's a good lesson in life. Colleagues, clients and bosses can observe how people behave in an audience.

AUDIENCE BEHAVIOR BACKFIRES

There can be unexpected consequences. Craig Harrison, owner of the website Expressions of Excellence, is a speaker and trainer who knows firsthand how audience behavior can backfire.

"I was conducting a sales training for an athletic equipment company in the Midwest. For the most part it went well, except for the four guys at the back table who were making wisecracks and being disruptive. I decided not to call them on their misbehavior and thought it was payback for something I did in seventh grade.

"After my program, the vice president of sales thanked me for the presentation and how well I handled these guys and said, 'What they don't know is that we're planning a reorganization and have to let go of some people. These guys weren't team players. We didn't know who we were going to fire; now we do.'" This isn't seventh grade; bad audience behavior has grown-up consequences.

How can *we* ensure good audience behavior? Simple: *Work the audience ahead of time!* As a professional speaker who has spoken to hundreds of audiences ranging from thirty to three thousand, I've been my own warm-up act. When we warm up the audience, they are receptive to our presentation and us. In a nutshell, talk to audience members *before* you are introduced to speak.

One of my clients hosted a casual 7:30 a.m. breakfast for their people. Although I wasn't scheduled to speak until 10:00 a.m., I offered to greet them at the breakfast. That the attendees were welcomed set the tone for the two-day session, and I connected on a personal level—and ended up with valuable material for my presentation!

Additionally, have a prepared introduction that requires the audience to turn off their cellphones and other interrupting accessories.

REMEDIES FOR ROADBLOCKS

The people you're meeting are not strangers. You have something in common with them. Maybe it's your profession, your community, your membership in a nonprofit organization or your membership of a board of directors. Or maybe it's a sales presentation to potential clients.

Casually introduce yourself to individuals. Look at their

name tags. Make a comment or an observation or ask a question about the information.

- "Nice to see you." (Accompany this with a firm handshake, eye contact and a smile.)
- "What brings you to the event?"
- "Oh, I'm originally from Chicago. Where did you go to high school?" (This question precedes the "Where did you go for pizza? Hot dogs? Italian beef?")
- "Great tie. I see you're a *South Park* fan, too. Cartman was my favorite character, but now I like Kyle."

GREETING AND MEETING

As the presenter you can be the greeter at the door as attendees enter the room, which I have done. People were so surprised and pleased to be "welcomed" into the conference luncheon, especially by their speaker. Or walk into the audience as they are being seated and greet them. Move around the room. You don't have to talk to each person, but do make sure you are in each section. Do include others by initiating eye contact. Get to the back of the room because the people who go for the seats in the last few rows may need the most "warming up."

It's my policy to chat with people who have seated themselves in the last four rows. That's when I have the most fun. "So you sat here for a quick getaway? You look like you have a good sense of humor. Could you help me and laugh at the punch lines?"

At a major IT security conference several years ago, there were two guys in the last row furiously working their Black-

Berrys. "You know, you can't do that during my presentation." One of the fellows just stared. "Oops!" I said, "that's my inner teacher talking."

Who knew his mom was a first-grade teacher? She must be good; her son put away his BlackBerry!

The people with whom you have chatted will pay attention because you're now a person, not just a presenter, and there's now a personal connection. The audience members who saw you talk to others get that same sense.

You have engaged your audience. They are now ready to listen to you. You have set the tone.

TIPS FOR TERRIFIC TALKS

- *Know* your audience. Ask the program chairperson several questions:

  Who will attend?

  How many will be in the audience?

  What is the audience demographic?

  How is the program billed?

  What is the goal for your program?

  Who else is on the program and/or your panel?

  What are the needs of the group?

  Why were you invited?

- *Read* the group's newsletter, trade journals, program brochure.

- *Visit* the group's website.

- *Interview* several people who will attend.
- *Prepare* your material. Get comfortable with the Power-Point visuals if you plan to use them.
- *Send* your introduction ahead of time, with the correct pronunciation of your name spelled phonetically.
- *Practice* so you are familiar with the three key points, subpoints and vignettes that support your points.
- *Attend* the group's receptions; they will appreciate your presence, and you'll get more material to personalize your presentation.
- *Greet and meet* members of the audience.

You have just had conversations with audience members. Continue that conversation from the platform when you deliver your presentation. Talk *with* the audience, not at them.

FREE SPEECH PAYS OFF

"I've been chastised by friends when I mention that I'm speaking for free at an event. They believe that you should always be paid for your time, regardless of the activity," said Dan Schawbel, author of *Promote Yourself* and founder of Millennial Branding. "One of my colleagues even said, 'Why aren't you being paid, you're crazy.'

"A few years ago, I was at a point in my speaking business when I was trying to get represented by a national speakers' bureau so that I could grow that aspect of my career. No one would take me.

"Later, I was invited to speak at my alma mater, Bentley

University, for a group of students who were interested in how to find a job upon graduation. There were about forty students listening to my presentation and a handful stayed afterward to ask me additional questions.

"A few months later, one of the students in my audience, Amanda Healy, contacted me. She now had a job at CA Technologies, a large B2B technology company, and was reaching out because they were looking for a speaker to talk specifically about social media and personal branding—my specialty.

"I contacted the speakers' bureau to tell them about that speaking engagement and they immediately added me on their roster because this opportunity proved my worth to them. Although I originally spoke at Bentley for free, the outcome was that I achieved the next level in my speaking career."

Sometimes the best-intentioned advice of our friends is not right for us. If Dan had not been generous with his time and expertise, this career-changing opportunity would not have happened. Dan continues to keep in touch with Amanda and serve as her mentor and friend.

Sometimes the rooms we work and work in we do as a volunteer. The rewards are unplanned and even more precious.

OPENING LINES

Don't start with a joke unless you wrote it and are great with delivery. Many people will have already heard it or read it in an email. Start with a story/vignette that happened to you or one you observed or that you were told in conversation or overheard. *Do not* tell a story that you've heard often or that another speaker has used. It is his or her material, not yours. You run the risk of retelling a vignette the audience already knows. Boring and not smart. And it demonstrates a lack of creativity, authenticity and preparation.

Tell your own vignettes. The "stories" are everywhere. Observe. Listen Write them immediately. Start telling these fun, ironic, odd occurrences to your friends. Observe their reactions. Brainstorm with yourself. Go to your favorite thinking place with a spiral index card book (any drugstore has them). Write one vignette per index card. Or use your smartphone note-taking app to capture the story.

Once I was aerobic walking, talking to myself, and voilà—a concept and the title of a chapter ("How to Work the Techno-Toy Room") popped into my brain. Because I kept paper and pen in my fanny pack, I wrote it down immediately or I would have lost the thought.

Technology has had an impact on this former Luddite. Now I always carry my cell phone on aerobic walks. As soon as I formulate an idea, I call myself and leave the information on my machine's second mailbox. That way I don't struggle deciphering my writing and the intonation is intact.

Wearing my Bluetooth has another advantage. Often I am practicing my upcoming presentation or working out a concept for a book or my blog aloud, which makes me look to others like I'm talking to myself. Now I always wear my Bluetooth so people will think I'm on the phone!

Be ready for ideas at all times. Use your phone or small digital recorder to record a voice memo or take small pads of paper everywhere! I still keep a memo pad in my purse.

Gather your own material, and your presentation will be unique and yours alone. Include research stats and comments from the experts, and give proper attribution to all sources (otherwise it is plagiarizing). This shows you did your homework.

Treat your audiences as the intelligent people they are. You may know a lot about web design, financial planning, a new surgical procedure or stress management, but don't act patronizing.

Customize your program for the needs and the members of the audience. I was on a program for Darden Restaurants with Secretary Colin Powell, who took the time to do his homework and made his presentation relate to his audience of restaurant managers. So should we all! And I took notes, learned and was smitten with General Powell's down-to-earthiness.

If the thought of a presentation to clients, potential clients, colleagues or community is so uncomfortable, join a Toastmasters group. Or start one in your company. The rewards will be well worth the time you invest.

And if you work your audience before you speak, you will be a hit!

HERE'S LOOKING AT YOU . . .

While Bogie is credited with that famous line, it does pass for a toast *Casablanca*-style. In our personal and professional lives we will be asked and expected to give toasts, be it for a wedding, a retirement dinner, a company celebration, an anniversary or a bachelor party. Whether it is business or social, proposing a badly conceived and poorly delivered toast is, unfortunately, unforgettable.

Here are some commonsense guidelines to delivering a toast that makes a great impression in any room.

Magnificent Seven Toast Tips:

1. It is *not* about us. It's about the honoree. Limit the "I's."

2. A toast is not a roast. So we must be careful about the stories we decide to share and the private information revealed.

3. Being tipsy during a toast could make us trip up our words, say something we should not say and put a damper on the occasion.

4. Memorize your no-more-than-three-minute toast (never read it); make eye contact with the guests who are your audience.

5. Remember the "appropriate" test: Is this what you'd say in front of your boss or grandpa?

6. Avoid foul language.

7. Start with your best story.

A good toast has the right balance of humor and honorific. Plan what you will say and use a story or stories that support the purpose of the toast. Be sure that there is eye contact with the honoree and the guests. Having notes in your hand is okay; reading them word for word is not. Be sure you practice using the microphone. I recently coached a father of the groom on the drafting of his toast. My suggestion for the best ending: "Ask people to lift a glass and join you."

GREAT OPENING ACTS

Being asked to introduce a speaker is another moment that can make an impression on the audience and contribute to our careers. It's fair to ask the speaker for information that he or she would like included. Some speakers will supply a bio, but that's not an introduction.

The introduction is about the speaker, not the introducer. It relates the speaker to the audience and positions him or her as the expert and honored presenter. The purpose of an introduction is to set up the audience to want to listen to the speaker. We do that by presenting relevant accomplishments and the relation of the speaker to the topic. The right tone of voice is one that indicates respect for the speaker and foreshadows the benefit of listening to the presentation.

The introduction should not be more than two minutes, and it should be practiced so that the words feel comfortable and shine the light on the speaker. Generally speaking, adding in your comments about the topic, your stories about the speaker can take time and take the focus away from the presenter.

We need to prepare and practice before we stand and deliver it so that presentations, toasts and introductions do deliver and that we make the right impression.

SOME ADDITIONAL THOUGHTS

Listen to other speakers. The people who do it most often are standing at the pulpits in churches, temples and synagogues.

On occasion I flip through the channels when I want to see what's on TV. That's how I discovered Pastor Joel Osteen of Houston's Lakewood Church. Listening to his

words and watching his delivery is instructive as well as in-
spiring. Pastor Osteen is a wonderful storyteller and sermon-
izer whose humor is self-deprecating. The "conversation" he
has with his parishioners and television audiences makes his
points of wisdom universal.

Attend company programs where your CEO is speaking.
If you are the CEO, attend the conference board sessions or
industry conferences.

Listen to tapes of the great orators. Go to comedy clubs
and observe the stand-up comics. Take a class in comedy
or improvisation. Watch Comedy Central and situation
comedies. *The Big Bang Theory* is a current favorite because
the writing is brilliant and delivery is perfect. Attend local
speaker series talks. Go to your local National Speakers Association's meetings.

At the CEO/executive level, work with a speech coach. I
have worked with executive speech coach Dawne Bernhardt
for almost two decades. Dawne had me define my goals and
vision as a speaker before she would offer feedback. Her
manner of giving feedback is so gracious that you're inspired
to self-correct immediately.

Go to live performances and observe how entertainers
"work" their audiences. Mandy Patinkin, now of *Homeland*,
formerly and always Inigo Montoya, is master at the banter.
The Divine Miss M (Bette Midler) taught me a microphone
technique I now use. And Billy Crystal's use of the handheld
microphone to create voices and sounds is instructive. Idina
Menzel, who's "gleefully" not too "wicked," worked her audience by speaking with us. But please note, as a presenter
you do not have license to "pick on" any audience members
as the entertainers do. I saw a speaker do this at a national
convention, and it was most unseemly and infuriating.

If you talk with your audience beforehand, you will

never need a gimmick or have to do shtick to capture their attention.

Caution: Millennials and Generation Y audiences were weaned on technology. "Don't try to wow these generations with technical expertise or artistic abilities in your Power-Point slides or handouts; just show them you know how to play," advises Cam Marston, who speaks on demographic shift.

By the same token, if you refer to a blog, explain what that is. Even though there are, to date, more than three hundred million of them, some members of your audience may not know what a blog is, much less have read one. Following my own advice, a blog is a web log/dialog journal of thoughts.

Caution: Do not sound overcoached or overpracticed. Your words will lose their authenticity.

ROANE'S REMINDERS

★ Hone your public-speaking skills.

★ Work your audience by greeting, meeting and conversing with them prior to your program.

★ Introduce yourself. Use name tags for conversation; move into and around each section of the audience.

★ Prepare for your presentation.

★ Start with an attention-getting observation, vignette or statistic.

★ Collect stories daily. Fun, interesting, odd and ironic occurrences happen all the time.

★ Customize your presentation for the audience.

★ Listen to other speakers and the great orators.

★ Observe entertainers to see how they engage the audience.

★ Practice your presentation so that it flows like a conversation.

★ Join Toastmasters to gain confidence and comfort with public speaking.

★ Work with an experienced, qualified speech coach.

★ Allow for spontaneity as long as your on-the-spot addition supports the topic.

Advisory:

★ Drink only room-temperature water (ice constricts vocal cords).

★ Avoid dairy and chocolate before a presentation as they are believed to cause extra mucus.

★ Be sure your phone is turned off!

14

WORKING THE RULES OF ETIQUETTE: GOOD MANNERS EQUAL GOOD BUSINESS

Mention the words *etiquette* or *good manners* and the most boring or vacuous conversation or meeting becomes highly charged. Why would such old-fashioned terms create such lively interest? One reason is that manners and etiquette are disappearing. I wrote that twenty-five years ago and the situation has dramatically deteriorated over the past decades.

Another reason is that the preponderance of techno-gadgets provides ample opportunity for misuse and rudeness. Our current 24/7/365 world offers our constant connectivity that has obliterated what we call common sense and common courtesy.

Many people are too "busy" or preoccupied with "more important things" to practice common courtesies—responding to RSVPs, extending a thank-you, making good introductions and treating others with courtesy and respect. Some people, it seems, were never taught the "niceties"—thoughtfulness and consideration. Yet bad manners can be deadly—both to the reputation and to the bottom line. It's not nice to hurt people's feelings or offend sensibilities and it's not good business practice, either.

The opposite is true as well. "If you have a great product, a commitment to service and treat your customers and employees with common courtesy, the market share will take care of itself," says Tom Peters, guru, author and speaker.

How are we, in general, *supposed* to behave at a party, reception or convention? The answer: *very well!*

But what is behaving well? The expectations are much the same as those that parents and teachers have of children:

1. Know the rules.
2. Observe the rules.
3. Do so graciously.

If you don't already know the rules of formal etiquette and business etiquette, it's wise to learn them. Many good references are available online, in bookstores and libraries.

The problem is that so many of the rules have changed that even people who were taught in various "white-glove" schools of etiquette often don't have any idea what the current rules are. Experts have scrambled to write books on new etiquette, business etiquette, social media etiquette, teen etiquette, Internetiquette, gadget etiquette—you name it! Clearly, things have changed. There is such a dearth of proper behavior that companies offer etiquette courses.

A local camp offers etiquette classes for tween campers. There's a five-week class offered in my community for seven- to eleven-year-olds. There are teas for toddlers and tykes to expose them to proper behavior. Each room (the wedding, funeral, party, etc.), has its own customs and rules. We ought to know them no matter how old we are.

ETIQUETTE AND MANNERS

Etiquette is defined as "the usages and rules for behavior in polite society, official or professional life." Certain basic rules are still accepted as the norm, and it behooves us to know both the *old* etiquette and the *new* etiquette. The executive suites of corporate America require it.

But knowing the rules of etiquette is not enough. What we're really after is manners—that wonderful combination of courtesy, caring and common sense.

There is a difference between knowing the rules of etiquette, being a person of manners and understanding the manner in which we relate to others. Some people follow every rule of etiquette but have a manner that is condescending and/or patronizing.

There is an old story about a Washington hostess who noticed that one of her guests used the wrong fork at a formal dinner and pointed out this error to him in front of the other guests. She knew the proper etiquette but showed a lack of good manners. Why? *Hosts with good manners don't embarrass their guests.*

In contrast, when Lady Astor's guest picked up the wrong fork, she picked up the wrong fork, too, so that he wouldn't be embarrassed.

People with good manners also treat others with respect. Knowing the rules is one thing; caring about people and treating them with consideration is something else.

Bob Beck, president and founder of Robert Beck Consulting Group, LLC, whom I met when he was executive vice president at Bank of America and hired me for a series of presentations, has often been asked whom he credited with giving him the most help in his career. People want to learn the name of this important mentor. "My mother," Bob said.

"She not only taught me that I could do whatever I tried but also how to treat people *courteously*."

Courtesy is the cornerstone of good manners. According to my *Standard Collegiate Dictionary*, "To be courteous is to be polite while having a warmer regard for the feelings and dignity of others."

This is reflected in our use of the techno toys, cell phones, radios and even the car stereo! It's how we behave with clients, coworkers, friends, family and strangers.

If people are comfortable with us, our presence at any event will be valued. And we will be remembered—for the right reasons.

How we behave in every room we enter contributes to our reputation. People talk. In what seems to be this "it's all about me" decade of viral marketing, we must be careful not to create bad buzz. The word on the Internet spreads farther and much faster than a wildfire.

John Rosemond, a psychologist and syndicated columnist, wrote that manners and character are inseparable. He quoted the esteemed rebbe, Rabbi Menachim Mendel Schneerson, who extolled the virtue of a solid foundation of character. Manners matter and they say volumes about our character and us.

"OPEN DOOR" POLICY

Or should I say the "*Hold* Open the Door" policy, which is one we ought to embrace because it's good manners and good business. It helps in building, maintaining and growing a solid reputation. And that can only be positive. It's not just men who should hold open the door for women; it's something we should all do for each other. Attorney Francine Ward told me, "When I'm going through a door, I turn around to see who's behind me—male or female—and I hold the door open for them." It's such a thoughtful gesture.

One of my mom colleagues said that she worked very hard to teach her son good manners. "I'm always so appreciative of the person who thanks my son and comments on his good manners." Point well taken.

TECH CRUNCH TIME

Jon Orlin, executive producer of TechCrunch TV convinced me to attend TechCrunch Disrupt in 2010, a three-day event in San Francisco's Tech Town area. I arrived a bit late, as did a fellow who was nice enough to hold the door open for me. We started a conversation about finding parking—always a topic of interest—and exchanged cards. Kris Duggan is the founder of Badgeville, now the leader in gamification. That year his company won Tech Crunch Disrupt Audience Award. When I received the e-blast, I sent Kris a congratulatory personal email and heard right back from him. Every time they won an award or were mentioned in the media, I sent a note and always received a response. When Badgeville hosted their first Engage event, my RSVP must have been one of the first. Though I only knew Kris, I met other interesting people. I even heard Brian Solis—whom I follow on Twitter—speak and had a chance to converse with him.

It's wonderful to watch the growth and success of one of the well-mannered good guys who practiced the "hold open the door" policy.

MANNERS MAVENS

The bad news is that the rules have changed—and continue to change at warp speed.

The good news is that it's easy to get help. You can search online for it. The changing rules of etiquette have spawned a whole new industry. Books, columns, seminars and even software programs and websites on etiquette are readily available. There is a great demand for expert consultants who can show us the acceptable conventions for social and business behavior, because people want to know. That is one of the reasons my presentations have been sought after in the business world. People want and need the reminders.

Letitia Baldrige claims that manners are 99 percent common sense and 1 percent kindness.

THE RSVP

RSVP stands for *Répondez s'il vous plaît*. This translates from the French as "Please respond." (And if you don't, you may not get invited again—at least to my house.)

A social invitation requires a response. That's all there is to it. To compensate for a general deterioration in etiquette, response cards are often included in invitations. These days, people have added phone numbers and email addresses, just so they can figure out the guest tally and how much food to order. (Notice I didn't say "to prepare"!)

E-vite and other online invitation sites ask for an RSVP and even offer a "maybe" category. They automatically "nudge" us with reminders, and that's a good thing.

The problem with a "regrets only" RSVP is that you mistakenly assume that those who haven't called in regrets will attend. It's far better to get a confirmation from those who intend to show up.

It seems there is an epidemic of no responses to all forms of invitations. It can be attributed to indecisiveness, commitment phobia or a desire among invitees to wait and see if they receive a better invitation to do something else. Savvy, thoughtful people respond whether or not they can attend and don't leave hosts dangling.

RSVP FOR BUSINESS

RSVPs for business events, meetings and association luncheons are a bit different. The expectation is that you will preregister and prepay or will call in a reservation. For many events you have the option of registering and prepaying online. And you are expected to attend if you reserve. You generally do not have to call to say you won't be able to attend unless you've already responded and committed to being there.

It's not good manners or good business to be a drop-in. I have attended many luncheons where too many "busy" people (*much* too busy to bother making a reservation) showed up at the door at the last minute. The food count was thrown way off balance—and so was the luncheon's chairperson! Leftovers for an army (or worse, a shortage of shrimp puffs) is every host's nightmare.

If you find out at the last minute that you'll be able to attend after all, at least call the morning of the event to let them know you're coming.

Several clients told me horror stories of commitment

phobes who never respond lest they have to show up. One woman told me that at least ten people sent in RSVPs for her wedding and did *not* show. The cost was about $1,250—and several friendships!

To RSVP shows good manners, good business, consideration, breeding and respect.

INTRODUCTIONS

Many people feel awkward about introductions because they remember being taught that there was one right way to do it—and they can't remember what that one right way is. So they stand there, with two people whom they want to introduce, stammering, "Uh . . . Jon, meet Susan . . . uh, no . . . Susan, Jon. My friend . . . uh . . ." Much of the warmth goes out of an introduction when we don't feel comfortable.

It helps if there is a reception line. If you see one, head directly for it and introduce yourself to the host. Give some information about yourself that he or she can pass on as you are introduced to the next person in line. If there is no reception line, take a deep breath and rely on the strategies we've discussed. If you spot people with "host" badges, introduce yourself to them and hope that they will introduce you around. It's appropriate to ask to be introduced to someone you must meet.

Letitia Baldrige makes introductions very simple in her *Complete Guide to Executive Manners.* She says that the most important thing to remember about introducing people is to *do it*, "even if you forget names, get confused or blank out on the proper procedure."

This may sound old-fashioned, but feeling confident about introductions is always in style.

> ## Ms. Baldrige's Guidelines for Introductions
>
> **"Introducing people is one of the most important acts in business life."**
>
> 1. Introduce a younger person *to* an older person.
> 2. Introduce a peer in your own company *to* a peer in another company.
> 3. Introduce a nonofficial *to* an official person.
> 4. Introduce a junior executive *to* a senior executive.
> 5. Introduce a fellow executive *to* a customer or client.

The idea is always to introduce the "less important" person to the "more important" person. (We know these people aren't really less or more important on a human level, but we're dealing here with arbitrary societal conventions.) What if the CEO is younger than the person you want to introduce? Use common sense and assess situations on a case-by-case basis.

Some examples:

- "Mr. Cummins, I'd like to present my daughter Cynthia. Cynthia, this is Mr. Sherwood Cummins, the president of our company."

- "Mr. and Mrs. Arnaz, I'd like to introduce to you a fellow executive from Standard Oil, Timothy Anderson. Tim, this is Mr. and Mrs. Desi Arnaz, good friends of my parents."

About using people's titles she says, "When introducing people of equal standing, you do not have to use a title unless you are introducing an older person, a professional or someone with official rank." In other words, you would use the titles of Dr. Skolnick, Senator Boxer, Sir Paul McCartney, Father Larry Lorenzoni or Rabbi Artson—but the two new vice presidents might be simply Jennifer Warner and Michael Berringer.

When introducing a public official, use his or her title even if he or she no longer holds the position. You would say either "Mayor Brown" or "former mayor Brown," "President Clinton" or "former president Clinton."

When we want to make the right impression, we need to be aware and to do our homework. Because we live in a multidenominational society, we should know the difference between the minister (called Reverend); the priest (who goes by Father, be he Catholic or Episcopalian), the mullah (called Mullah); and the female Episcopalian priest (referred to as Mother). If we don't know the correct title to use, we should just ask. People will respond.

My brother Michael told a story of attending a mass and asking the Franciscan Cardinal George of the Archdiocese of Chicago a question. He referred to the cardinal as Your Eminence, which is how you're supposed to address him—correctly and with respect.

Proper etiquette is important in introductions, but we shouldn't become such slaves to it that we lose our warmth or our humor. The most important thing is that people know you *want* them to meet one another. When in doubt, just give the names and some indication of who the people are and what they might have in common. And say so with respect and regard and enthusiasm.

Never, ever "shorten" someone's formal name unless he or

she invites you to do so. My name is Susan, not Sue. I know Roberts, Davids, James and Judiths who do *not* go by Bob, Dave, Jim or Judy.

E-INTROS ARE E-Z

How many times have you thought or said, "You really ought to meet Joe Jones" to another colleague? If they both weren't in the same room, the introduction often didn't happen. That's no longer the case.

We now get to benefit from the technological advances in communication and can send an e-introduction. The email (or text) is sent to both parties and the introducer writes a few sentences about each person and what they have in common and why they should connect.

Kelli Grant, a journalist for CNBC.com, is superb at e-introducing the people she knows. She has harnessed the power and spirit of what we do in person and transferred them to the online world where the room has no physical boundaries.

NAMING NAMES

People like to be remembered—*by name.* But it's not easy to remember everyone, particularly if we meet a lot of people.

The classic name nightmare: You're at a reception for a local charity; it's attended by about two hundred people and is held in the ballroom of a local hotel. A man approaches you and says, "Craig, it's so good to see you again!"

Your mind races and a bead of perspiration forms on your brow. You don't have a clue who this person is.

What to do? Pretend you don't see or hear him? Obviously not. The best solution is to tell the truth, preferably with some humor. You might try: "Forgive me. It's been such a busy day, I barely remember my own name." Or "Please, help me out. I've just gone blank—it's genetic."

Who's going to say, "No, I want to watch you squirm until you remember my name"?

By the same token, don't let people squirm to remember *your* name or who you are. Always state your name clearly, immediately and with energy. Give the other person some idea of who you are or how you may have met.

Memory expert Dr. Joan Minninger, author of *Total Recall* (a memory book, not a movie), offers some tips for remembering names. The first is to *decide to remember.* She recommends that we say our name and repeat the other person's name while shaking hands—because this physical gesture makes for kinesthetic reinforcement. Looking for an unusual physical characteristic and focusing on it also helps connect the name with the face.

And, finally, for those of us who did not grow up in California (where everyone seems to be called by his or her first name), there's the problem of what to *call* people. Do we use the first name; the Mr., Mrs. or Ms. form; or the formal title?

Option 1: Use the formal title (Dr. Turner, Pastor Osteen, Ms. Lee, Secretary Kerry, Supervisor Gonzalez). People who want you to call them by their first names will invite you to do so. "Please call me Jim." If they don't offer the first name, stick to the title.

Option 2: Ask. "Do you prefer to be called Dr. Keane?"

My mother was ninety-two and still called her doctor by his title, although she had several decades on him. To her, that was a matter of respect.

GLOBAL NAME GLITCHES

The world is our global workplace. We may be doing business with clients halfway across the world. Or we work for firms and companies with global offices. According to David Ricks, a professor of international business at the University of Missouri–St. Louis, quoted in a 2006 *Wall Street Journal* article, "American companies' forced friendliness can be offensive in countries where clients and customers bristle at the use of first names."

THANK-YOUS

Fewer people write thank-you notes these days. In fact, they seem to be almost rare. But it's an extremely gracious gesture and one that is appreciated and memorable. In this day of texts and instant messages, a handwritten note is a treasure, and sets you apart from the crowd. Think of how you would feel if you'd hosted ten people for dinner. Wouldn't it be nice to get a note from someone thanking you for all you'd done to make the evening pleasant?

A former professor and educational consultant said, "If I take the time to plan the menu, shop, clean the house, cook, serve the dinner and clean up, that may take four to six hours! My guest certainly has a few moments to write me a two-sentence note or card to say thank you."

With the desire to be memorable and stand out from the crowd so prevalent, sending handwritten thank-you notes makes a lasting, memorable and positive impression. I'm delighted to see that finally the importance of handwritten notes is receiving media attention and that I've been joined by venues from the *Wall Street Journal* to university career centers and myriad blogs, extolling their virtue. In fact, in 1993, I included examples of well-written and poorly written thank-you notes in *The Secrets of Savvy Networking*.

My history with the handwritten thank-you (a friendly letter format) goes back to my days as a language arts teacher where I taught my students proper letter and note writing. A vice president of an investment firm told me he used the samples in *Savvy Networking* to write notes because he was in a gifted class and wasn't taught the fine art of the hand-written thank-you. Oy.

To email or to write? Handwritten notes are becoming a lost art, and some people complain that it takes too much time to write thank-you notes. But most manners mavens agree that a handwritten note is more valued. It reflects personal care, thought and time expended. An email should be sent as a quick acknowledgment, followed by the handwritten note or card.

Bonus: For a limited time, people who mail me a note will receive a package of formal thank-you notes. My address is in this book at the "For Those Desperately Seeking Susan" section or on my website, www.susanroane.com.

FAST FEEDBACK

Email is a vehicle for truly "expressed" appreciation. Don't get me wrong, I still believe in the value of handwritten notes. Cait (Charlie) Burns was an account manager in New York when she expanded my thinking. She pointed out that sending an email enhances communication. "You send the email to someone you met that says, 'It was nice meeting you and chatting about the problems in the reservation system.' It makes it easy for the recipient to respond by hitting reply and sending one sentence. Now you are in a two-way conversation, which most likely wouldn't have happened with just a note. I then write the note as well."

When we take the time to personalize our notes, we distinguish ourselves from the crowd and become memorable.

One of my teacher friends sent her son to my special Language Arts Summer Gifted Class, where I was teaching thank-you-note writing in business and friendly letter formats. One day she called laughing and said, "Thank you so much for teaching my gifted son how to write a note. He's at camp and for the first time ever I got a note from him. It was in perfect friendly letter form . . . asking me to send money!" She sent him money. How could she not!

A grandmother of my acquaintance told me how she "taught" her college-student granddaughter the importance of a thank-you note. "Two Christmases ago I sent Wendy a check as is my habit. *Not* a word! Last year, I sent *nothing*. Wendy called and told me she had not received her usual check for Christmas. 'Really, dear, when I did not receive your thank-you for my Christmas gift, I assumed you did not want or need my money.' Wendy apologized profusely. But I sent nothing. That year she was more attentive to her old grandma. When this year's Christmas gift arrived, she called immediately *and* sent an exquisite note."

Reprinted with special permission of King Features Syndicate.

MISCELLANEOUS MANNERS (THREE TIPS)

1. People expect that we will "bring something to the banquet." That means, at the very least, energy, enthusiasm, conversation, information and humor. Approach people with a smile, a handshake and an open, upbeat greeting. And look them in the eye. Invite people into your conversations once they get started.

2. While most places prohibit smoking, some do not. Don't let your good time go up in smoke. Smoking is a burning issue. We may have the legal right to smoke in some places, but this may not be prudent.

3. Judging people by their appearances can be a grievous error. Overly casual apparel may be worn by your best potential client. As one of my Big Four consulting firm clients said about a fellow wearing a sweater among the "suits," "We don't judge him. He doesn't have to dress for success; he already is one."

It's important to consult the manners mavens to keep abreast of changing patterns in etiquette, but it's even more important to be a person of manners—one who genuinely cares about other people and makes an effort to make them feel comfortable. Manners are a combination of common sense and kindness.

Do the gracious thing, the thing you would like done if you were in the other person's place—whether you are responding to invitations, making introductions or extending a "thank-you."

The bottom line: Be nice, and be thoughtful and considerate of others, especially in the "techno-toy room."

ROANE'S REMINDERS

★ Good manners equal good business.

★ We are never too busy to bypass common courtesy—which is having a regard for the feelings and dignity of others.

★ Don't save nanoseconds. Invest time in the "niceties."

★ Know the rules of etiquette:

Table manners

Introductions

Guest and host behavior

Cyberspace

★ RSVP. Don't ever show up without having done it. Don't forget to attend. And don't wait for better offers.

★ Don't presume informality: Wait until it is offered.

★ Thank-you notes are a sign of acknowledgment, appreciation and manners, which may follow a thank-you email.

★ Send thank-yous for the tangibles—gifts, checks, meals—and for the intangibles—ideas, leads, referrals, advice, support and listening.

★ Never shorten someone's name unless told to do so. ("Please call me Dave" is the invitation to do so.)

☺ Go! ☺

15

WORKING THE COCKTAIL PARTY WITH PLEASURE, PURPOSE AND PANACHE

You're all set. You've reviewed the roadblocks and applied the remedies. You've focused on the potential benefits and prepared your presence, attitude and your strategies. You're ready to converse with just the right balance of chutzpah and charm, and you know your manners as well as your etiquette.

Now it's time to take your wealth of knowledge and your enthusiasm for mingling out into the world. In the next few chapters, we will focus on five of the rooms that are now at your feet: the cocktail party, the reunion, the trade show, "techno-toy room" and yes, the world!

The cocktail party is a mainstay as a business and a social function. Surviving them is good; making the most of them and having a good time in the process is even better!

Cocktail parties are gatherings of about two hours where drinks and finger food are served and guests are expected to stand and circulate. There are three basic types of cocktail parties:

- Social
- Business
- Fund-raiser (charitable, civic, political, etc.)

People have wanted detailed "mingling maps" so they can plot out their footsteps. Maybe a GPS? When you're prepared, you can observe the room and feel confident that no map is needed. Just bring your good manners, conversation and genuine interest in others, whether they are standing near a wall or at the dessert table.

THE SOCIAL COCKTAIL PARTY

The social cocktail party is more popular now than ever because it is a simpler process than a sit-down dinner and can more easily be used to reciprocate social obligations. You can return invitations without hiring a staff of twenty or spending a week making food. Calling a caterer is my preference.

Heavy sit-down dinners are less common because we have become a nation of "grazers." We want a sliver of this and a taste of that. We love to nibble and nosh, to experiment and combine different kinds of foods.

The social cocktail party may have a theme or be an "occasion" party based on holidays or other specific events. It might celebrate an engagement, a housewarming, retirement, company IPO, Halloween, Valentine's Day or maybe the host/hostess simply felt like having a party and inviting his or her friends to meet one another. I hosted a cocktail party at a local restaurant for my friends and colleagues. The theme: a "book mitzvah," a party for my "firstborn," *How to Work a Room*, for its thirteenth anniversary. I even had napkins to match, a cake in the shape of a book decorated like the cover, a cantor and chopped liver flown in from New York! My guests talked to each other as they noshed and nibbled.

If there is a written invitation, you will probably be asked to RSVP and you *must* definitely do so. For my party— which required a "head count" for the restaurant, I called three people who had not replied to my invitation. Will they be invited to my next soiree? Not a chance.

If your hosts request specific attire (costumes, casual, black-tie optional, etc.), adhere to it. It's their party, and they've put some effort into planning it. Don't let them be the only ones in the room wearing a black tie or a costume.

Your first stop will be to say hello to the hosts. It's their job to meet, greet and introduce you to others. Good hosts always have a vignette or two about each guest that makes introductions easier and more interesting.

My friend, author and speaker Robert Spector, gets an A+ as a host. At his and his wife Marybeth's twenty-fifth anniversary party, Robert made sure their guests met one another. His introductions contained information about each person that created a common bond. *How* he made the introduction made you want to continue the conversation after he excused himself.

After you have begun to meet people, remember that parties are for *mingling* and *circulating*. The hosts have invited you so that you can meet their other friends. It's rude to latch on to one person and sit in the corner with that person for the rest of the evening.

A tip to hosts: Placing the food and beverages at different locations around the room encourages guests to circulate.

At the social cocktail party, you can always fall back on "How do you know Arlynn [the host]?" for a conversation starter.

Even though the party may be purely social, you, of course, never leave home without your business cards. You never know! Keep a supply of them with you. You might meet your biggest client of the year, your new best friend or someone who can coach your daughter's soccer team. Remember: This isn't the time to wantonly pass out business cards as if you're dealing blackjack.

Even if the encounter is completely social—or perhaps even romantic—business cards are a better and safer way to exchange information. Although some people will still scrawl phone numbers or email addresses on used napkins with old golf pencils or hunt around in a purse or wallet for deposit slips, others will simply add their information into the mobile contact base on their phones.

And remember: Thank the hosts before you leave.

THE BUSINESS COCKTAIL PARTY

Business cocktail parties come in several varieties:

1. The no-host reception before the professional association meeting
2. The office party, which may celebrate anything from the company's IPO to a retirement dinner or a holiday
3. The business social, which is often sponsored by the chamber of commerce, the convention and visitors bureau or some other civic organization

The No-Host Cocktail Reception

The no-host reception is usually forty-five minutes to an hour long and precedes a business luncheon or a dinner meeting. You register for the reception when you register for the meeting and generally there's a no-host bar.

This is a time for members to reconnect with one another and to meet new people who have been brought as guests. It's also an opportunity for you to bring guests who might be interested in joining the association. If you are a guest, it's a time for you to find out about the organization. For both members and guests, it's a great opportunity to interact.

There's usually no official host at these events, but there may be a greeting committee. Introduce yourself to someone on the committee. They should find at least one other person to whom they can introduce you, and then you're on your own. Warm up your smile and begin to work the room!

Conversation starters are everywhere at these events. If you're a guest, you can ask questions about the organization and the various ways of participating. If you are already a member, this is a time to renew acquaintances and meet new people in your field. You will also want to extend yourself to guests and new members so that they feel more comfortable and welcome.

The Bonnie Raitt/Susan RoAne Method of Mingling

Bonnie Raitt sang, "Let's give them something to talk about." She graciously allowed me to use her name when I told her about the Bonnie Raitt/Susan RoAne method. "If it helps people, that's fine with me."

Former secretary of state Madeleine Albright wore

"brooches." When her circle "broached" difficult issues, she provided the conversation piece that started the discussions.

Men have worn ties that gave us "something to talk about." Looney Tunes, Mickey Mouse, Jerry Garcia, *South Park* and holiday ties open up conversations. I found a great Three Stooges tie for my brother Michael, the lawyer—Moe, Curly and Larry faces with the names Dewey, Cheatem and Howe, attorneys at law. He told me the "boys" are quite the conversation starter. Nyuk! Nyuk!

Remember, these gifts of gab must be "opened"! When you see a unique lapel pin, brooch or tie—say something! You are being invited to say hello!

> *Being approachable is just as important as approaching others, and a smile and eye contact are essential.*

Don't forget that your focus here is *business*—with a social flair, to be sure, but it's still important to do your homework and work the room so that you make new contacts and strengthen old ones.

This kind of cocktail reception is usually followed by a sit-down meal, a program and announcements. So even when the reception is over, you have another opportunity to meet people during the meal.

THE MEAL: SIT DOWN,
YOU'RE ROCKING THE BOAT!

The first rule: Do *not* sit with people you know. If you just wanted to spend time with your friends, you could have gone out for a pizza. This is a chance to meet seven to nine new people, all of whom have something in common with you. Don't miss the opportunity!

The second rule: Be the table host. Introduce yourself to the group at the table and ask the others to go around the table and do the same. This is a risk, but the rewards are great. The person you really want to talk to could be sitting on the other side of the table rather than next to you. If you hadn't gone around the table and introduced yourselves, you might never have known anything about that person. After the meal is over, there will be time for a more private conversation, and you will have him pinpointed. The other people at the table will appreciate this opportunity to introduce themselves.

The dress for these occasions is usually what you would wear to the office, but it can get a bit tricky around the holidays. I once attended the holiday party of a local professional association. I was wearing a dressy suit; one of the other women wore a strapless long gown. One of us was dressed inappropriately. I never figured out which one. When in doubt, make some subtle inquiries.

THE OFFICE PARTY

The office or company party is a different kind of animal from the no-host reception before a professional association meeting. *It is business*, despite the trappings that may confuse us—music, formal invitations, dancing, drinking and so on.

If clients are in attendance, you are also a host—whether or not you own the company or firm. I was first asked to give a presentation to members of a law firm because they had hosted a party for clients and potential clients, and the attorneys had talked only to each other! It's a costly waste of time and money that happens all too often. And it's one reason I continue to be invited to speak to professional firms. *Act like a host* so your guests will feel welcomed.

Remember the cautions about alcohol consumption, appropriateness of conversation and humor and the need for business greeting etiquette even if your coworkers have forgotten them.

One of the most fun parties was thrown by my buddy Guy Kawasaki for a celebration of Garage.com. Guy, prolific author and former chief evangelist at Apple, featured in the *San Jose Mercury News* as the man who "works" Silicon Valley (to which I would add "like a mensch"), was the most congenial host. He spent time with each guest, the Garage.com staff and the venture-capital gang. Guy made sure we all had T-shirts, books, lots of food and fun! In fact, I have his APE T-shirt based on his new book on self-publishing, *Author Publisher Entrepreneur.*

The office Christmas/holiday party is notorious for bad behavior. I've heard many stories of inebriation, sickness, flirtations and dalliances that have caused people to lose promotions and, sometimes, jobs. *The office holiday party is business.* Go to have a good time in the spirit of the holiday season, but don't exceed the bounds of taste or reason. But do attend.

Dancing and relaxing are definitely *not* out of line. But

leave the "dirty dancing" for a nonbusiness occasion. (If the event is a dinner-dance, you may want to take a few dance lessons if you are not comfortable on the dance floor.) This is a good chance to chat with colleagues in a less pressured setting. It may also be a great time to give kudos to those who have helped you or who have been particularly encouraging or supportive.

Spousal Support

Spouses who attend office parties should be treated as individuals in their own right and not just as appendages of the person who works with you. It's not easy being a spouse at an office party, and the person who makes an effort to meet and chat with spouses is always appreciated. Try to find out what the spouse's interests are instead of talking only about or to your colleague and the work you share. In fact, not including a spouse can be a huge mistake that backfires.

Remember, today most spouses work, are involved in the community and have interests that may match your own. The spouse may be a CFO, a tireless fund-raiser for the local art museum or a physical therapist who can tell you the best exercise to relieve your backache. In this small, small world, the spouse may have attended your alma mater. Be nice and inclusive.

One behavior that easily includes the spouse in your conversation is to glance at him or her as you speak. It's rude to have eye contact only with your colleague and lock out the spouse. *Be mindful of how you talk to your own spouse.* No one wants to listen to put-downs, digs and comments reflective of *Family Feud.* Sadly, I have observed this behavior firsthand, and it was very disconcerting and uncomfortable.

The Business Social

The business social is often called the "after hours," or mixer, and it's become a staple of many convention and visitors bureaus, chambers of commerce and other professional and civic organizations. It's an event made to order for creating visibility and meeting other businesspeople in your city.

These functions are usually held about once a month and are open to members and their guests. People who attend them have in common:

- Membership in the organization
- Business interest in the community

These common bonds represent a wide range of conversation starters!

Research shows that it's easier to remember a person's profession than it is to remember his or her name. At the business social, people usually talk about what they *do*.

This is no accident. The business social is one of the best forms of free advertising anywhere—if you know how to work the room. I faithfully attended my San Francisco convention and visitors bureau business socials, and actually do much of my "hands-on" research at these events across the nation. The San Francisco Chamber of Commerce business mixers were my original research incubator for this book.

I've met people at these events who have become dear friends as well as valued associates. Early on, I gained more visibility than I could possibly have afforded through advertising, and great material for my books and talks. I've described working a room as what you do if no one left you an inheritance for the advertising budget.

The business social is not usually a place to finalize deals or sign contracts: It's a place to meet people, get to know them better and discover what you have in common and how you might support one another—even if it is "only" moral support. In spite of what some sales experts claim, it's an opportunity to establish rapport, not to close a sale. You're "opening a relationship."

People do business with people they know, like and trust. Again, etiquette, manners and courtesy are the keys.

No matter how clear your focus, the impression you create depends on your ability to communicate a genuine interest, a sincere generosity of spirit and likability.

In this brave new world with new rooms to work, we are invited now to meet-ups, tweet-ups, fans of Mashable gatherings and LinkedIn local get-togethers because online pals want to meet face-to-face at business socials. There are more opportunities than ever to meet and mingle in person.

THE FUND-RAISER: YOUR MONEY OR . . .

The third type of cocktail party is the fund-raiser. Its purpose is to benefit a charity or community organization. Or it may be to "honor" a politician or political hopeful by raising funds for the campaign coffers.

Carl La Mell, as the CEO and president of Clearbrook, must attend many of these events. Due in large part to his style of fund-raising and gathering support, he took Clearbrook and expanded it from a base of $12 million to a base of $28 million. He says, "After working a full day, I rarely *want* to go to a cocktail party or reception. But once I am there, I'm ready to do my job *and* have a good time."

When *we* are having a good time, our enthusiasm generates enthusiasm in others. They want to be around us, to do business with us and to contribute to our causes.

"Yes, once you do your homework, you can target the room," La Mell says. "But absolutely *never* ignore people. Each individual is a potential connection, and you have to treat everyone with regard."

Again, it's authentic interest and gracious manners that get the response.

La Mell's point is echoed by others: "Make the connection and do not belabor your point. Following up in a social way is a soft sell and establishes rapport."

PARTY POLITICS

At a political fund-raiser, everyone has to donate money in order to attend. The reasons for donating money to a candidate are as varied as the number of people in attendance, but everyone has in common an interest in the candidate or the organization's success.

Often there's big-name entertainment, but the real "draw" is a chance to meet the candidate or officeholder. If the politician is working the room properly and you are not hanging out behind the curtains, *you should get that chance.* Make the most of it. Put yourself forward in a gracious way, introduce yourself and say something memorable—and brief. The politician wants to meet and connect with you, but he or she may need to do the same with hundreds of people in only a few hours. A short, unusual quip will make you stand out in the sea of faces.

We assume that all politicians have mastered the art of working a room. After all, the phrase *working a room* came to us from politics. But this isn't always the case. Politicians have all the same roadblocks we do. They, too, are 93 percent shy. It's just that their very survival depends on remedying those roadblocks. And they wouldn't be where they are if they hadn't had some success in doing so. Often they have a "handler" who introduces them to individuals in a crowd and is a political wing-man or -woman.

Can you imagine a politician who heeded Mother's Dire Warning "Don't talk to strangers"? That's a politician who can barely pay for his meal, let alone buy television advertising! And how would you like to be one of that politician's constituents? Until you'd been properly introduced, you couldn't even tell him about the pothole on your street.

A former San Francisco mayoral candidate told me, "The fund-raiser in my honor was much easier because people who attended were supportive. The issue for me was balancing two to four conversations at once with people who wanted several words *alone* with me. I believed I owed each person that time and tried to do just that. And it was tough. The event that honors someone else is different. You have to judge the event and the people and not overstep your bounds. It is poor campaign form to get up and move from table to table when you are *not* the honoree. We need to exhibit manners and respect for protocol and for other people."

His comments are instructive for us nonpoliticians as well. If we table-hop to work someone else's room, it may backfire; we could lose a friend, a job or a piece of business.

Former San Francisco mayor Willie Brown is a masterly mingler. What can we learn from this master of working a room? Beyond the obvious charmers—engaging in eye contact, smiling, touching, shaking hands, offering humor, speaking and listening to each individual, laughing—there is a special warmth and sense of caring, and *he looks like he is having a fantastic time himself.* Connecting with people didn't appear to be a chore for him; it appeared to be fun.

When we honestly enjoy other people's company, we hardly have to think about how to work a room. All the "right" things come naturally, because we *want* to make people feel comfortable and cared for. They respond to that and to us.

La Mell's Latest Advice for Working Fund-Raisers

1. Know who you have to see.

2. Make sure they do *not* know that it's your goal to see them.

3. Ask to be introduced when possible.

4. Do not talk about business. Make the connection, set rapport and make sure they know who you are.

5. Do not overstay your welcome. You cannot monopolize any one person.

6. Depending on the response to you, get the business card.

7. *Follow up!*

KNOW-IT-ALLS

We've all encountered a know-it-all. No matter what we say, he or she already knows it. It kills a conversation. According to Brian Palmer, president of National Speakers Bureau, "When someone says something you know or know a piece of, resist the urge to nod vigorously, say 'yes, yes,' interrupt and signal that you already know about what they're talking. It shouldn't be important to show how allegedly smart you are or how much you know. When you really listen, the odds are increased that you'll say something truly interesting."

SCRAP SNAP JUDGMENTS

Caveat: We cannot know people in sixty seconds. Unfortunately, technology has foisted us into a split-second society. We make snap judgments. In *Blink*, Malcolm Gladwell referred to the "thin slices" of exposure research. Dr. Nalini Ambady, professor of psychology at Tuft University, found that "the degree to which thin slices of experience help us navigate modern encounters is 'up for debate.'"

According to Dr. Paul Eckman, professor of psychology at the University of California Medical School, San Francisco, "The accuracy of a snap judgement depends on what we're sizing up."

Another side of this prism is revealed by Dr. Ivan Misner, founder of BNI, in his book *Truth or Delusions: Networking in the Real World*. One of the truths that we must bear in mind before we make snap judgments: "We don't know who they know." To dismiss people because of our instantaneous reactions is a mistake. Dr. Misner further explains, "Never underestimate the depth of the pool your fellow networkers are swimming in."

My thought: First impressions are sometimes wildly inaccurate. We know our reactions to other's voice, comments, clothes and style. But we do not know of their good hearts, charitable ways, family connections or network. Or their evil ways and disrespect for coworkers or the law.

There is no such thing as the "One-Minute Mingler!"

ROANE'S REMINDERS

The cocktail party—whether social, business or fundraiser—is a perfect opportunity to meet new friends and new contacts, to reconnect with familiar faces and to have a good time.

Bring:
- Your business cards
- Your smile
- Your focus
- Your sense of humor
- Your wit, wisdom and interest in others
- Conversation starters: lapel pins, ties, jewelry, hats (when appropriate)
- Appropriate manners fit for the occasion

Observe:
- The layout of the room
- Gifts of gab (and say something)
- The people, the groups, the flow

Lose:
- Prejudgments
- Snobbery
- Self-focus

WORKING THE REUNION: REELING IN REALITY

If you doubt that reunions are a major cause of weight loss in America, just ask anyone who has ever attended one. My twentieth high school reunion in Chicago prompted three weeks of starvation and many questions.

Why would any busy person leave her business and home for days to reconnect with the past? Why would any sane person fly two thousand miles to see high school classmates? My motive for going then was a combination of curiosity, friendship, business and lots of warm feelings for a very nice group of "kids" from Mather High School.

It was worth every moment of fear and trepidation. I had a terrific time, reconnected with old friends. A pleasant and *unplanned* by-product of attending my prior reunion with the "kids" was several speaking engagements with their companies. Go figure!

JUST GO!

At a reunion, the room is *not* filled with strangers! For some, this is a plus. You definitely have something in common with your old classmates—even if it's a dreaded algebra teacher of days gone by.

For others, having a history with these people is a drawback. The invitation to the reunion may unearth old pains and insecurities. (Who among us was truly secure and serene at age seventeen?) It may prompt fear about comparisons—professional, social, marital and monetary.

And always, always, there is the Pound Problem—for men as well as women. Gloria Steinem, founder of *Ms.* magazine, tells the story of her Smith College reunion and says that no one was as concerned about professional success, marital bliss, children or who had found the meaning of life as they were about *weight*. The first thing everyone said to her was "You're so *thin*!"

The thought of voluntarily returning to celebrate the days of yesteryear can be chilling! But don't let a few extra pounds or lost hairs stop you from saying yes to the reunion invite.

Will everyone want to probe your personal life, searching for imperfections? Will they want to see your last six bank statements? Hear all about your first date after the divorce?

Probably not. With the advent and growth of Facebook, you may already have reconnected online with former classmates and have shared "catch-up" information.

The fact is people are planning reunions because we want to see each other in person. One reason is that baby boomers are reaching the age for forty- to fifty-year reunions. Generation X has hit the thirty-year reunion stage; Generation Y has hit the twenty-year reunion. Another reason is that despite all the terrible trepidations and worst fears, despite the months of dieting and starvation and aerobics, and despite the time and expense that is usually involved, most people have a good time at their reunions and would do it again tomorrow! Or in another ten years.

NATIONAL NOSTALGIA

The reunion is a social event with a long history. Family reunions are proliferating because we live in an age where people want to connect with family, friends and roots. Whether it's your high school, university or summer internship, just go!

Besides, now you know how to work a room. You may come away with a whole new group of friends, people whose presence is fresh and exciting but who also knew you "when."

Reconnecting is powerful—especially when we don't have to fill in the beginning, and people know our families as well as knowing us.

Last, but certainly not least, you may discover some wonderful business contacts among your old gym or geography buddies.

REUNION REFERRALS

My primary purpose in attending my reunions (I've had several) was to reconnect with old friends and, frankly, to see what had become of people since we last saw one another.

Business opportunities aren't limited to your former classmates. If you are traveling to your hometown, give some thought to other potential contacts there. For me, scheduling a book signing, a presentation or an appointment with a Chicago-based corporation or association-meeting planner was an added bonus. Your current network of colleagues may suggest people you could contact in your hometown.

I took business cards with me to my reunion in Chicago. Even if you attend only to socialize and see classmates, it's far better to exchange cards—which are still necessary—than to write your address or phone number on a used napkin. Some people will have a phone with a database for on-the-spot inclusion. It's important not to be consumed by the potential business aspects of a reunion or you risk creating the impression of a "hard sell," which is off-putting. But reunions are an excellent opportunity to reconnect and interact—and people prefer to do business with people they know, like and trust. Now, with email, Facebook and LinkedIn we can offer our cards and easily stay connected.

Prepared to do business as well as have a wonderful experience, I got both! Old friendships were renewed by talking about "the good old days" and were enhanced by the added dimension of talking about our business/work lives.

I just returned from another Mather High School reunion that was wonderful: friendly, fun and warm. Although Chicago's May weather wasn't warm, it was worth the time, effort and investment to see my former classmates.

If you're interested in business as well as pleasure at your reunion:

- Visit the reunion website or Facebook page.
- Plan ways to initiate contact and follow through.
- Contact people before the reunion to be sure they are attending. That shows your interest in seeing them. They may even be part of the reunion Facebook page.
- Practice an upbeat, interesting, concise reintroduction.

Don't overwhelm people with your information; just let them know what you do as part of a casual conversation—when it's appropriate. There is no point in offending people with a poorly timed "hard sell." Besides, *the first reason to attend any reunion is to reunite, reconnect and have fun.*

ATTITUDE

Go with the intent to have fun, and don't fret about what people will think of you. Remember, the best way to overcome self-consciousness is to concentrate on making others feel comfortable. *No one* attends a reunion without some second thoughts. Be genuinely interested in classmates opens conversations.

ROMY AND MICHELLE'S HIGH SCHOOL REUNION

If you need some encouragement, rent the cult classic *Romy and Michelle's High School Reunion*. You will meet some characters who will make the cast of players at your reunion seem low-key. Multitalented actor Alan Cumming's portrayal of the nerd becoming a dot-com billionaire is a classic.

Keep an open mind. A lot of nice things happen to people in ten, twenty, thirty years, and it's a good idea to give your old classmates a clean slate. Barry probably doesn't throw spitballs in board meetings the way he did in history class. Rory may have sworn off hurtful gossip nineteen years ago.

And remember, you have nothing to prove. Be yourself and enjoy.

NAME TAGS

Be sure to sneak a peek at the name tag just in case you don't recognize someone. Mercifully, some of us are late bloomers. You may want to glance at your yearbook before the event, the reunion Facebook page and visit the reunion website to see if photos are posted.

"NEW" FACE TO PLACE

Sometimes a name tag doesn't help us place the face, and for good reason. Pat Teal, literary agent and a dear friend, went to a reunion of sorts. When she was approached by a woman who greeted her like an old friend, Pat looked at her but drew a blank. "You have an advantage over me. You know me, but I can't place you," she said apologetically. The woman reminded Pat of her name. Indeed, "Betty" was a longtime acquaintance but still was unrecognizable.

Pat later learned that Betty had had a face-lift, which explained why she couldn't place her face!

Moral of this story: If you can't place the face, even with a name tag, it may be that your recognition skills are fine, but the face is new!

Caveat: One greeting we must avoid at any event, but especially at reunions, according to personal trainer Jonathan Cummins, who attended his twentieth reunion, is, "'Hey, do you remember me?' It's uncomfortable. It's easy enough to reintroduce yourself and not embarrass anyone."

FOCUS

Identify the people to whom you definitely want to talk, but be open to serendipity. Those are our unplanned rewards for showing up. That could mean a business referral or a romance or a friendship renewed. You never know what you'll find out about your old friends or their interests.

Who knows? You may even fix up your son with your classmate's daughter! Or your brother with a classmate's sister or your father with a classmate's mother. Or recruit a classmate to work for your pre-IPO company. Or get a job lead for your son or daughter. Or yourself!

One focus to avoid is proving to people how much you've changed or, worse, how successful you are. These tactics usually backfire and aren't much fun anyway. The people who use them are off-putting.

Concentrate on the pleasure of connecting with old friends in new ways. Don't worry if you've lost some hair or gained a few pounds in ten or twenty years. Most of us (certainly, those of us who have matured) know that it isn't the cover that counts; it's the contents.

A "BOONE" TO MANKIND

Thanks to word of mouth, the Concord telephone grapevine and the viral buzz of forwarded emails, the seventy-fifth anniversary of Boone Elementary School in Chicago's West Rogers Park was a hit. Over fifteen hundred former students formed a line around the block to get into a building that, in the past, we couldn't wait to get out of! And what a celebration it was.

Classmates from all decades and all parts of the country attended. Some of our teachers were there as well. I brought my seventh-grade picture and my sixth-grade report card, signed by my teacher who later became principal. When I laid eyes on the lovely, charming and regal Martha Koelling, my sixth-grade teacher, I was instantly flooded with pleasant memories. I reintroduced myself and showed her my report card that she had signed. She looked at it, smiled and with her classic twinkle, said, "Susan, I didn't give you that red check for 'not keeping profitably busy.' Your brother must have added it later." That solved that mystery!

Then I went to the gym—which seemed so very huge at thirteen—to discover it was now so very small. The fellow standing at the entrance looked vaguely familiar. I snuck a peek at his name tag and was delighted. He was the brother of a friend whom I was trying to find! I introduced myself, showed him the class photo of Alice and me and asked where she was. Spencer Karlin said his sister Alice wasn't there, and he filled me in on the past decades.

It was one of those serendipitous, meant-to-be moments. Had I not visited the gym before going to the cafeteria, I would have missed seeing him and the joy of reconnection to his sister, my friend, Alice Powell. Since then we see each other several times a year and stay in touch. I'm so grateful that I saw her brother and said something and found Alice.

CARDS

Bring your business cards. They are a practical way to exchange information and build your Millionaire's Rolodex or friends and family database, even if all your contacts are purely social. You may be connected and have "friends" on Facebook, but having a card provides an easy way to locate street address and phone number.

It's important to exercise good judgment and good taste when handing out your cards. I was told of a man who at a reunion arrived late and moved through the banquet, dropping a handful of cards at each table. I doubt that he received any business from such a tacky tactic. And he annoyed a lot of folks.

A family friend used the suggestions in this chapter for her thirtieth reunion of Denver High School. "At my other reunions, I was fairly quiet. This time, I prepared, read, had some questions and conversation ready. I had nothing to lose, so it was easier to approach classmates I recognized and those I didn't. It was a blast!"

HUMOR

Bring a healthy sense of humor. If you can laugh at whatever gaffes or goofs you make, people will be more comfortable with you.

No one liked being the butt of jokes or sarcastic remarks back in high school, and they are even less likely to enjoy it now. Bring stories of your life, friends and family and news about former teachers.

TALK TO EVERYONE

Our tastes and values have changed in one, two or four decades, and so have *we*. Other people have changed, too. Move around the room and speak to everyone. This cannot be over-emphasized. You never know what treasure you'll find. The nerd of yesterday could be the nice guy of today . . . and tomorrow. And there are cliques. One clique of our "girls" was known for being stuck up then, and they stuck together at our prior reunion. But at the last reunion, there were no cliques. The women and men of Chicago's Mather High mixed and mingled and were delightful!

A tip from a colleague who plans to retire this year: Don't ask, "What are you going to do?" to potential retirees. It puts them in an uncomfortable position. Instead tell them congratulations and wish them well. Perhaps share a story of another friend who retired.

FOLLOW UP

Reunions are a wonderful networking opportunity both for friends and for business associations—but only if you follow up. It doesn't matter how significant your connection over the punch bowl was. If you don't follow up, the opportunity is lost. Emails, texts, "friending" on Facebook, calls, notes and LinkedIn are some of the many ways to stay in contact.

There may be a postreunion online gathering. If not, you could spearhead one.

That's just as true for social connections as it is for business contacts.

Take a few minutes to send an email, a post or online message or to write a note to the people with whom you had particularly pleasant experiences. Let them know, at the very least, that you enjoyed seeing them again. If you snapped a photo of them, email it with a short note. If you want to go a step further and renew the relationship, suggest getting together. And if you discussed business, by all means send them a link to your website or your brochure if they asked for it—and any other information you think they might find interesting.

IN SOUND COMPANY

Reunions sometimes are planned by companies and former colleagues. Arthur Andersen employees have been invited to attend such gatherings with their former colleagues via Andersenalumni.net and they recently celebrated the firm's 100th anniversary. Another example, 85 Broads (an homage to the address 85 Broad Street) was started in 1997 by former Goldman Sachs investment banker Janet Hanson to organize other female Goldman Sachs employees into a network to stay connected. It has grown into a network of currently over thirty thousand members in ninety-two countries and twenty-six graduate and undergraduate classes helping to support women in the workplace.

If invited to a reunion, go. These are people with whom you have a common bond; a place to start the conversation. You never know where it will lead.

PAYING OUR RESPECTS

There are some "reunions" we attend that have a serious, even a sad, purpose. Yet our presence is important and may speak volumes about who we are, our priorities and our respect for others. Attending a funeral, wake or life celebration service is never easy.

We often worry about what to say and sometimes don't attend because of that worry. I interviewed people in bereavement for *What Do I Say Next?* There were some who felt abandoned by friends who "disappeared" and others who were grateful for the support of friends, colleagues, coworkers and bosses.

What we say isn't as important as our presence. A simple touch on the arm and an "I don't know what to say. My thoughts are with you" is comforting. Sometimes it's a story we have of the person that reflected their character, interests and humor. When we share the story, it gives the bereaved a measure of comfort.

Remember: Avoiding a hospital visit, memorial service or funeral because *we* are concerned about *our* discomfort is unacceptable.

In our multicultural workplace and world there are varying customs. To feel more comfortable, ask your friends and coworkers for advice. Search for the answers on the Internet.

Are these rooms to work? Absolutely not! But reuniting with an old friend or former coworker at a wake, when we are all paying our respects, can reconnect us in myriad ways.

ROANE'S REMINDERS

★ RSVP and say yes.

★ Go to your reunion.

★ Prepare ahead of time as you would for other parties/events.

★ Do your homework.

★ People have grown up, changed and are interesting.

★ Reunions are a chance to reunite with old friends and reestablish longtime connections.

★ Connect with people as they are today.

★ Connections with classmates can blossom into renewed friendship, romances and/or business.

★ Build your personal and business network with longtime pals.

★ Relax and enjoy yourself while you are there.

★ Follow up your new connection to old classmates.

★ Remember, you never know what can happen.

★ Have fun!

17

WORKING THE TRADE SHOW OR CONVENTION: THE TRADE-OFFS

Trade shows and conventions are the Olympics—the supreme test of your ability to work a room or, more accurately, many rooms.

Not only do trade shows and conventions feature almost *all* the types of events we've discussed—business meetings, "social" gatherings, cocktail parties, dinners, lunches, individual encounters and sometimes even reunions—but there are usually *hundreds* of these events, all crammed into the space of a few days to a week.

Some of the events on the schedule will be called "social," but make no mistake—this is business and requires the ability to work a room.

And it is work! Just ask anyone who has ever staffed a booth—standing! Or anyone who has walked through miles and miles of exhibits. Most women agree that the difficulty of these activities increases in direct proportion to the height of their heels.

But take heart. With a bit of planning and strategizing, trade shows and conventions can also be a tremendous amount of fun. After all, you have invested money, resources and time in order to connect with people.

HASH TAG TALK

Currently many conventions have a hashtag, which is designed to give everyone a way to find out information about the trade show or convention. It also will provide a way to learn what's being offered, suggested or assessed. Be prepared to be part of that conversation via Twitter.

"Meeting your colleagues and friends is the most important aspect of a convention," said Tom Peters, author and management guru. Conventions and trade shows provide opportunities for face-to-face interactions, over a cup of coffee or beverage of choice, which cannot be duplicated.

Whether you attend the trade show or convention as an exhibitor, a potential buyer, a representative of the facility where it is taking place, a member of the organization or simply as an interested party or the spouse of one of these people, certain strategies will help you get the most out of the event.

PREPARING OUR PLANS

Most of us want to use our trade show/convention time (and money) wisely. Getting what we came for is important not only to us but to our employers. The folks who paid for us to be there expect success. And if we're self-employed and have shelled out the money for the conference, booth, materials, airfare and expenses ourselves, the event had *better* be profitable. Regardless of your role at the event, preparation is crucial. It should start long before you get on the plane.

The time to start preparing is *not* when the plane touches down or when we get our first peek at the convention hall. First of all, it's easy to be overwhelmed by the sheer volume of

things—the number of people to see, booths to visit, meetings to attend, parties to drop in on, and by the immense
physical distances to be covered. It's not unusual to attend
six to eight events in the course of a day—and that's before
the evening cocktail parties, dinners, hospitality suites and
late-night get-togethers.

Conventions and trade shows require a three-pronged
approach to planning:

1. Planning for the office to run smoothly while you are
    away
2. Planning for the time spent at the event
3. Planning for follow-up

Don't Leave Home Without . . .

With all you'll have to do at the trade show or convention,
you don't need to be worried about what's happening back
home—whether you remembered to cancel your dental appointment, whether your clients are getting everything they
need, whether someone is feeding your cat (and children!).
For parents there's even more to plan.

Make a list of the things for which you are responsible
at the office and at home. You may have to delegate some
projects or trade off some tasks, reschedule appointments
and train someone to handle your tasks and office phones
the way you want them handled. With today's laptops, tablets and very smart cell phones—wired and WiFi options—
staying in touch with the office is easy.

At home, your preparation may include lining up baby-
sitters or house sitters, finding someone to care for your

plants or pets, alerting your neighbors that you'll be gone, determining which bills need to be paid and getting someone to take in your mail.

Making these preparations not only lets you leave in comfort and enjoy the convention but also ensures that you won't come back to an overwhelming mess.

THINKING AHEAD TO THE EVENT

You can eliminate a million distractions by anticipating your own needs at the convention—and the needs of others.

First, get the facts straight—the dates, place, times, locations and accommodations. Most groups post an advance schedule of events on their websites, and some include a map of the exhibits. If you can, plan your route through the convention hall in advance so that you can see the people you want to see without walking extra miles.

Be sure you understand the financial arrangements. Does your company prepay the costs? Is there an expense account for entertainment? Do you cover costs and present receipts for reimbursement? If you are self-employed, financial arrangements and allocations must be built into your business's budget.

Second, you need to understand exactly why you are attending this convention. Are you there to investigate the latest trends, developments or products? Are you being sent to gather data or information from the seminars or to land new accounts? Will you be expected to report back? How detailed will your reports need to be? Is this a crash course for *you* to increase your skill, knowledge and effectiveness? It's important that you make these determinations before you go.

Perhaps you are attending this conference simply to increase your visibility or your contact base. Much of what is learned and accomplished at a convention may be done informally. Sometimes I've learned more chatting with a colleague or mentor over coffee than I would have by attending six seminars. We can always buy the tapes, but it's the casual conversation in the hallway (or at the lobby bar) that may be valuable and the most informative.

Third, plan your clothing. What you take will be determined by the location of the convention, the time of year and finding out what the weather is likely to be by checking the Weather Channel (www.weather.com). Check the schedule to see if you'll need clothing for a meeting, an afternoon barbecue, a pool party, two cocktail hours and a formal dinner on the same day.

Take clothes that are appropriate and comfortable. Remember, this is business. Shoes should be *especially* comfortable. You won't be able to work the show as effectively if you are hobbled by blisters or if your feet are screaming for a rest. You won't have as much fun, either.

Fourth, be aware of the culture, norms and expected behaviors of the industry, profession or company. A convention of the National Restaurant Association will have a different character than a trade show for preschool educational toys or SXSW (South by Southwest). Different types of people will be present, and different behaviors will be expected. Know the world you're about to work.

Fifth, schedule your travel arrangements so that you have some time to relax and recover from jet lag before you "hit the floor." Don't plan to land at 2:00 p.m. and attend a 3:00 p.m. meeting. With air travel as it has become, that would be unwise. Why arrive harried and out of breath at the airport, the registration desk or the meeting when you could have a better time being gracious and serene? For the National Speakers Association convention, I arrived in Philadelphia two days early to see the Barnes Collection and to relax before the convention started. And have at least one Philly cheesesteak.

And while we're on the subject of travel, remember that unforeseen circumstances always occur. Suitcases, boxes of materials and airplanes often travel to different destinations. The late comedian Henny Youngman told this classic story: Checking in for a flight to Des Moines, the seasoned traveler told the airline employee, "Please send this red suitcase to Omaha, the blue one to Newark and the box to Miami."

"Sir," the surprised employee replied, "we can't do that."

"Why not? That's what you did last week!"

Funny . . . sort of. Unless you are the traveler in question. Take your luggage . . . please! At least take a carry-on with one change of clothing and underwear, plus toiletries and important papers.

Finally, remember the basics. Prepare a positive attitude. Know your focus—your purpose and goals for attending the convention or show. It helps to have a written plan. Work on your self-introduction and several conversation starters appropriate to the event.

Allow for serendipity—the "you never know" unplanned opportunities that happen because you showed up.

FOLLOW-UP IS CRUCIAL

Bring everything you will need to record expenses (there are now apps for that), take notes or record seminars, collect and organize business cards and gather follow-up information.

Bring your laptop or tablet, business-card scanner, smartphone and adapters and extra batteries.

Include yourself in your follow-up plans. Most people forget to plan for "regroup and recoup" time when they get home, but I have found this to be invaluable. Build in time to unpack, do laundry and just spend some downtime before launching back into the routine. You've been in a completely different world, operating at a high pitch, and both need and deserve a minivacation—even if it's only a morning or an afternoon. In this fast-paced, nanosecond world, time for regrouping rejuvenates.

There's Gold in Them Thar Booths

The booths at conventions and trade shows are places of golden opportunities, whether you are a buyer or seller. The whole point of booths is to bring large numbers of buyers and sellers together for their mutual benefit.

Whether you are behind the booth or in front of it, the *real* work occurs before you leave your office. Again, planning is the key. "Organization, attention to details and the ability to see the overall picture are essential to the planning and preparation," claims a Bay Area event planner.

"Preplanning is essential," says Susan Friedmann, the trade show coach and author of *Meeting and Event Planning for Dummies*. "Take the time to learn about the association or the exhibit sponsor so that conversation flows more readily. It's too easy to talk to other purveyors or long-term clients. The goal is to establish new relationships. Also, reinforce for the staff that we cannot prejudge other attendees and must exhibit manners and extend our social graces to everyone."

Fake Flash Mobs

The trade show or exhibit floor may even be the scene of entertainment at different booths. According to the *Wall Street Journal*, one of the new trends are fake flash mobs designed to ramp up the energy, grab your attention and perhaps promote a product or service. If you see a group converge in the aisle and start to dance, don't be surprised.

Walking around the convention requires concentration and persistence. Faced with so many choices and so many people to see, it's easy to tune out, talk to whoever is around and turn the show or convention into a continuous party. Stay focused and take short breaks if you need them.

But there's a catch. A marketing strategy must be planned before you attend. That plan must also include the tactics and activities that will be used and the goals established in terms of numbers of prospects and qualified leads, especially if you're an exhibitor.

For attendees, the trade show is a chance to research, assess and qualify products and services. It is also an educational experience, an opportunity to learn the state of the art and a way to exchange information instantaneously—face-to-face.

Being aware of the benefits helps us work trade shows and conventions more effectively and expedite business from both sides of the booth.

WORKING THE BOOTH

Staff training is *paramount*. Staff needs to be well informed about the product or service they are selling, about the competition and how to draw business to the booth.

When they know only about their product and haven't bothered to research the competition and attendees who are potential buyers, they lose sales.

Homework works. It produces good connections, satisfaction, sales and good feelings for everyone involved.

THE THREE E'S

The people behind the booths should also exhibit the Three E's—energy, enthusiasm and electricity—according to Pam Massarsky, the lobbyist for the Chicago Teachers Union, who has worked both sides of the booth.

Your staff should prepare interesting tidbits as conversation starters. Since everyone at the show or convention will have a name tag, your people might open with a question or comment about the company and/or its location. They should also prepare questions about the attendees' needs or the suppliers' products and services. *And listen to the answer.* "A smile for each trade show attendee is a good start," suggests Pam.

"May I help you?" is *not* a good opener for the exhibitor. It gives the attendee a perfect chance to say, "No thanks, I'm just looking." That closes the discussion, and anything the exhibitor says after that might be construed as a "hard sell." According to Daniel Pink's *New York Times* best seller, *To Sell Is Human*, "Pushing too hard is counterproductive."

"May I help you?" should be asked only at candy stores— where the customers are presold. If you walk into Fannie May's or See's, you're not looking for a Whitman's Sampler. You're there to buy Fannie May's or See's, where the choice is between Tipperary bonbons or walnut squares!

A firm handshake, a smile, warmth and an upbeat (practiced) self-introduction will make the initial contact easier and more effective.

Make sure you are facing the trade show traffic. Never should booth staff have their back to the attendees. Nor should they be so engaged in conversation with each other that they inadvertently ignore attendees. People are simply not going to approach and interrupt two people in an intense conversation. I have seen this happen too many times and always address it in my trade show programs.

"*O.K., step away from the laptop and hold up your end of the conversation.*"

STICKY SITUATIONS

My clients have shared several perplexing trade show scenarios. While starting a conversation with a potential customer may not be easy, concluding it can be equally as difficult. The best way to end the conversation is to initiate a handshake, thank the person for coming to the booth and offer some literature and your card. "If you have any questions or I can further help you, please let me know" are the words that accompany your card. Don't forget to ask for his or her card, too, even if the conference has the computer chip name tags you can zap and add to your contact base.

One of my technology security clients found that his booth often attracted the "I know more than you do" guest. The best way to diffuse the know-it-all is to say, "That's certainly another way to look at it."

For those staffing trade show booths, when you're speaking with a visitor—a prospective client—and another person approaches your booth, don't ignore them. It takes no time to acknowledge their presence. Smile and say, "Please wait, I'll be with you soon." At MacWorld a not very savvy exhibitor ignored me both times I visited his booth. People will understand when you're busy talking with another interested visitor. The trade show is for meeting prospects not ignoring them.

Walking (or Working) the Floor

When you walk around to see other people's exhibits, you'll want to be at your best. Here are some tips for conserving energy so that you can sparkle while you mingle and converse.

- Map out your route before you begin so that you are sure to see the people you must see.

- Don't try to do too much in one day and arrive at the last booth looking (and feeling) as if you've just run a marathon.

- Make a list of people you want to see and things you want to do and carry it with you.

- Carry a small notebook, tablet or smartphone with you to jot down information and ideas.

- Resist the temptation to take everyone's brochures, tchotchkes and handouts. You could be schlepping an extra fifty pounds by the time you work your way around the room.

- Stick as closely as you can to your normal regimens for food and exercise.

Honoring your own routine is very important. If you are used to working out each day, you may begin to wilt if you don't incorporate this into your routine. Some conferences schedule early-morning runs to accommodate joggers—and they are also a good place to meet people. Many conference facilities have tennis courts, weight rooms and saunas on the premises. Be aware of what kinds of foods and eating schedules allow you to function best. If you need a big breakfast, have one. But if you are grumpy in the morning, it might be a good idea to order from room service. Take care of yourself.

"CONVENTION"AL CHARM

At trade shows and conventions, business isn't always conducted around the booth. The "social" aspects of these events are just as important. I put *social* in quotation marks because if you are at a trade show or convention, *you are working*. But that doesn't mean you can't enjoy yourself, meet new people, reconnect with those you know and extend yourself to everyone around you.

These events are made to order for increasing your database of contacts.

- Sit with people you don't know at dinners and luncheons.
- Take the initiative and introduce yourself to the people at your table.
- Ask them to do the same, just as you might at your local professional association dinner meeting.

The "social" parts of the trade show or convention can be just as much fun, and just as profitable, as working the convention floor or attending the sessions.

TRADE SHOW TEMPTATIONS:
TRYSTING AND TIPPLING

There are a few social aspects of the trade show or convention that bear some warning.

The trade show tryst is a touchy issue. Miscommunication can make for uncomfortable situations. Be conscious of the verbal and nonverbal messages you send. Be clear about what you want and what you don't want. Your boss sent you in good faith to represent the organization. Will an "indiscretion" get back to him or her—or to the other people in the office? Or to spouses? How would this be received? How would *you* be perceived? Yes, you have a personal life and are entitled to privacy. But at a conference you are still on company time. Maybe my mother's "convention"al wisdom has a place here: "May all your 'affairs' be catered."

"Aline," a meeting planner, told me that she knew who among the association members were "involved" with whom. While she had guaranteed a number of rooms based on pre-registrations, the hotel insisted there were fewer rooms used. To prove their point, the hotel would send the registration lists. Sure enough, people arranged to share rooms upon arrival, and she knew who they were. To her credit, Aline kept the information to herself. Darn!

Drinking is another delicate subject. Sloppy behavior is usually offensive and can mean losing a client or even a job. Know your limits. Women are not expected to "keep up with the guys" at cocktail hour. So don't. One insurance company hired me to do a program because the sales staff misplaced the collection of business cards they accumulated during an exhibit. Why? Too much fun and alcohol blurred their judgment and cost the company $50,000, a mistake they did not want repeated.

Convention behavior requires alertness, an ability to listen and comprehend and the capacity to give out information *selectively*. If liquor impairs any of these three areas, you will be less effective.

DAD'S RULE

In this day and age of YouTube and Instagram, we must be careful about behaviors that can be recorded, uploaded and viewed by thousands.

My father had a rule: None of his salespeople could drink before 6:00 p.m. at the conventions and they had a two-drink limit. He, on the other hand, positioned himself at the bar by 10:00 a.m. with orange juice on the rocks. He bought screwdrivers for everyone, acting as the congenial host and listening carefully to what everyone said. By the end of the day, he had learned much information about the industry and about his competitors. By sticking to straight OJ, Dad controlled the information he gave out—and he never, in sixty years, caught a cold at a convention!

Let common sense be the rule of thumb. Attend the sessions, learn, make personal and professional contacts and connect with clients. Take notes, buy CDs/DVDs, visit the exhibit hall and analyze the products for your boss. *Then* decide what you want to do for relaxation.

That doesn't mean you can't have fun. You can. A convention is a *balance* of work and play. Don't be a stick-in-the-mud, but remember that conventions can easily turn into three-day office parties—and some office parties can come back to haunt you.

The balancing act here is to keep your sense of humor without losing your perspective.

SPOUSES: TIRED OF GETTING
SCHLEPPED ALONG?

It's not easy to go to an event where you are identified only as someone's spouse. Unless you are blessed with an abundance of the dynamic duo—chutzpah and charm—and make it your business to *start* fascinating conversations that are of interest to you, they don't always happen.

At one time, most of the spouses at conventions were wives who didn't work outside the home. All that has changed. Many spouses who attend conventions have their own careers and businesses.

Joyce Siegel attended medical conventions and meetings for more than fifty years and observed this shift. "More and more, we saw on the name badges that the doctor is female and the spouse is male. Over the years the programs offered to us changed. Flower arranging and fashion shows were replaced by estate and tax planning and time management."

Spouses must know how to work a room, too, so that they feel their time has been invested wisely. A friendly spouse can help create rapport with clients and colleagues. My mother did that whenever she accompanied my dad to his paper-product conventions.

But some spouses enjoy socializing more than others. What does *not* work is to bring (or be) a sullen spouse, one who doesn't really enjoy either mingling or the convention itself or who may be shy and uncomfortable in crowds. These spouses can often support their husbands or wives best by staying home and doing the things they do enjoy.

Spouses Have Impact

Spouses are an important part of convention conversations. You will want to be polite, inclusive and attentive to the spouse of a colleague, associate or potential client because that not only makes good business sense, but it's also smart, savvy and thoughtful. By the same token, people notice how we speak to our own spouses and guests.

Again, we can include the spouse or significant other with our eye contact. Directing a question or observation directly to him or her is appreciated. Then we *must* listen to the answer. Making spouses or significant others feel comfortable and included is wise . . . and nice.

Spousal Support

It is unwise and unkind to ignore spouses. Speaking at conventions has given me an opportunity to hear what spouses have to say about the way they're treated.

At a presentation for spouses of midsize bank CEOs, a woman shared a cautionary tale. "My husband has a senior vice president who acts as if I don't exist. He speaks directly to my husband and never looks at me. Who does he think spends time with his boss? My plan is to make sure he never gets promoted." Be very nice to spouses, significant others and their children.

Remember: A spouse or significant other can put in a good word on your behalf or a word that isn't!

ROANE'S REMINDERS

The trade show or convention is a unique opportunity to increase your base of contacts, build relationships, buy and sell products and services and have fun. Where else could you find so many rooms to work in one place at one time? This is the big time, the marathon, the ultimate challenge to those of us who value the ability to work a room.

To get the most out of it and keep from being overwhelmed, plan the following in advance:

★ The smooth running of the office while you are away

★ Your work at the convention itself

★ Your follow-up

Working a booth or an entire trade show is just like working a room—only more so! Rise to the challenge, seize the golden opportunity and have fun!

More trade show tips:

★ Visit the website.

★ Devise a plan.

★ Arrange for appointments and hosted dinners ahead of time.

★ Invite clients and potential clients to visit your booth.

★ Stick to your eating and exercise regimen.

★ Attend sessions (it's a great way to get conversational tidbits).

18

HOW TO WORK THE TECHNO-TOY ROOM

The "techno-toy room" has morphed into a megamansion. This chapter is about how, when and where to use—and not use—the latest gizmos and gadgets and the etiquette that speaks volumes about our behavior. Every day new "toys" debut touting faster speeds, smaller sizes (except for the huge plasma screens) and new ways we can use them to both connect and interrupt our lives.

It saddens me that the subject still has to be covered, but the gross errors in judgment in using the technology have increased so much that they're commonplace and make the issue one that must still be addressed. It's another facet of how to work, and how *not* to work, a room. In Albert Einstein's words, "I fear the day that technology will surpass our human interaction. The world will have a generation of idiots."

In 1991 I wrote about cell phone abuse. It's over two decades later and the horror stories have increased exponentially with the speed of light. Electronic gadgets have made our lives easier, but they are also making our lives more complicated.

GOOGLE GLASS: HALF EMPTY OR HALF FULL?

Maxwell Smart is so yesterday; we are beyond talking into our shoes. The future is here. With the creation of Google Glass, we can talk into our eyewear. There are people in San Francisco, New York and other major outposts of techie nerd status wearing this new tech toy. It's a "wearable computing device, looks a lot like a visor and mimics the functions of a smartphone (gets directions, makes calls, takes photos) and only the wearer can hear," according to Taylor Hatmaker of ReadWrite. For now it's mostly tech bloggers and Apple's Explorer Club who own the latest devices.

I planned to write about Google Glass and then thought I wouldn't. But when *Saturday Night Live* did a skit on it, followed by a Stephen Colbert segment and coverage in both the *Wall Street Journal* and the *New York Times* all within the same week, I was convinced.

There are etiquette and legal/privacy issues yet to be addressed. Will Google Glass be the newest, latest, greatest digital device to own? At $1,500, maybe not yet. At least not for most of us. That all may change. Who knows!

THE NOISE "TOYS"

Unfortunately, in the expanded techno-toy universe, we are still giving signals in social space that "you don't exist" because my music, my smartphone, my text messages and email and my video games are more important, according to Dr. James Katz, director of the Center for Mobile Communications, Rutgers University. We not only listen to our tunes, but we also tune out friends, coworkers, strangers and family in every room. If you're a parent, you know that firsthand. At the same time, we get to increase our risk of hearing loss. Earbuds inject more intense sound. According to the Hearing Health Foundation, "One in five Americans have hearing loss in at least one ear, 20% of the U.S. population aged 12 years or older has hearing difficulties, 26,000,000 Americans between 20 and 69 have high-frequency hearing loss due to exposure to loud noise."

"All loud music is bad, whether it's rock, rap or classical," says audiologist Dr. Gail Whitelaw. We should not impair our hearing nor impede our social interactions.

TAKE TWO TABLETS AND "POKE" ME IN THE MORNING

I'd be remiss if I didn't address the invaluable contribution of the iPad and Android tablets (Nexus, Samsung, Kindle Fire, et al.). They are the stars of the techno-toy room and have had a tremendous impact in many arenas of life. According to TabTimes.com, tablets are being used in an increasing number of businesses often replacing laptops and notebooks.

But it's the impact to education and to those who have special needs that makes the apps for these gizmos so remarkable. A segment on autism on *60 Minutes* showing how an app for the iPad allowed a young man to finally communicate with his mother brought tears to my eyes.

Speech and language pathologists are using iPads to work with children who have a variety of problems. According to Marin-based speech and language pathologist Kathy Fowler, "What's so valuable is that the apps are designed to give our clients the instant feedback they need so they can immediately hear their errors and learn to self-correct. And it's fun for them because the apps are colorful, animated and their pictures can be inserted into video clips. They think they're using the iPad as a reward, but it's really the work they need to be doing to address their problems."

These tablets and the apps are fascinating for kids of all ages. With them they develop motor skills, hand-eye coordination and critical thinking. I've watched two-year-olds play games with great ease. Still and all, my favorite use is the most practical: as captivating (while educating) babysitter!

ATTENTION-GETTING DEVICES

Living in Marin County (north of the Golden Gate Bridge) affords me the constant opportunity to laugh at the ironic and moronic situations of life. I constantly read and hear about the refreshing concepts, precepts and principles of Eastern cultures, like "being in the moment" and "being mindful." But now I hear these phrases roll off the lips of the people who profess to be "in the moment" and are wearing a cell phone on their belt or Bluetooth on their ear and/or checking for emails and texts—to be in the *next* moment! Give me a break!

PLEASE, BE CAMERA-SHY

I love my phone's camera, each and every one of its five megapixels. But it's a techie toy that ought to come with some warnings. It's handy and easily captures those no longer called "Kodak moments." However, there are some times when taking that snapshot is not a good idea. More questionable is the posting of these photos without permission. It makes sense to think before we shoot or post.

And then there's the photo viewing. We used to invite people over to see our vacation slides, photos or movies (depending on the era) and could be politely turned down. But now it's "Let me show you my photos of (my cats, dogs, home, children and, yes, my vacation). The phone appears out of nowhere and you're stuck.

This recently happened to me at a dinner party where I was held hostage by a man whose conversation deteriorated into a show-and-tell . . . and show and tell . . . and show and tell some more. I endured sixty-eight photos and it was painful.

In his honor, I've created the "Five Photos and You're Finished" rule. Unless someone asks to look at more of the photos on your phone, stick to five and put it away!

"Eat your lunch, and then we'll see about giving your phone back."

"LOCK 'EM IN A CELL" PHONE!

While road rage is all the rage, cell phone and smartphone outrage has hit the national boiling point. People who are distracted while driving cause car accidents. According to the National Highway Traffic Safety Administration, drivers who use handheld devices are four times more likely to get into crashes. Everyone has a story of rude, inappropriate, thoughtless cell phonies.

Our cell phones are fabulous tools when used correctly. When you give someone your cell phone number for follow-up, especially for a job interview, be sure to carry your cell phone with you and, more important, *turn it on*. A friend of mine, who prided herself on being unattached to her cell phone, didn't and missed out on five job interviews—a costly error in judgment.

CELL PHONE TURN-OFF

People can lose business by *not* knowing how to work a toy in a room, especially if there is an important meeting in that room. When Leigh Bohmfalk, currently a senior vice president of a major national bank, was the director of marketing at an Internet start-up company, she had to hire a new public relations firm that would get a $35,000 per month account. For the third meeting, she arranged for its vice president to meet her CEO. "Not three minutes into the meeting, Mr. PR's cell phone rang and he took the call! With that he lost an account worth almost half a million dollars a year!" (That's when a half-million dollars was a lot of money. To me, and probably to most of you, it still is.)

GENERATION TEXT AND/OR TWEET

Text messaging, used for both our social and professional lives, is an extremely convenient way to send a brief message. However, *texting* during most meetings, events or a gathering of colleagues, clients or friends is not a way to work the room. The subtext being messaged is "Someone—or anyone—else is more interesting than you are."

Christine Hawkins was delighted to get a ticket for the musical *Wicked* while on business in Chicago. She was seated next to a young girl who was texting her sister seated on the other side of the theater. "It distracted me during the entire play because of the light on the keyboard."

We now tweet at meetings and conferences where they have "live tweeting" using a hashtag (#) so people can share what they're learning. It's not only acceptable; it's encouraged. But tweeting during a play, a wedding or a client dinner is still inappropriate.

Rule of thumb: Avoid using any gadget that has a distracting light when in a darkened theater or room not only because the light is disturbing but also because it's downright rude. Maybe theater, ballet and opera announcements need to include the text message taboo as well as the "turn off your cell phone" reminder before the performance begins.

A client told me that her daughter was *texting* while they were having dinner. "I don't care if she's a married woman with children, she's still my daughter. I told her it was rude to text while we're talking. She's a good person who knows better. Maybe now she'll think twice before she 'texts' when she's with other people—including her mother!"

If we want to show people they are important to us, let's give them our undivided attention.

THE (GADGET) GENERATION GAP

A recent item in Leah Garchik's column in the *San Francisco Chronicle* made me smile. She reported that author James Patterson attended a premiere at SFJazz Center. After the director asked people to "silence their pagers," the young man next to Patterson asked him what a pager was. Yep! There's a definite gadget generation gap.

I couldn't help but think that young man probably has never seen the window crank in a car! That's the handle exclusively used to roll down windows before electric windows existed. My twenty-year-old Miata has window cranks, which, I might add, get the job done quite well.

In 1991 a pager went off in the dramatic play *Cobb* at a local theater. The audience was stunned. Because that was over two decades ago and pagers are ancient history, I decided to delete the story. That was until last weekend when I attended a play in Chicago, *The Pianist of Willesden Lane* at the Royal George Theatre. In the most intense scene, even after the "turn off your cell phone" announcement, someone's cell phone rang. Not just rang but also played a few bars of a tune. It proved that even boomers and senior citizens can be out of tune and rude!

SHOUT IT OUT

Cell phone usage is intrusive everywhere. The manager of a small boutique said she "has no choice but to be included in someone's personal conversation when customers answer their phones in the boutique." And she doesn't *want* to be included. "Their conversations are none of my business."

Not only are we hearing people's personal business, we

sometimes hear business information that should be private. Another problem is that in too many cases people try to "assist" the transmission of their conversations by shouting their words across the digital domain. As if that helps!

Bonus: Still and all, Alexander Graham Bell's telephone was an amazing invention that changed how people were able to communicate. Because some of us are not as comfortable using the phone as we'd like to be, I've provided access to the chapter "Facing the Phone Fear Factor" in my book *Face to Face* as a thank-you for buying and reading *How to Work a Room*. Copy and paste the URL (http://www.susanroane.com/articles/room_Bonus.html) into your browser or scan the QR code with your phone scanner app.

MASS IGNORANCE

I once attended a funeral mass for a teenager. In the middle of one of the prayers the unthinkable happened: Someone's cell phone rang. Fortunately it was only a ring and not a downloaded ring tone tune. But my heart sank! How could anyone be that self-absorbed, self-important and rude? The thought that washed over me was a prayer. I prayed that the parents and family of this young man did *not* hear that phone.

Maybe the person just forgot to turn off the phone. The reality is that our phones do *not* belong with us in a religious sanctuary. At the very least, they shouldn't be turned on, not even on vibrate. Especially not at a funeral service. The techno toys have no place in these rooms, which are sacrosanct. When we're caught transgressing the boundaries of good taste, the impression is both poor and indelible.

Bluetooth Ache

There's another techie toy to help us offend others. While Bluetooth has many excellent benefits, it also has its place, and that isn't at a memorial service. Here in Marin County, one of the mourners paid her "disrespect" by walking into the chapel wearing her Bluetooth. People noticed immediately, which may have been her intention. But they were offended by her blatant disregard and disrespect. People talk; that's how I learned about this Bluetooth blueprint of bad behavior. Let's not ruin our own reputations.

Houses of Cell Phone Worship

By now every minister, rabbi, priest and their parishioners have stories of cell phone transgressions. How they handle such distractions is another story. The Jewish New Year is a holy day. The rabbi was just finishing a very solemn passage when a congregant's cell phone rang. Because it was a smaller sanctuary with great acoustics, we all heard it and gasped. The late rabbi Alan Lew looked out at the congregants, smiled and said, "It must be a call from G-d wishing us a Happy New Year!" We laughed. To his credit and quick wit, the rabbi addressed the issue and relieved the tension with his humor.

Cell phones, MP3 players and tablets have no place in houses of religious worship—unless you are waiting for heart surgery or performing it.

SELF-IMPORTANT CELL PHONE QUIZ

Have you answered or used your cell phone or other devices to talk, send a text, check Facebook or tweet:

1. In a movie or a play?   Yes ❏   No ❏

2. In a meeting?   Yes ❏   No ❏

3. During a business lunch with a client?   Yes ❏   No ❏

4. On a date?   Yes ❏   No ❏

5. During a funeral service?   Yes ❏   No ❏

6. During a religious service?   Yes ❏   No ❏

7. a. At a wedding (yours)?   Yes ❏   No ❏

   b. At a wedding (someone else's)?   Yes ❏   No ❏

8. In a lecture hall?   Yes ❏   No ❏

9. In a restaurant?   Yes ❏   No ❏

10. At a party?   Yes ❏   No ❏

11. In a job interview?   Yes ❏   No ❏

If you answered yes to any of these, please reread this chapter!

"It keeps me from looking at my phone every two seconds."

To focus and pay attention to the person in the room is respected, remembered and revered. When we turn off our cell phones and remove earbuds in meetings, meals, family gatherings or other social occasions, we are implicitly saying, "You are important!" That's the memorable way to work a room.

MULTITASKING MANIA

One does not have to be a teenager to be Velcroed to his techie toys. BlackBerrys were dubbed "CrackBerrys" for good reason. People were "addicted" to them. Now we use our thumbs to text. I bet that carpal *thumb* syndrome will become a legitimate medical disorder in the near future.

We must exercise caution when we decide to check our email, Facebook and Twitter surreptitiously while lunching with a client or cousin. People know we are doing it. That's no way to work a room.

Be very careful multitasking while you drive or walk. You could get hurt or get a ticket. In New York, I see people crossing at midtown intersections while checking for messages. I worry that one day there will be fatalities of those who paid attention to their emails and tweets rather than the Don't Walk signs.

Over dinner in New York, Sally Minier, now owner of Sweet Sally's Bakeshop, admitted that she was one of those addicted to her BlackBerry. "While I was walking here to meet you, I was busy checking my messages, not paying attention to where I was walking. And I fell into a pothole!" Luckily, she wasn't injured. Except by my laughter at the table. She wasn't the first and won't be the last.

We are multitasking and therefore multiplying the potential mistakes, accidents and problems for ourselves and for others.

A personal plea: If that "room" you're in happens to be a car, please don't text and drive. If you're a passenger, remind the driver not to do it. Both of your lives are at stake.

LOW-TECH/NO-TECH TOYS

There are distractions that are low- or no-tech as well. It's as simple as turning down, preferably turning off, a talk-radio station when a colleague, friend, coworker or family member is in the car. Unless it's the NBA championship game that you *both* want to hear, the message is, "You just aren't important or interesting enough." And that is *no* way to work any room—even if the room is your car.

How we correctly use the gizmos and gadgets of the twenty-first century is determined by respect, regard and consideration of others. We just need to "play fair" in the techno-toy rooms we enter! And make sure we turn off those toys so that other people at the events, parties and meetings aren't impacted or inconvenienced by our use of them.

ROANE'S REMINDERS

Do

- Use your cell phone, iPod or Bluetooth appropriately.
- Become familiar with your cell phone's vibrating option.
- Leave your cell phone in the car or office or at home when it is not appropriate to have it with you.

Don't

- Use your cell phone during church or synagogue.
- Use your cell phone during an important meeting.
- Use your cell phone during a funeral service.
- Use your cell phone in your child's school program.
- Use your cell phone during a date.
- Use your cell phone during a movie, play or opera.
- Use your cell phone during a job interview.
- Use your cell phone during a wedding ceremony or family celebration.
- Use your cell phone in a hospital room.
- Use your cell phone in a restaurant.
- Shout loudly to help transmit the sound. It doesn't help and it annoys the rest of us!

19

HOW TO
WORK THE
DIVERSE ROOM

The variety of rooms we work have a common thread: diversity. People in the room (be it for a convention, trade show, meeting, community gathering, bar mitzvah or company barbecue) will be different from us and from one another. Being comfortable with people who are diverse in myriad ways and developing skills of conversation so that what we do and say are appropriate make good business sense.

After one of my presentations in Florida, a salesperson in the hospitality industry told me that moving from Washington, DC, to Sarasota was a cultural shock. "In order to do business I was forced to develop my conversation skills, patience and memory! If I didn't ask about the daughter's soccer tournament or Grandma Rose's garden, doors were closed to me. I was not used to this kind of exchange and had to slow down and become an interested listener in order to succeed in my new territory."

Some of the differences we will encounter are geographic; others are race, religion, country of origin, cultural, abilities/disabilities, interests, gender, gender preferences and the hot topic: age. The bonus of diversity: We get to learn from people who are different.

Newsflash: The workplace has always held occupants of varying ages. And the young entering the workplace rooms have always had new and different skills and mindsets. One reason the verbiage has increased is that there are more media venues looking for news items about age-related issues. Another is that the baby boomers, by sheer numbers, are creating the generational conversations. And the young, aggressive, self-assured "free agents" confidently zigzag their careers while redefining loyalty and taking career risks unparalleled in prior generations in the workforce. This young group of Millennials is different in that it grew up with more technical savvy than social savvy.

TURNABOUT IS FAIR PLAY

A recent report showed a program where high school students sign up to tutor senior citizens on their computer and tech-toy skills. GE had a mentoring program in 2000 where young tech-savvy employees tutored senior executives. Citibank now has one.

The older and the young each have much to contribute to the equation. It boils down to Aretha Franklin's classic refrain, "R-E-S-P-E-C-T"—of people's skills, expertise and experience. We all need to be open to learning from different sources. Mary Haring taught me about the blog post communication protocols. She had to "school" me several times. I'm so grateful she didn't give up after the first time.

"HIRE AUTHORITY"

Because only the incompetent think they know everything, it's not embarrassing to admit a missing skill set. That's why I eat in restaurants and have an alteration person who expertly tailors my clothes. This book is being revised once again—using No. 2 pencils with good erasers! Becky Gordon, who is skilled in using the computer and in editing, is translating the majority of my hieroglyphics. (Don't email me about my antiquated methods. I have heard it all. It works for J. K. Rowling, Nelson DeMille and me.) Many people have looked at me pityingly for my lack of techiness. Trust me, this method of draft writing has no impact on book sales!

When my website went up years ago, in order to view it, I had to hire a fifteen-year-old high school student to find it. And to teach me how to do the same. His skill and facility with the computer and the Internet were astounding. He taught me and I was grateful.

Reverse mentoring abounds! I have learned so much from my former assistant of three years, Nicole Wells Johnson, who is also a professional organizer. In return I was delighted to be the greeter at her wedding. Nicole said, "Having you, the author of *How to Work a Room* and the Mingling Maven®, as our wedding greeter was so special and made so much sense. You made our guests feel welcomed from the moment they approached the chapel." Looks like I have a third career as a wedding greeter, should I want one.

The free agent does what he or she does best and should be doing, and hires out the other tasks! That's why small-business owners have professional organizers, bookkeepers, accountants, graphic artists, attorneys, search engine optimizers, experts and advisers. That's how our SOHO (small office, home office), diverse, free-agent community survives and prevails.

BUILDING BRIDGES, BONDS AND
BUSINESS RELATIONSHIPS

Talking to different people is interesting but sometimes difficult. We shouldn't be patronizing or rude. There is the chance that the person in the room who is different from us could be our best contact. You never know!

The best advice is a gem from Sharon Gangitano, who researched American multicultural studies. Her advice, as an African American woman, for conversing both professionally and personally with people of diverse backgrounds is simple:

> *"Talk to those different from you . . . as you would talk to those who are like you!"*

We have more in common than not. Respect and focus on those commonalities and celebrate the differences. Most people have interests and talents, went to school, have parents or are parents, have kids and once were kids. We all want to be safe, have a nice roof over our heads, be free of financial worries and have our health. Some of us love the movies, others participate in sports, while still others of us support the arts. Many people read books and have favorite authors. Others have favorite television shows. And most of us enjoy a good meal!

Sedi and Nader Sami closed their San Rafael establishment, Spotless Cleaners, to observe the Persian New Year (No-Rooz), which is the first day of spring. Sedi told her customers about the traditions, customs and foods of this joyous holiday, which is celebrated by Persians of all religions.

A few days later I was speaking for a law firm when one of the attorneys mentioned she came from Persia. I was able to wish her a Happy No-Rooz. We then had a livelier, more interesting conversation due to a connection made because Sedi had shared her holiday.

Learning about other cultures contributes to the connections we can make and relationships we can build in any room.

We have more in common than not. In the rooms where we work, as well as the rooms we visit for the conferences, meetings, board retreats or parties, we'll meet people with visible differences. We should not ignore them or avert our eyes.

LISTEN UP!

Some people will be different in invisible ways. Maybe it is English as a second language, accented by the first, or a case of carpal tunnel syndrome that makes a too-firm handshake painful. Or, maybe, a hearing loss that is not profound but is severe enough so as to make events with perpetual noise difficult. According to the Hearing Loss Association of America, one in three people over sixty will experience some hearing loss. That person could be your next mentor or client.

If you're talking to someone at an event and you see them cupping their ear or notice a hearing device, take heed.

Tips for Talking to the Hearing-Impaired

- Face each person as you strike up a conversation.
- Enunciate but do not overpronounce.
- Add facial expressions.
- Don't cover your mouth or face with your hands.
- Listen patiently.

There are additional tips from Lisa Goldstein of the University of California Berkeley School of Journalism, printed in the *San Francisco Chronicle*: "Don't speak louder. Don't assume all hearing-impaired know sign language. Don't assume the person not responding is ignoring you. They may be deaf and ignoring you!"

I know at least twenty men and women who have either total loss of hearing in one ear or partial loss in both ears. Too many years of rock and roll and noise have taken their toll. Wearing earbuds in our ears is taking a toll on our hearing as well.

At business or social events, talk to the person on crutches or in a wheelchair. Since the car accident that caused her to become a quadriplegic, Lori Sneed, whose dad, John, and I met on a plane years ago, has maintained and sharpened her wit. She has had to deal with the "curious." People will often talk more loudly to her. "I have told several waiters that I cannot walk, but that I hear perfectly well."

The Silicon Valley, Silicon Alley, Highway 128 and all other high-tech corridors are populated by smart people from many different countries. These CEOs may speak in accented English, which requires us to listen more attentively—and to be patient. Go to an event in Silicon Valley and English is spoken with accents from Spain, China, India, Taiwan, England, Israel, South Africa, Latin America and Japan, because our workplace is global and the rooms we work are diverse.

THE VIRTUAL, DIVERSE ROOM

Whether our virtual room is a chess tournament, a gourmet recipe chat room or an online video game, it's a diverse room because there are no geographic barriers. Whether you're playing Words with Friends or World of Warcraft, which has over eight million subscribers to date, you're in a very diverse room. "We range in age from a fourteen-year-old player to a sixty-two-year-old lawyer on the East Coast. There are both male and female players from many countries. While the conversation is lighthearted small talk, and even some 'trash' talk, hateful comments are not tolerated," said James E., a self-described geek.

They never should be. And silence is approval.

Good advice: What to say when a racist or other offensive comment is made came from a June 2006 *New York* magazine article on urban etiquette: "You must be joking . . . though it's not really that funny." And refrain from smiling.

TECHNO FRIENDS

A benefit of working the virtual, diverse room is that we get to meet people from across the globe. They are people we may never meet or even talk to in real time, but our electronic communication creates a heartfelt connection and friendship.

We also need to try to be "multitechnolingual." By that I mean that we need to make an effort to speak in a variety of other modes. Toni Boyle, author of *Gremlins of Grammar* and a Boston-based writer and editor, suggests there is an easy way to determine someone's preferred method of communication: Simply ask them. How quaint! "Mrs. Jones, how would you prefer I follow up—phone, email, text, instant message or snail mail?" (If Mrs. Jones works for the United States Postal Service, you may want to avoid the phrase *snail mail*.)

If my younger friends and clients are text messaging, then it's incumbent on me to do the same. If your boss or aunt expects to *hear* from you, pick up the phone. If Great Aunt Bess wants to see you, arrange for a visit. It behooves us to be multitechnolingual to communicate in any room.

AVOID GENDER BENDERS

Connie Glaser is an expert on gender communications and author of *Gender Talk Works*: *7 Steps for Cracking the Gender Code at Work*. She suggests that we pump up our listening skills to both men and women at every event. "Astrid Pregel was the first female Canadian consul general posted to Atlanta. Because she didn't have a distinctively female name, people assumed the new consul general was a man. Pregel noticed that when she attended receptions, people didn't listen when she introduced herself—not realizing who she was. But she was always introduced very clearly prior to her presentations. Once she would finish her remarks, the (mostly) men who had been dismissive *before* the speech would rush up to her with their cards—looking sheepish. Bottom line: Be sure to listen carefully to both men *and* women in the rooms we occupy.

AGE GAUGE

CPA Lana Teplick observed the young techie from a client company who visited her office to help with a computer system. "He acted as if we were inept on purpose. Remember, we do all the accounting work for his computer company and would never expect the principals to know all tax code changes."

Her advice, so that "we can all get along" in the workplace or in any room we work or walk into, is this: "Be patient. We all have different skills, a lot to learn from each other and we are trying our best."

And attitude is everything. We need to approach opportunities, challenges, rooms and people with interest and enthusiasm. Add to that ideas, words and stories that reflect "what's happening," and we have communication that counts.

REMEMBER: Patience is an antidote.

ROANE'S REMINDERS

★ Be nice to everyone! You never know from where or when the next job, client, tickets to the play-offs or friend will come!

★ We can be diverse in many ways: age, country, culture, religion, race, gender, interests.

★ Celebrate our differences.

★ Lose the judgments based on physical appearances or disabilities or accents.

★ Look for commonality.

★ Talk to those who are different from you as you would to those who are the same.

★ It's good business and good behavior to be open to all people.

★ Focus on the event/venue/theme, which are the common factors.

20

WORKING THE WORLD: TRAINS AND BOATS AND PLANES

It's a fact of life: People who know how to work a room create more opportunities, produce more results and have more fun.

You have the skills now and may have started enjoying the benefits already. Why limit your ability to work a room to meetings, dinners, cocktail parties, business lunches and formal social engagements?

Why not make every situation you encounter a room and *work the world*? The worst that can happen is that you enjoy life more, and the chances are good that you'll also make new friends and add to your number of business relationships. The casual conversation with a stranger could just "make your day" or theirs. One of the traits of people I interviewed for *How to Create Your Own Luck* is that they talk to people they don't know—everywhere.

BAGGAGE CLAIM CONVERSATION

You never know who you're going to meet or where. Having dinner in San Francisco with Matteo and Cindy Novelli and their young son, Alessandro, may have looked ordinary to the casual observer. It was anything but that.

We met a year and a half earlier in the baggage claim of Charles De Gaulle Airport. As I waited for my luggage, I noticed Matteo had an iPhone, and in very poor college French, I asked him about it. Fortunately for me, he answered in English. I told him I was visiting family who lived near the opera house. And once again it was proven to me that it's a small world. Matteo invited me to join them in their cab and our conversation continued. We exchanged emails and stayed in touch. On their trip to the United States, they planned to visit California and I sent my "what to see in San Francisco" list.

Dinner in San Francisco may have looked ordinary, but it started in an unlikely place—as a baggage claim conversation between strangers that has been continued via email and face-to-face over sushi!

THE CORNUCOPIA OF CONTACTS

What is a room? Whatever you *make* it! It can be:

- The airplane, airport terminal or baggage claim
- The golf course
- The bus stop
- The pool

- The bowling alley
- The doctor's office
- The bleachers or box seats at the ballpark
- The nightclub or theater
- The wedding reception
- The jogging track
- The supermarket
- The health club
- The department store
- The bike shop or bike path
- The sushi bar
- The barbershop
- The video arcade
- The hardware store
- The bank
- The playground
- The bookstore
- Anywhere you go

You don't go to these places in order to "work" them, but as long as you have to stand in line at the supermarket or wait for your latté or wait for a plane, why not have a pleasant conversation? Will it bring you a business deal? Who knows? That's not the point. *The point is to extend yourself to people*, be open to whatever comes your way and in the process, have a good time. You never know!

THE LUCKY LAYOVER

After thirty hours of travel from San Francisco to Johannes-burg, I was tired and facing another three hours before my flight to Cape Town. I had a question about the flight and asked the woman who sat next to me in the gate area. She could have easily just responded yes or no and ended it there. But Dr. Fahmeeda Moosa asked me where I was from and if I was going to ride in the bike race in Cape Town as she was. (That Sunday thirty-nine thousand cyclists descended on Cape Town for the world's largest timed bike race.)

We talked until we boarded. Based on my baggage claim luck, I looked for her there when we landed but to no avail. The next day we bumped into each other in the lobby of our hotel and hugged hello, so happy to see each other. We then saw each other on the day of the race when I wished her good luck.

On the surface, we have nothing in common—we're in different professions, she has four daughters, we're of differ-ent religions and from different cultures, we're different ages and live in different hemispheres. But Fahmeeda's warmth and openness to this weary solo traveler started a conver-sation that continues in this boundaryless room called the Internet.

We all have multiple opportunities to meet people any-where in the world we happen to be. Even if it's only for a brief moment, a pleasant exchange can make their day or yours.

Obviously, you have to exercise some caution. There are certain parts of town you probably don't want to work—

especially at night. But what could it hurt to strike up a conversation with the man who works in the appliance store or chat with your dry cleaner? You might just learn how to use that complicated DVR function or learn about a great app to download on your phone or get introduced to the costar of your movie. Seriously, that happened.

THE BARBER OF CIVILITY . . . AND MATCHMAKING

When actor John Turturro was getting his hair cut he told his barber, Anthony Silvestri, about his movie script and said Woody Allen would be perfect for one of the roles. As recounted in the *Wall Street Journal* (May 3, 2013), a few weeks later he received a call from Mr. Silvestri saying Woody Allen was interested and to give him a call. It just so happens Woody Allen was also his customer. It's a small world after all. You never know where the conversation will lead or which people can help lead it.

"PUBLIC" SPEAKING

How we talk to people and treat them in public can be overheard and oft repeated. When we are curt, patronizing or rude to service people, others hear, and that's a risk we should not take.

There is no reason to speak to the shoe-repair store owner, the copy center employee, the waitress or the barista unkindly. No matter how "rushed" we are, we have to take the time to be polite in those rooms where others work. Period. End of story.

A friend who owns a speakers' bureau told me she attended a party in the Napa Valley. She was chatting with a newly retired couple who had just sold their dry-cleaning establishment in Silicon Valley and they had many interesting stories about it.

Once they discovered my friend owned a speakers' bureau, they became very animated. "Two of our longtime customers are speakers. One couldn't have been nicer. The other was pompous and insulting. He would brag that he could 'buy and sell us' with his monthly income from two presentations." And then they told her his name.

As the world is a mini–mingling market, of course my friend knew him. She had attended a party where "he was drunk, loud, obnoxious and behaved inappropriately." How he treated this couple confirmed for her that his "party" behavior was *not* a onetime accident; it was his bad behavior MO. "I could never recommend him to speak for one of my clients. Could I ever trust he knows how to behave? No way."

It behooves us to think before we speak!

THE POWER OF WORDS

Choosing our words wisely is . . . wise. I relearned this lesson from eleven-year-old Annika Skov when I smiled and told her dad, Pete, "Annika manipulated her Grandma Susan to do a somersault on a low bar. I executed it perfectly, but it was followed by a horrific dizzy spell." Upon hearing me say this, Annika smiled at Dad, then smiled at me and said, "I didn't manipulate you; I convinced you."

And so she did. Remembering the dizzy spell, I realized that sometimes we shouldn't say yes when we ought to say no—or no, thank you. No more somersaults for me.

THE PLANE TRUTH

Planes are great places to meet people. You have a captive audience. I met a significant person in my life on a plane from San Francisco to Los Angeles. Father Larry Lorenzoni and I spent an hour chatting, laughing, comparing publications and enjoying a meeting of the minds and spirits—on a higher plane, of course. What if I hadn't taken the risk and spoken to him? I might not have had this wonderful friend in my life for twenty-five years. He will have celebrated his ninetieth birthday by the time this edition is published.

Caution: We do have to pay attention to verbal and non-verbal cues and honor people's need *not* to converse if that's their preference. If someone is working or reading, our desire to chat could be an unwanted interruption.

ARENA AROMA

Chicago's Garrett Popcorn Shop is famous for its freshly made caramel corn, popcorn and cheese corn. Everyone walking by the shop inhales the aroma and conversation pops! Some of us think they use a popcorn-scented spray to attract customers. It works!

At a Boston Celtics game, a different scent started a conversation in an entire section of the arena. One woman was wearing so much perfume (or toilet water) that Lana Teplick's eyes began to water. Once the woman left at halftime, everyone in the section began to talk about her, the smell and their reactions. "People usually didn't talk at these fast-paced games because we kept our eyes on the ball," said Lana. "Her overbearing use of 'toilet water' changed that. People talked with each other from five rows away. When we realized she wasn't returning for the second half, we were 'old friends' who cheered. I remember the scent and the event as if it were yesterday."

"Common scents" suffering created a new "scents" of conversation at a basketball game! To paraphrase the famous Brylcreem commercial, "A little dab will do ya."

COMMON GROUND

What's unique about working the world is that there is always a clear common ground. Wherever you are, the people there with you are in the same situation. Remember, the roof is the introduction even if the venue is in an open-air forum.

If you're on the golf course, the common interest is golf. Mark Mayberry, a professional speaker, is an avid golfer who swings into conversation about golf as he travels across the country. "A game of golf provides an opportunity to learn about your partner's honesty, temperament, sportsmanship and attitude, and it's a great subject for conversation." The *Wall Street Journal* featured an article in which golf course etiquette, rituals and manners are being taught along with swings, putts and focus. The Executive Women Golf Association has chapters across the country because women are linking on the links in growing numbers. Golf is closing many gaps and gulfs.

If you're at the jogging track, the other people there will probably be joggers as well—or are thinking about becoming joggers. If you're at the ice cream store, everyone else will be just as interested in a cone, a scoop or a sundae as you are. You might even compare notes on flavors. On more than one occasion, we talked to other restaurant patrons about their orders, recommended dishes and even shared desserts. What fun!

APP-TITUDE

The newest item to "share" is the latest, greatest app you discovered. It's a topic of conversation that can happen anywhere. I learned about PicCollage at a Stanford football game tailgate. People are apt to talk about their apps anywhere.

"COUNTER" INTELLIGENCE

The contacts you make while working the world may or may not evolve into friendships or business associations. You may never see these people again. Even if you don't, you've brightened your own day and someone else's with the encounter and have earned Planet Points!

Sometimes these connections are profound, and sometimes they are fleeting but pleasant. When travel consultant Lisa Miller was doing research on the best mountain bike to buy, the manager of a local bike shop introduced her to another biker who also happened to operate a bakery.

A few weeks later, she needed a birthday cake for a friend. She decided to visit his shop, and he was behind the counter. "Ordinarily, I would have smiled, placed my order and left, *wishing* I had said something to him. But this time, I took a deep breath and reintroduced myself. He did remember meeting me in the bike shop. The reward for taking a risk: great service and a delicious, free cookie!" There are tasty rewards for taking risks!

TRY SOMETHING NEW

One way to expand our networks is to go out in this world to try something new. That way we get to meet another group of potential friends and clients, and work new worlds. Joining a new church, synagogue, health club, poker club or book club can create feelings of apprehension.

Much like the results of the students in the bowling research previously mentioned, doing something with a new group of people can be fun and contribute to our well-being.

Joining the Bay Club Marin was a big decision that caused me trepidation: new classes, new teachers, a new environment and new classmates. I was nervous even though I wrote this book! But I decided to smile at everyone and make small talk as comments popped into my head. I was pleasantly surprised. People were shy and cautious at first, but they smiled back.

Over time, instructor Sergio Paganelli's warmth and personality turned our aerobic and Latin dance class into a community. That's a benefit I hadn't anticipated and so very much enjoy. It's ten years later and I can safely say that some of my best friends are my dance classmates.

There are many small steps we can take and create what Dr. B. J. Fogg identifies as our Tiny Habits.

ROANE'S REMINDERS

★ The world is a cornucopia of contacts and communities.

★ How we speak to people in public can be overheard.

★ Four walls no longer define a room; it can be *anyplace*.

★ Don't wait; initiate.

★ Casual conversation can contribute to our base of contacts and business—and pleasure.

★ Chance encounters can change our lives.

★ Smile and say something; even "Hi!" or "Hello!" works.

★ Seize the moment. You'll be glad you did.

21

"ROOM"-IN-ATIONS

Working a room—where we meet and connect with people—allows us to build relationships and our "Millionaire's Rolodex." Being a magnificent mingler is only part of the equation. We must also be savvy networkers, understanding that it's a lifestyle, not merely a workplace activity. The idea is to meet people, connect and build relationships.

This chapter is comprised of action steps we ought to take before, during and after going to any group gathering. They are short, direct and doable.

RANDOM THOUGHTS

The Action Plan:

- RSVP. Say yes and show up.
- Arrive with a positive attitude and smile.
- Prepare: Do your due diligence.
- Avoid eating garlic and onions before an event. Better yet, don't eat them at all. Enough said!
- Dress appropriately for the occasion. If you're not sure, *ask*.
- Pay attention to people.
- Don't wait for the perfect opening line. Smile and say, "Hello!"
- Listen with your ears, eyes and face.
- Prepare a self-introduction.
- Plan small talk topics.
- Have three items/news/stories prepared for conversation.
- Understand that selling is not networking. Nor is networking . . . selling.
- "Single task" to do anything well.
- Be a conversational chameleon; adjust and adapt to each person.
- Scrap snap judgments; don't judge tomorrow's book by today's cover. (First impressions are everlasting and they are often wrong.)
- Be a two-timer: Give people a second chance.

- Turn off your phone ringer. Take off your Bluetooth. Do not check your emails or texts while talking to someone.
- Exit conversations graciously.
- Ask for business cards. Look at them and "honor" them before you put them away.
- Offer your card if not asked. "May I offer you one of mine?"
- Be considerate of others in every room (restaurants, concerts, plays, movies, operas and mass transit).
- Watch your children and your pets . . . please!
- Do that which you say you'll do when you said you will do it.
- Treat people of all ages with respect (you never know who that person's cousin, parents, neighbor, grandson, aunt, godfather or friend is).
- Be judicious about tweets, posts, emails and texts! They are admissible in court.
- Reintroduce yourself to people, smile and say both your first and last name.
- Be sure to follow up by sending an email or text.
- Send an invitation to LinkedIn. Do not send its boilerplate invite—create your own to personalize it.
- Revisit and reprogram your self-talk.
- Arrive in a timely manner.
- Talk to the people who are standing alone.
- Bring them along to meet others.
- Offer your hand to shake.

- Let people know if you have a problem (carpal tunnel syndrome, arthritis, a cold).

- Use your OAR when you converse: Observe, ask, reveal.

- Caveat: Don't overshare—ever. TMI can backfire.

- Do not interrogate; asking too many questions is off-putting.

- Have a focus; don't be blinded, only guided, by it.

- Allow for serendipity—your reward for showing up.

- Junk the jargon and dump the buzzwords.

- Update profiles in social media regularly.

- Learn the rules of etiquette of every room, site or organization and culture.

- *Never* treat people like prospects. Treat them like people.

- Fact-check before you tweet, post, blog or email.

- Be a matchmaker: Introduce people both in person and online.

- Introduce people with enthusiasm and information.

- Avoid scanning the room while speaking with someone.

- Don't correct people's grammar in public.

- Apologize if you misspeak; accept responsibility. Say "I apologize" or "I'm sorry." Ditch "My bad." It's bad.

- Don't leave people twisting in the wind. If you can't, won't or don't—say so. It isn't easy, but it's considerate.

- Acknowledge gifts of time, information, support, referrals and advice.

- Stay in touch with people when you need nothing from them.

- Act like a host: Be a good guest.

- Be different. Send a handwritten note (by your hand, not a computer).

- Send a real sympathy card via U.S. mail right after you send the condolence text.

- If behavior and actions do not support words, they subvert them.

- When is it too late to connect or reconnect with a long-time acquaintance, classmate or friend? Never.

- Remember that rooms, events and gatherings are filled with *nice* people, over 90 percent of whom may be uncomfortable and would welcome your conversation.

- Take the risk. The rewards are boundless.

THIS IS YOUR LIFE

Each of us has similar stories and examples of how circumstances and connections evolved into something professionally and personally beneficial and wonderful. It doesn't happen by accident; it happens because we see an opportunity, exert energy and take a risk.

It's said that "you can't give a smile away; it always comes back." According to Nancy Irwin, a Los Angeles–based psychotherapist, "A smile from a stranger can change a person's entire mood." The same is true of a kind word.

Seize the moment wherever you are. Smile and say something—anything! As with everything else, it will get easier and you'll get better at it if you "practice, practice, practice." Who knows? You might find yourself in the Carnegie Hall of Conversation.

The best benefits life has to offer are relationships with other people. In a sense, "working the world" is just another way of saying "living life to the fullest." Rewards go to those who take the risks. Those who are willing to put their egos on the line and reach out to other people create a richer, fuller life for themselves.

This book is about reaching out, which it has been about for twenty-five years. Being able to work any room can bring you personal and professional rewards, happiness and success.

Many silver anniversary warm wishes to you as you connect with people, work the world and live your life. May it bring you what you desire.

ENDNOTE

The world is rapidly changing, but no matter what technological advances are in our future, what won't change is that we will still have to attend events in both our professional and personal lives. These events give us the opportunity to meet new people, connect and build lasting relationships. Remember, with practice you will be able to successfully manage the mingling.

Don't think of it as "work"; think of joining a room full of "you never know" opportunities. Have a focus, but be open to serendipity.

Remember also that 93 percent of adults think of themselves as shy. That means the majority of people at any convention, conference, confirmation or casual professional or personal gathering are uncomfortable.

Now, when that invitation arrives, add it to your calendar, RSVP and *go*!

DISCLAIMER

With apologies to Burl Covan, my high school English teacher, and to other lovers of the language, who prefer correct, not "common," usage. Please know that this book was submitted in traditionally correct English and grammar. I added no unnecessary serial commas. And to my former language arts students, if you see any errors in grammar, punctuation or spelling that are different from the rules of English that I taught you, it's not my doing. It just ain't me, babes!

THE TEN COMMANDMENTS OF CONNECTING: THE GOSPEL ACCORDING TO ROANE

I. THOU SHALT PREPARE

- Attitude
- Focus
- Self-introduction
- Conversation
- Business cards
- A smile and handshake

2. THOU SHALT ATTEND

RSVP and go!
Act like a gracious host.
Be a good guest.

3. THOU SHALT TRY THESE STRATEGIES

- Read name tags.
- Go with a buddy.
- Talk to wallflowers.
- Approach and be approachable.
- Smile.
- Allow for serendipity.
- Listen.
- Extricate courteously and circulate gracefully.
- Follow up.
- Call, email or send "thank-yous."

4. THOU SHALT SAY SOMETHING—ANYTHING

- Don't wait; initiate.
- Take the risk; the rewards are thine.
- Listen with interest to the response.
- Smile and make eye contact.
- Pay attention.

5. THOU SHALT MIND THY MANNERS

- Learn old and new etiquette and brush up on thy manners.
- Acknowledge others.
- Treat *everyone* nicely.

6. THOU SHALT AVOID THE COMMON CRUTCHES

- Don't arrive too late.
- Don't leave too early.
- Don't drink too much.
- Don't gorge at the buffet table.
- Don't misuse the buddy system by joining thyself at thy hips.
- Don't misuse thy cell phone.

7. THOU SHALT REMEMBER THE THREE E'S

- Make an *effort*.
- Bring thine *energy*.
- Exude *enthusiasm*.

8. THOU SHALT DRESS APPROPRIATELY

Unsure? Ask!

9. THOU SHALT REMEMBER THE THREE C'S

- Courtesy
- Charm
- Chutzpah

10. THOU SHALT BRING THY SENSE OF HUMOR (NOT JOKES)

- Use the AT&T Test: appropriate, timely and tasteful

FOR THOSE DESPERATELY SEEKING SUSAN

A Speech Is Within Your Reach!

If you want to book best-selling author and in-demand keynote speaker Susan RoAne for your meeting, retreat or convention:

 "Work" my website: *www.susanroane.com*

For daily tips, ideas, and information:

Follow Susan on Twitter @ susanroane
or @HowToWorkARoom

Mail:

The RoAne Group
320 Via Casitas, Suite 310
Greenbrae, California 94904

Voice mail:

415-461-3915

Email:

Susan@SusanRoAne.com

For books and
audio books:

Your local bookstore
online bookstore
www.powells.com
www.amazon.com
www.barnesandnoble.com
www.800ceoread.com
www.bookpassage.com

Titles:

- *How to Work a Room*
- *The Secrets of Savvy Networking*
- *RoAne's Rules: How to Make the Right Impression* (audio)
- *What Do I Say Next?*
- *How to Create Your Own Luck: The "You Never Know" Approach*
- *Face to Face: How to Reclaim the Personal Touch in a Digital World*

For more information as well as complementary articles, posts and a free ebook, visit www.howtoworkaroom.com. To ask the Mingling Maven for free chapters of my other best sellers or for coaching, visit www.susanroane.com.

A SAMPLING OF
SUSAN'S CLIENTS

CORPORATIONS

Anheuser-Busch
Arbonne International
AT&T
Bell Canada
Boeing
Cartier
Century 21
Coca-Cola Leadership
Darden Restaurants
Discovery Toys
Equity Residential
Exxon Corporation
Hershey Foods (now Hershey Company)
Infiniti
Keyspan (now National Grid)
Kraft Foods
Lockheed Martin

Lucent Technologies
Monsanto Chemical Company
Ohio Edison
Pfizer
Procter & Gamble
Prudential Real Estate
Rohm and Haas Company
SuccessFactors
Time Warner
Trainer Communications
Waste Management of North America

ASSOCIATIONS

American Automobile Association
American Bankers Association
American Payroll Association
Associated General Contractors of America
Association of Government Accountants
College and University Professional Association for Human
    Resources
International Council of Shopping Centers
League of California Cities
National Asphalt and Pavement Association
National Association of Catering Executives
National Association of College Stores
National Association of Secondary School Principals
National Association of Television Producers and Executives
National Association of Realtors
National Court Reporters Association
National Football League

National Restaurant Association
National Tour Association
New Jersey Association of Mortgage Bankers
Professional Insurance Agents
Public Library Association
Society of Consumer Affairs Professionals
Society for Foodservice Management
Toastmasters International
Women's Council of Realtors
Women's Fund of Omaha

CONSULTING FIRMS

A.T. Kearney
Booz Allen Hamilton
Deloitte & Touche
Ernst & Young
KPMG
PA Consulting (UK)
PricewaterhouseCoopers
Watson Wyatt Worldwide

FINANCE

Bank of America
Black Economic Council
Chase Manhattan
CitiGroup
City National Bank
Edward D. Jones

Georgia Society of CPAs
Goldman Sachs
Managed Funds Association
Moss Adams LLP
Treasury Management Association of Chicago
United Nations Federal Credit Union
Wells Fargo Bank
Zurich Financial Services

LEGAL

Buchanan Ingersoll & Rooney
Crosby, Heafey, Roach & May
Latham & Watkins LLP
Lewis and Roca
Paul Hastings LLP
Pitney Hardin
Quarles & Brady LLP
Robins, Kaplan, Miller & Ciresi LLP
White & Case, LLP
Williams Kastner & Gibbs

MEDICAL/HEALTH CARE

American Association of Healthcare Consultants
American Association of Medical Society Executives
American College of Physician Executives
American College of Surgeons
American Physical Therapy Association
California Nurses Association

Doctors Hospital, Columbus, GA
Health Care Executives of Southern California
Kaiser Permanente
Lutheran Hospital, La Crosse, WI
Ochsner Health System, New Orleans
Pfizer
Sutter Health
UnitedHealth Group
University of California, San Francisco, Medical Center

ACADEMIC

Chatham University
Harvard Alumni Association
New York University, Summer Publishing Institute
Northeastern University
Northwestern University Council of One Hundred
Regent University, Executive Leadership Series
University of California, Berkeley, Haas School of Business
University of California, Los Angeles, Anderson School of
   Management
University of Chicago, Booth School of Business
University of Hawaii
University of Illinois MBA Program
University of Phoenix
University of San Francisco School of Law
University of Southern California
University of Texas School of Law
Wharton School, University of Pennsylvania
Yale School of Public Health

GOVERNMENT

Association of Government Accountants
Federal Executive Boards
Occupational Safety and Health Administration
Texas Workforce Commission
United States Air Force
United States Navy
U.S. Department of Treasury (Bureau of the Public Debt)

MEETINGS INDUSTRY

American Society of Association Executives
Greater Washington Society of Association Executives
International Association of Conference & Visitor Bureaus
International Special Events Society
Meeting Professionals International
National Speakers Association
Professional Convention Management Association

TECHNOLOGY

American Software Users Group (ASUG.com)
Apple Inc.
Autodesk, Inc.
Avnet, Inc.
Intel Corporation
Oracle Users Group
RSA Security

MISCELLANEOUS

Churchill Club
Commonwealth Club
Eden Crescent, Durban, KwaZulu Natal, South Africa

YIDDISH GLOSSARY

The following are some of the Yiddish terms I've used in this book, plus others that you may have heard, know and find useful and/or amusing. I thought you would enjoy these definitions as modified from Leo Rosten's *The New Joys of Yiddish*. I've added some expressions that are "Yinglish."

Bris   "The covenant"; a ritual circumcision ceremony observed on a boy's eighth day of life.

         ("At a bris even I got squeamish when the mohel picked up the instruments.")

Bupkes   Insultingly disproportionate remunerations to expectations and/or efforts (said with scorn, sarcasm or indignation). And used on situation comedies.

         ("Can you believe this Fortune 100 company wanted me to coach their executives for bupkes?")

Chutzpah   Classic usage: gall, brazenness, nerve.

         ("It takes a dose of chutzpah to initiate conversations.")

RoAne's usage: courage, gutsiness.

> *("The crook embezzles from the company and then requests a farewell party! That's* chutzpah!*")*

Dreck — Trash, junk, that of inferior quality; a vulgar term not to use around my mother—or yours.

> *("When the* Wall Street Journal *has described some of what is available in cyberspace as* cyber-dreck, *it must really be awful!")*

Dreidel — A four-sided spinning top played at Hanukkah.

> *(It takes skill to spin a dreidel.)*

Fe! or Feh! — An exclamatory expression of disgust and distaste. (Now an acceptable English term on Words with Friends).

> *("They are serving pasta with scallops and kumquats?* Feh!*")*

Hakn a tshaynik *or* Hocking — To rattle on loudly and insistently (like a tea kettle) but without any meaning. Shortened version: "hocking" has come to mean bothering.

> *("Stop hocking me about putting away the groceries.") Source:* Born to Kvetch *by Michael Wex.*

Kibbitz   To joke, fool around; to socialize aimlessly.

("The group in the corner of the room was kibbitzing over coffee.")

Klutz   A clod; a graceless person.

("Run a marathon? I am such a klutz I'm lucky if I can walk off a curb without spraining my ankle.")

Kosher   Fit to eat; ritually clean, trustworthy, proper, ethical.

("Using email to fire a person is not kosher. [Neither is bacon, shrimp or lobster.])

Kvell   To beam with immense pride and pleasure.

("The happy parents were kvelling at their son's bar mitzvah.")

Kvetch   To fuss, gripe, complain; the person who does that.

("Brenda is constantly kvetching about everything.")

Maven   An expert; a knowledgeable person.

("Malcolm Gladwell explains that mavens are experts who help create a tipping point.")(I'm pleased I trademarked the Mingling Maven®.)

Mazel tov!   Good luck; congratulations.

("I am so pleased that you were promoted. Mazel tov!")

Megillah   Anything long, complicated, boring. It's based on the biblical story of Queen Esther.

("Tell me the results of the negotiations. I don't want to hear the whole megillah.")

Mensch   An honorable person of integrity; someone of noble character with a sense of sweetness as well as of what is right and responsible. To call someone a *mensch* reflects deep respect.

("Mark Chimsky, my dear friend, is a real mensch!")

Mohel   The person who circumsizes the eight-day-old Jewish baby in the ritual *bris*.

("The mohel is regarded as a technician [and he better be a darn good one] and is the butt of many borscht belt comedian's jokes, yes, including the one about collecting tips instead of fees.")

Nosh   To eat between meals; a snack, a small portion, a nibble.

("I prefer to nosh and nibble than to eat three meals.")

Nudge   To pester, nag; to give a surreptitious reminder of a job to be done; the person who is a nag.

("He kept nudging her to stop smoking.")

Oy vey!   A lament, a protest or a cry of delight. It expresses anguish, joy, pain, revulsion, regret, relief.

("Oy vey! It is such a tragedy to lose a home in a fire. Thank heaven the family is safe.")

Plotz   To feel so tired, excited or bursting with emotion, you could fall over.

(When I saw the bill for the wedding reception, I almost plotzed!)

Pupik   The navel or belly button.

("Don't let the lanyard with your name badge extend to your pupik," advises Joan Eisenstodt.)

Schlep   To drag, pull or lag behind. Someone who looks bedraggled and *schleppish*.

("Don't schlep all those packages; you'll hurt your back.")

Schmooze   Friendly and gossipy; prolonged conversation; act of chatting *with* someone. (*Schmooze* is not defined as "a way to get what you want in a business situation.")

("Ira and Michael schmoozed for an hour at the party." Incorrect: "Ira schmoozed Michael at the party.")

Schnorrer   A cheapskate; a freeloader.

("Talk about timing, that schnorrer, Lowell, always manages to be in the restroom when the bill arrives.")

Shivah   The seven solemn days of mourning for the dead when Jews sit *shivah* in the home of the deceased.

("During my father's shivah, relatives, friends and his business associates from his sixty-four years in the paper industry came to pay their respects.")

Shpilkes   Nervous energy; to be "antsy." Feeling like you're sitting on pins and needles.

(Larry can't sit still for two minutes he has such shpilkes.)

Shtick   A studied, contrived piece of "business" employed by an actor (or salesperson); a trick; a devious trick.

("Watch him use the same shtick *on this new client.")*

Shvitz   To sweat; steam bath where one goes to sweat (off a few pounds).

("When describing a very humid summer day in New York that made her sweat, Katie Couric said shvitz *was a favorite word to say [rather than do].")*

Tchotchke   A toy; a trinket.

("I refuse to buy people tchotchkes *that just collect dust.")*

Tumult   Noise; commotion.

("The noise level was so high that the tumult *interfered with conversation.")*

Tush   Derriere (a cute term); bottomed out.

("One cannot work a room on one's tush.*")*

Yenta

Classic definition: A gossipy woman who does not keep a secret. It may also refer to a man who does the same. Newer usage (since *Fiddler on the Roof*), a matchmaker.

("I do expect that in the next production of Fiddler, *Yenta will sing 'Networker, Networker . . . make me a match.'")*

FREQUENTLY ASKED QUESTIONS

Here are eighteen questions I have been asked frequently over the last two decades.

1. HOW DO I APPROACH PEOPLE?

Go to the person standing alone or to a group of three or more. Smile. Comment on the situation you have in common.

2. HOW DO I REMEMBER NAMES?

Focus on the person instead of your to-do list. Listen to the pronunciation. Repeat the name. Look at the person and read the name tag.

3. HOW DO I BECOME MEMORABLE?

Be:
- Energetic
- An interested listener
- Inclusive
- Engaging

Tell:
- Good, true stories

Have fun.

Be lighthearted.

4. HOW DO I INCREASE MY SELF-CONFIDENCE?

Be prepared. Read the paper . . . and *People* magazine. Have three to five stories, news tidbits and questions prepared. Practice stories and casual conversations. Talk to people at the health club, in the checkout line, in line at the refreshment stand.

5. HOW DO I OVERCOME SHYNESS?

Know that 93 percent of us feel we are shy.
Decide to work through shyness.
Observe the behavior and manner of an outgoing person you admire.
Emulate that person.
Take an acting and/or improvisation class.
Join a book club or discussion group or an organization in your area of interest (see question 4).

6. HOW DO I BREAK INTO A GROUP?

Choose a *lively* group of three or four people. Stand on the periphery. When acknowledged verbally or by eye contact, step into the group and ask if you may join them. Comment about the conversation. Do not segue to your own agenda.

7. HOW DO I GET OUT OF A CONVERSATION?

Gracefully. Interrupt yourself. Shake hands, summarize the conversation ("It was fun [informative]. Glad we had a chance to meet [talk].”). Move one quarter of the room away to another person or group.

8. HOW CAN I TELL IF THE OTHER PERSON WANTS TO MOVE ON?

Observe facial expressions and body language and listen for verbal clues. If you make it easier for the other person to move on, you will be remembered well.

9. HOW CAN I GET PEOPLE ON MY AGENDA?

They may have no interest in moving our agendas forward. That is not why they showed up at the event. We can only get people into conversation. The ongoing conversation, over time, allows for shared agendas.

10. HOW CAN I MAKE A BUSINESS CONTACT WITH-OUT APPEARING TO COME ON TO A PERSON OF THE OPPOSITE SEX?

Be friendly, open. Dress appropriately. Shake hands; no other touch is proper. Monitor language—no off-color comments, swear words or double entendres. No sidelong glances; avoid the once-over.

11. HOW DO I MOVE FROM SMALL TALK TO BUSI-NESS?

Carefully. Small talk is the *most important* talk as it is how we learn about people and their interests. “Big” talk is earned—over time. Listen for a cue to segue.

12. HOW DO I BREAK THE ICE?

Melting the ice is a great skill of masterly minglers. The comments and questions relate to the event, venue, sponsoring organization. Start with a big smile and eye contact, which makes you "approachable" in any room.

13. WHAT'S THE BEST WAY TO GET THE BUSINESS CARD OF SOMEONE I THINK WILL BE AN IMPORTANT CONTACT?

Ask for it. "Do you have a card?" "May I please have one?" If you don't get asked for your card, you can ask, "May I offer you one of mine?"

14. HOW DO I RESPOND TO AN EMAIL THAT IS CRITICAL AND INSULTING?

You don't. If an issue needs to be addressed, pick up the phone! Avoid the "duel by email." I received an email from a stranger who, based on the photo on my homepage, wrote, "Way too much make-up on, Babe." He was out of line. There is no reason to respond to someone who is inappropriate, offers unsolicited advice or is insulting.

15. HOW DO YOU TALK TO A BIG KAHUNA (CEO, CFO, POLITICIAN, AN IMPORTANT MEMBER OF THE COMMUNITY)?

Introduce yourself and say something about them, their works, or contribution, or talk to them about the event, the venue, or the company. Then politely excuse yourself so that they may greet other people who want to meet them as well.

16. WHAT DO YOU DO WHEN A PERSON MISPRONOUNCES YOUR NAME?

Tell a story in which you use your name, clearly enunciate it rather than outright correcting Miss-Pronouncer.

17. I HAVE CARPAL TUNNEL SYNDROME. WHAT DO I DO IF SOMEONE WANTS TO SHAKE MY HAND?

Explain the situation. People will understand if you give them a reason, and it's more polite than just not reciprocating.

18. CAN I SEND A GROUP THANK-YOU EMAIL?

Only if the group sends one gift. Group thank-yous are as impersonal as the letters that arrive addressed to "occupant."

READERS' GUIDE
FOR BOOK
CLUB DISCUSSION
GROUPS

To inquire about having Susan RoAne visit your reading group or book club via phone or Skype, contact her at Susan@SusanRoAne.com.

The following questions are offered to stimulate a discussion about how and why it's important to be able to work a room and how the participants will endeavor to implement strategies from this book.

These questions/observations can be posed by the group leader to a full group or small group to enhance participation.

1. What do you do as a host for an event or party?

2. Take two minutes to draft a seven- to nine-second self-introduction. Go around the room and have each person introduce him or herself to the group.

3. How do you prepare yourself for events?

4. What would be the top three specific benefits to you if you could work rooms easily? Rank them.

5. What is your biggest deterrent? How do you deal with that?

6. What three suggestions/strategies do you plan to adopt? Why?

7. Identify a magnificent mingler whom you know. What do they do? What could you "borrow"?

8. What's the most successful way you've started a conversation?

9. What graceful exit have you experienced?

10. If you consider yourself part of the 93 percent who self-identify as shy, how have you adjusted in social business situations?

11. What online social media sites have you joined? Your favorite? Why?

12. How have they contributed to you? Your career?

13. Any tips you would share with the group for remembering names? Any awkward situations when you forgot a name? How did you recover?

14. How do you handle your cell phone at events/gatherings?

15. Have you encountered a "sleaze"? What did they do to be one?

16. What's the most beneficial, positive outcome you've had from attending a business event?

17. How does an event with a greeting committee differ from others? (Would you sign up to be one?)

18. How do you choose which business events to attend?

19. How do you prepare for small talk? How do you move it to business conversation?

20. How will you follow up events once you have collected business cards?

21. Do you consider yourself shy? An introvert? What do you do to manage social settings?

22. What's your biggest pet peeve about going to events?

23. Any relationships—business or personal—that started by meeting a stranger at an event?

24. What is the one thing you will no longer do as a result of reading this book?

25. What is your top tip takeaway from *How to Work a Room*?

REFERENCES

Baldrige, Letitia. *Amy Vanderbilt's Everyday Etiquette*. New York: Bantam, 1981.

———. *Letitia Baldrige's Complete Guide to Executive Manners*. New York: Rawson Associates, 1985.

Brogan, Chris. *Trust Agents*. Hoboken, New Jersey: John Wiley & Sons, 2009.

Butler, Pamela E. *Self-Assertion for Women*. New York: HarperCollins, 1992.

———. *Talking to Yourself: Learning the Language of Self-Affirmation*. Charleston, South Carolina: Book Surge, 2008.

Byrne, Robert, ed. *637 of the Best Things Anybody Ever Said*. New York: Fawcett Crest, 1987.

Cain, Susan. *Quiet: The Power of Introverts in a World That Can't Stop Talking*. New York: Broadway Paperbacks, 2012.

Carducci, Bernardo. *Shyness: A Bold Approach*. New York: HarperCollins, 1999.

Cohen, Stephanie. "Balancing Blockbusters and Ibsen." *Wall Street Journal*, May 5, 2013.

Dubois, Shelley. "There Are No Superhero CEOs." *Fortune/CNN Money*, December 3, 2012.

Garchik, Leah. *San Francisco Chronicle*, April 19, 2013.

Givens, David. "The Animal Art of Getting Along." *Success* (April 1985):

———. "Social Anxiety: New Focus Leads to Insight and Therapy." *New York Times*, December 18, 1984.

Gladwell, Malcolm. *Blink*. New York: Little, Brown, 2005.

Godin, Seth. *Lynchpin*. New York: Portfolio, 2010.

———. *Permission Marketing*. New York: Simon & Schuster, 2007.

Hearing Health Foundation. *Hearing Loss in Older Adults*. New York, 2013

Kawasaki, Guy. *What the Plus!* ebook, 2012

Keyfitz, Nathan. "The Baby Boom Meets the Computer Revolution." *American Demographics* (May 1984): 23–25, 45–46.

Korda, Michael. "Small Talk." *Signature* (September 1986), 78.

Leland, Karen. *Ultimate Guide to Pinterest for Business*. Irvine, California: Entrepreneur Press, 2013.

Lyubomirsky, Sonja. *Myths of Happiness*. New York: Penguin Press, 2013.

Minninger, Joan. *Total Recall: How to Boost Your Memory Power*. New York: Pocket, 1989.

Misner, Ivan. *Truth or Delusion? Busting Networking's Biggest Myths*. Nashville: Nelson Business, 2006.

Morris, James. *The Art of Conversation*. New York: Cornerstone Library, 1976.

Murphy, Katie. "The Right Stance Can Be Reassuring." *New York Times*, May 5, 2013.

Pink, Daniel. *To Sell Is Human*. New York: Riverdale Books, 2012.

Prodromou, Ted. *Ultimate Guide to Twitter for Business*. Irvine, California: Entrepreneur Press, 2013.

Reynolds, Gretchen. "Live Longer and Better." *Parade* magazin, January 27, 2013.

Rivas, Teresa. "Name Game Hits a Global Roadblock," *Wall Street Journal*, May 30, 2006.

RoAne, Susan. *The Secrets of Savvy Networking*. New York: Warner Books, 1993.

———. *What Do I Say Next?* New York: Warner Books, 1997.

———. *Face to Face: How to Reclaim the Personal Touch in a Digital World*. New York: Fireside, 2008.

Rosten, Leo. *The New Joys of Yiddish*. New York: Washington Square Press, 2003.

Schwartz, David J. *The Magic of Thinking Big*. New York: Cornerstone Library, 1987.

Sintumuang, Kevin. "Google Glass: An Etiquette Guide." *Wall Street Journal*, May 4–5, 2013.

Skenazy, Lenore. "American as Cheese." *Psychology Today* (May/June 2013): 75, 77.

Sullivan, Bob, and Hugh Thompson. *The Plateau Effect: Getting from Stuck to Success*. New York: Dutton Publishing, 2013.

———. "Brain, Interrupted." *New York Times*, May 5, 2013.

Tannen, Deborah. *That's Not What I Meant*. New York: Washington Square Press, 1987.

Young, Kimberly. "Internet Addiction Quiz." University of Pittsburgh, Center for Internet Addiction Recovery, 1995.

Zimbardo, Philip. *Shyness: What It Is, What to Do About It*. New York: Addison Wesley, 1990.

———. "Get a Daily Dose of Friends." *AARP* (February/March 2013), 41.

ROANE'S RECOMMENDED READING AND LISTENING LIST

Black, Joanne. *No More Cold Calling.* New York: Warner Business, 2006.

Boyle, Toni. *The Gremlins of Grammar.* New York: McGraw-Hill, 2006.

Carducci, Bernardo. *Shyness*: *A Bold Approach.* New York: HarperCollins, 1999.

Carr, Gina and Brock, Terry. Klout Matters. New York: McGraw Hill, 2013.

Cialdini, Robert B. *Influence: The New Psychology of Modern Persuasion.* New York: Quill, 1998.

Clark, Dorie. *Reinventing You: Define Your Brand, Imagine Your Future.* Boston: Harvard Business School, 2013.

Friedmann, Susan. *Meeting & Event Planning for Dummies.* Hoboken, N.J.: John Wiley, 2009.

Glaser, Connie. *Gender Talk Works.* Atlanta, Ga.: Windsor Hall Press, 2006.

Godin, Seth. *Lynchpin.* New York: Portfolio, 2010.

Kawasaki, Guy. *Enchantment.* New York: Penguin Books, 2011.

Leland, Karen. *Ultimate Guide to Pinterest for Business.* Irvine, California: Entrepreneur Press, 2013.

Misner, Ivan. *Networking Like a Pro.* Irvine, California: Entrepreneur Press, 2010.

Pink, Daniel. *To Sell Is Human.* New York: Riverdale Books, 2012.

Prodromou, Ted. *Ultimate Guide to Twitter for Business.* Irvine, California: Entrepreneur Press, 2013.

RoAne, Susan. *Face to Face: How to Reclaim the Personal Touch in a Digital World.* New York: Fireside, 2008.

———. *How to Create Your Own Luck.* Hoboken, N.J.: John Wiley, 2004.

———. *The Secrets of Savvy Networking* (audio book). New York: Audio Renaissance, 2006.

Scheele, Adele. *Skills for Success.* New York: Ballantine, 1999.

Schawbel, Dan. *Promote Yourself.* New York: St. Martin's Press, 2013.

Weinberg, Tamar. *The New Community Rules: Marketing on the Social Web.* Sebastopol, California: O'Reilly Media, 2009.

INDEX